GOING FISHING

THE STORY OF THE DEEP-SEA
FISHERMEN OF NEW ENGLAND

GOING FISHING

THE STORY OF THE DEEP-SEA FISHERMEN OF NEW ENGLAND

By

WESLEY GEORGE PIERCE

Illustrated by the Author

Gloucester Fishing Schooner *Kearsarge*

INTERNATIONAL MARINE
PUBLISHING COMPANY

CAMDEN, MAINE

1989

Published by International Marine Publishing
Company in cooperation with
The Peabody Museum, Salem, Massachusetts,
and the Boothbay Region Historical Society,
Boothbay Harbor, Maine.

10 9 8 7 6 5 4 3 2

Library of Congress Cataloging-in-Publication Data

Pierce, Wesley George.
  Goin' fishin' : the story of the deep-sea fishermen of New England
/ by Wesley George Pierce : illustrated by the author.
    p.   cm.
  Reprint. Originally published: Salem, Mass. : Marine Research
Society, 1934. Originally published in series: Publication no. 26 of
the Marine Research Society.
  Includes index.
  ISBN 0-87742-251-6
  1. Fishing--New England.   2. Fishers--New England. I. Title.
  II. Title: Going fishing.
SH221.5.N4P54   1989
639.2'2'0975--dc20   89-35602
                                                          CIP

International Marine Publishing Company
offers software for sale. For information and a
catalog, please contact TAB Software
Department, Blue Ridge Summit, PA
17294-0850.

Questions regarding the content of this book
should be addressed to:

International Marine Publishing Company
Division of TAB BOOKS, Inc.
P.O. Box 220
Camden, ME 04843

*The paper used in this publication meets the minimum
requirements of American National Standard for
Information Sciences—Permanence of Paper for Printed
Library Materials.* ANSI Z39.48-1984.

TO THE MEMORY OF MY FATHER

PREFACE

MY paternal ancestors for five generations were fishermen. Father was a fisherman for many years and at the age of nineteen made his first trip as skipper, in the schooner *Archer*. I was born at Southport, Maine, in a house close by the sea, so my first breath was salt air. As soon as I was old enough to climb into a boat I went shore-fishing with an uncle, and a few years later went away from home, for the first time, mackerel fishing in the schooner *Astoria*, during the summer months. In the winter time I went to school. When I was fifteen, I went to the Western Bank, hand-line fishing for cod, in the schooner *Lady Elgin*. At the age of seventeen, while seining in the *Elgin*, she brought in the largest trip of mackerel (four hundred and twenty barrels), ever landed at Southport. I also went cook at eighteen and have been fishing out of Portland, Gloucester and Boston. I am familiar with the advancement made in new models of fast-sailing fishing vessels, and their change of rig, and also the advance made in new methods of catching fish. As much of this information concerning New England's first industry is rapidly becoming a thing of the past and likely to be forgotten, it has seemed to me worthwhile to record the daily life of the salt-water fisherman and how the fish were caught.

W. G. P.

Rockland, Mass.
January 4, 1934

CONTENTS

FOREWORD

Wesley George Pierce was born January 17, 1869 on Southport Island, which forms the western side of Boothbay Harbor, Maine. On the night he was born, his father was riding out a northeast gale as skipper of a fishing schooner on Georges Bank.

When George was fifteen, he went to the banks with his father in the schooner *Lady Elgin* as "salter's devil," carrying salt to the men in the hold kenching the catch. Too young to go out in a dory, he caught 1600 codfish that summer over the schooner's rail.

As he grew up, he fished in other vessels and from other ports. During his active life he saw significant changes in the fishing industry. From fishing over the schooner's rail, he went to dory handlining, to dory trawling and then to dragging for codfish, haddock, and halibut. He jigged for mackerel in the Bay of Chaleur and set seines from Carolina to Maine. He was in the crew which brought in the biggest catch of mackerel ever landed in Southport. The schooner's scuppers were literally awash. He sailed in stubby pinks and salt-fish schooners on long voyages to the banks, in fast fresh-fish schooners racing home from Georges for the best price on the Boston market, and in steam and diesel draggers.

Through all this, he was a close and thoughtful observer. He sailed with high-line skippers and knew what made a successful fisherman and a fast, able schooner. He knew every detail of dory fishing and dragging. He had been a cook and knew how to smoke mackerel by hanging them in the galley chimney, how to cook doughnuts by the bushel, and what supplies to lay in for a voyage. He knew the financial side of the business too—how the fish were sold, how the crew was paid and how much. He saw fog and storm, calm and gale, lee shores and quiet nights.

About 1930 he came ashore and worked in a shoe factory in Rockland, Massachusetts. Lecturing and writing articles for marine magazines, he developed an admirable literary style. The words and phrases of the year-round commercial fisherman reflect not only the details of the fisherman's life but his genuine feelings and attitudes with no Sunday supplement sentimentality. Furthermore, Mr. Pierce relates his own experience to significant changes in the fishing industry.

Many of his own drawings illustrate and clarify the text and have no small artistic merit.

The Marine Research Society of Salem, Massachusetts published *Goin' Fishin'* in 1934, recognizing its historical value; but by the 1980s it was long out of print, available only occasionally and at a high price from rare-book dealers. The Boothbay Region Historical Society, eager to preserve works of local history, obtained the generous permission of the Peabody Museum, successor to the Marine Research Society, to republish the book. International Marine Publishing Company, recognizing that its value far exceeded merely local or antiquarian interest, undertook to produce and market the book, thus preserving and making again available a work of historic, literary, and artistic significance.

Roger F. Duncan
Boothbay Region Historical Society

GOIN' FISHIN'

GOIN' FISHIN'

CHAPTER I

THE EARLY COD FISHERY OF NEW ENGLAND
1623-1835

FOR many years cod have been considered by fishermen the most important food-fish found in the waters of the North Atlantic. Of the many kinds of food-fish caught by New England fishermen, there are two classes — *ground-fish* and *school-fish*. Ground-fish are cod, haddock, halibut, hake, pollock, cusk and flounders of several kinds, including gray-sole, lemon-sole, black-backs, yellow-tails and dabs. These fish live *on*, and *near* the *bottom* of the sea, where they find their food supply. The school-fish are mackerel, menhaden (porgy), shad, butterfish, herring of several kinds, including ale-wives, bluebacks and "kyacks." Mackerel live mostly *on* or *near* the *surface* of the sea, where they find their food supply, and this is the reason for their schooling, for then they are feeding on tiny fish that live on the surface, some looking like very small minnows and others like small red spiders and called by the fishermen "mackerel feed."

The early explorers on their first visits to North America, found cod very plentiful all along the coastal waters from Hudson Bay and the Labrador coast on

NOTE.—For a very complete and scientific account of the New England fishing industries consult "The Fisheries and Fishing Industries of the United States," by G. Brown Goode, 5 vols., 4to, profusely illustrated, Washington, 1887. For a detailed study of fishing craft, particularly during the early period, consult "Report of the Shipbuilding Industry of the United States," by Henry Hall, Tenth U. S. Census, vol. VIII, pp. 1-45, 4to, illus., Washington, 1880.

3

the north, to Cape Cod and Long Island on the south. Cape Cod derived its name for this reason. Some of the early settlers of New England (including both the Pilgrims and Puritans) found food supply and a means of earning their living by catching cod in the near-by waters. Soon fishing hamlets sprang up all along the coast of Massachusetts which later on became towns and cities.

For many years the early fishermen went fishing in small craft that were built for them, such as the ketch, pinnace, chebacco-boat, and later on the pinky. At first they found plenty of fish such as cod, haddock, mackerel, etc., nearby on shore-soundings. Later on, when they had larger, square-sterned vessels of forty, fifty, and sixty tons each, they went off-shore to the different Banks found along the New England and Nova Scotia coasts, among them the "Middle Bank," "Jefferys' Ledge," "Cashe's Ledge," "Brown's Bank," "La Have Bank," "George's Bank," "Western Bank," "Banquereau," "Green Bank," and the "Grand Banks," off Newfoundland.

For more than a hundred years the early fishermen confined their activities to "shore-fishing," and then about "1730 the fishermen of Marblehead began to go off-shore on 'George's Bank,' but we have no records that show this fishery was long continued by them."

Between 1830 and 1850, Marblehead sent to the Grand Banks, hand-line fishing from the deck, for cod, on salt trips, a fleet of eighty vessels, all schooner-rigged and from fifty to seventy tons each.

Most of these vessels made two trips each season, starting in April and arriving home from the second trip late in September or early in October. The length of the trip, of course, depended on how the men found

I. A Pinnace.   II. A Chebacco Boat

the fish. If plentiful, a trip could be secured in two and a half months; if fish were very scarce, very likely it would take them three and a half months to catch a full fare of 700 to 1000 quintals.

Four months had to be passed each season on the fishing grounds in order to secure the bounty offered by the Federal Government for the encouragement of the fisheries, amounting to four dollars per ton on all vessels of ninety tons and under, no allowance being made for any excess of burden. Most of the "Bankers" built during the forties and fifties were vessels under ninety tons, so as to be entitled to the bounty. No bounties were paid on fishing vessels after the outbreak of the Civil War.

In the summer time many fishermen used an "oiled petticoat," made very full, with a "bib" in front. Some men had a "barvel," in shape much like a woman's apron made very full, but without a "bib." Both these garments were much cooler in hot weather than "oil-pants," and were also used by the men while working around the wharves packing fish.

All oil-clothes, pants and jacket, long coat, petticoat and barvel, are made from a good grade of unbleached white cotton cloth. When finished they are thoroughly soaked in the best grade of boiled linseed oil and hung up to dry; then oiled the first coat on the outside and when again dry, they are given the second coat, and show a fine, glossy surface which will shed water well.

Most oil-clothes are a light yellow color, when new, and turn to a darker shade with age. Some men prefer black oil-clothes which are made so by using a black oil.

In 1821, Gloucester vessels began going to "George's Bank" after cod and halibut. Only a few went at first, but the number increased each year, and by 1835 there

THE CREW OF THE SCHOONER "POLLY," HAND-LINE FISHING
FROM THE DECK ON GEORGE'S BANK. SHE WAS A "HEEL-
TAPPER"; NOTE HER HIGH QUARTER-DECK

was quite a large fleet. Most of them were pinkys. Tra-
dition says, "The first fishermen were afraid to anchor
their vessels on the Bank, for fear they would 'run
under' in the strong running tide." The reason for the
very strong tide running so swiftly on "George's," is
because of the shallow water on the Bank, it being
much nearer the surface than the surrounding bottom
off the edge of the Bank where there is deeper water.
This large body of water, at each ebb and flood tide,
must pass over the Bank in a given time of six hours.
The tide often runs so strongly that a vessel at anchor
will "hawse up," stern to the wind, when it is blowing
a gale.

The fishermen on "George's," fish from the deck of
their vessels, each man having one hand-line, and on
account of the swiftly running tide he uses a lead of

nine pounds to reach bottom. Each line has a spreader, with long "snoods and gangings," and two hooks. This is what the fishermen call "George's-gear." The fish caught on "George's Bank," are mostly very large cod and halibut, and during the early fishery both kinds were very abundant. When the fish were very plentiful, the fare was made up in about six weeks — that is, when they had "wet all their salt."

Cod caught with fresh mackerel bait were larger than those caught with salted clams (*Mya arenaria*) for the reason that a larger bait of fresh mackerel can be put on the hook than of clam, and the largest fish take the larger bait.

Fishermen's hands are preserved from the cutting of the fishing lines by a pair of "nippers" worn when hauling in the line. "Nippers" are made from woolen yarn and when finished resemble a large doughnut in shape, with a deep crease around the outside center. When at their work the men wear a suit of oil-clothes, pants and short coat, over their common dress, and during stormy weather a sou'wester. A pair of thick cowhide boots of a russet color, with soles an inch thick, pegged on with wooden pegs are worn, and sometimes rubber boots. This completes the outside clothing of the fishermen.

"George's Bank" is one of the roughest places in the world on which to fish, more especially so during the winter months, for then fierce gales, with snowstorms, prevail and many vessels have been lost with all hands. "In a single storm, on the night of February 24, 1862, 15 Gloucester vessels and 120 men were lost, leaving 70 widows and 140 fatherless children to mourn for the loved ones who would return no more."

There are several shoal spots on the Bank: "Cultivator Shoal," "North Shoal," and several others which always break during a heavy gale, and woe betide the vessel that breaks adrift, or parts her cable, drifting on to one of these shoals, for she is very likely to be lost with all her crew.

During the sixties, seventies, and eighties there was a large fleet of "George'smen," and many big trips were landed at Gloucester, one of the largest being made in 1875, by skipper Solomon B. Jacobs, in the schooner *Samuel R. Lane*, when he landed 123,000 pounds of large cod. Skipper Sol Jacobs was "high-line" for several years, and he brought to the "George's" hand-line cod fishery, the same energy that he did later on, when he entered the mackerel purse-seine fishery.

Gloucester has always been a fishing port, and from the very first settlement, its chief industry has been the fish business which was at its height in the eighties. For many years it was the largest fishing port in the United States, if not in the world. In late years Boston has surpassed Gloucester in the fresh fish business and since the building of the new fish pier near South Boston, more than two million pounds of fresh ground-fish are often landed by the fleet in one day; and on some days in the summer, an additional million pounds of fresh mackerel are also landed.

This enormous amount of fish is handled and sold by the dealers, and the next morning they are ready to buy more. Gloucester is still the largest fishing port in the United States, handling an enormous amount of pickled, smoked, canned, and dried salt fish of several kinds. She has a large mackerel canning factory and several smoke-houses where haddock, herring and halibut are smoked and cured by the thousands of pounds each season. There are several large "skinning lofts" where millions of pounds of salt dry fish are skinned, boned, and packed in boxes as boneless fish. Some of her new industries are the preparing of several kinds of fresh fish which are dressed, cleaned, boned and packed. Ready for cooking, these make a delicious table food.

There have been many changes in Gloucester's fleet of fishing vessels during the past fifty years. I can remember when she had more than five hundred sail of vessels in the various fisheries, such as mackerel seiners, cod and haddock trawlers, both salt and fresh fishing; halibut trawlers, George'smen hand-lining, hand-line dory fishermen, rip-fishermen, pollockers, herring-net fishermen, etc. All of these fishermen went in sailing vessels. Today, sail is a thing of the past, for steam, and crude oil engines, now drive their craft in place of sail.

A COD FISH

CHAPTER II

THE MACKEREL HAND-LINE FISHERMEN
SALT FISHING, 1626-1864

JIGGIN' mack'rel by hand-line over a vessel's rail was lively work when they were biting well. Mackerel are a most uncertain fish. Some years they are very plentiful; other years very scarce. Not because they have been caught up by the fishermen the previous year, but most likely they go somewhere else where the fishermen cannot find them, for they may be plentiful again the following year. It takes seven years or more for them to mature. Mackerel spawn in June, and by the time they leave to go south in the fall they are about six inches long. Fishermen then call them "Tacks." The second year they are spoken of as "Blinks," and the following years they are called "Tinkers," No. 3's, No. 2's, No. 1's, and extra No. 1's.

Every year, late in the fall, they leave the northern coasts of New England and Nova Scotia, and go south. Just how far and just where they go, is a mystery, for no one knows; but they go to the southward of Cape Hatteras, somewhere. In the spring they return and the first fish are generally caught off the North Carolina coast, in the vicinity and just north of Cape Hatteras. Sometimes, they are not seen until farther north, perhaps some fifty miles southeast of Cape May, about April 1st.

Mackerel move along northward during the spring and in June they are up around Block Island, Nantucket, Cape Cod, and along the Plymouth shore, where they spawn on the sandy bottom. After the spawning season is over these mackerel go along the

New England coast as far as the Bay of Fundy, during July and August.

There is also another great body of mackerel that swing off to the northeast, when they are up abreast of Sandy Hook, and it is supposed they go to the eastward of "George's Bank," bound for the Nova Scotia coast, where they are first seen schooling off Liverpool, each spring, about May 20th. These fish school at times while passing down the "Cape Shore," and along the coast of Cape Breton, then, when down by Scatari Island, they disappear and go on up into Chaleur Bay, and the Gulf of St. Lawrence. They are known as "bay" fish and you will read more about them later on in this chapter.

There is no doubt that mackerel have been going south each fall, and returning north each spring, for thousands of years. Who knows how long? They were here when the white man came to these shores, for it is a matter of record that, "Isaac Allerton, caught mackerel with a drag-net off the beach at Point Allerton, in July 1626." But, for the most part, mackerel in those early days were caught by hand-line "drailing" or "trailing," in the old-style "chebacco boats," most generally by two or three men fishing with long poles out over the side at right angles to the boat, with lines attached, on which were one pound leads, and quite a large baited hook. These men fished with their boats sailing along two or three miles an hour, for they had an idea that mackerel would not bite the baited hook unless it was moving through the water. Fishermen used this method for nearly two hundred years, until the advent of the "mackerel jig," somewhere between 1815 and 1820.

Several men claimed to have invented the "jig." I

do not know who was first, so will name no one, but I have heard old men say that the "jig" came into general use about 1820. After this date a new method was used by the fishermen to catch mackerel, for then their craft (boat or vessel) was "hove to" on the starboard tack, the jib let run down, with fore and main sheets well off, and with the wheel rolled hard down, the vessel would lay side to the wind and drift slowly off to leeward. It was about this time that "mackerel-toll" was first used to bring the mackerel up alongside the vessel. During the ten years from 1820 to 1830 the hand-line mackerel fishery flourished, and the industry increased rapidly. Many large boats and small vessels of several kinds, with various rigs, were built each year, so that at the end of the ten years there was a large fleet of nearly nine hundred sail along the New England coast.

Mackerel were very plentiful during those years, increasing each year, so that by 1831 this fishery had reached its height, and this was the banner year of all time; for during the season (April to November) the fleet landed an enormous amount of fish, 450,000 barrels, the most mackerel ever landed in the hand-line mackerel fishery, or for that matter any other. The next great mackerel year was fifty years later in 1881. By this time there had been a great change in the methods of catching mackerel, for the hand-line and jig had almost gone out, and the purse-seine had come into use. There was then a large fleet of seiners, perhaps 500 sail, and during the season of 1881 they landed 392,000 barrels, mostly dressed and salted; but some few thousand barrels were brought to market fresh. This large amount of mackerel, however, was 58,000 barrels less than the record year of 1831, when the fishermen caught *all* their fish with the jig and hand-line, *one at a time*, and dressed and salted all of them into barrels. During the years following 1831, the catch fell off very rapidly, so that by 1840 only about 50,000 barrels were landed, the lowest amount for many years.

The pinky was a great favorite with the early fishermen, and hundreds of them were built between 1750 and 1850. The pinky derived its name from her peculiar, high, sharp stern. Her shape on deck was much like a pumpkin seed, sharp at both ends, what we call a double-ender. Some of them had rather a bluff, full bow, built that way for fear they would dive in a head-beat sea; but for all their full bows many of them were fast sailers, and fine sea-boats in rough water and windy weather. Most of them were built of old growth white-oak, with copper fastenings and with proper care, if kept well painted, would last for many years. My grandfather owned and sailed a pinky for years, and went in her to Chaleur Bay fishing for mackerel. I remember seeing pinkys as late as 1900, and one of them, the *Hope*, was then 78 years old, as sound as a nut, and still good for service. Many of the fishing vessels built in the early days were built upon honor, and made to last a lifetime. The fishing schooner *Polly* was built in 1808, and in 1912 she was 104 years old and still in service as a coaster.

For several years during the thirties and forties, both cod and mackerel were very scarce off the New England coast, and many of our fishermen went to the "Bay," and Gulf of St. Lawrence, fishing in pinkys (some of them only 25 or 30 tons burthen) and in small, square-sterned vessels. Many of those small pinkys carried only four men for a crew, with a boy

The Pinky "Hope," Built in 1822

ten to twelve years old as a cook. His duties were not very exacting; simply to make a fire in the small fireplace, at meal time, to heat some water to make tea, to boil a pot of potatoes and cook some fish. Sometimes he made a "cod's-head chowder" or "haddock-tea," for a change. The men often cooked mackerel by hanging them on a wire in the chimney above the fireplace, where they cooked and smoked, both at the same time, and were very fine eating. They always carried their bread supply from home, in the form of "ship-biscuit," or "hardtack." It was a long way to go in those small pinkys, some eight hundred miles; but they went this long distance, caught trips of fish, and returned in safety and very few of them were ever lost or cast away.

In those early days the fishermen sailed their vessels by dead reckoning, using their best judgment, for they had only a mariner's compass and sounding-lead, as an aid to navigation. They had no patent log to give them their distance run; no quadrant or sextant, to find their position by latitude and longitude; no nautical almanac and no chronometer. The fishing skippers often had no log and would throw overboard a chip of wood at the bow and walk aft as the chip floated by with the vessel sailing along, and then judge her speed by walking fast or slow. This was a very primitive way of getting a vessel's speed. I have often heard my father tell how the skippers of those small vessels, who were bound to the "Bay," would run across the Bay of Fundy in foggy weather, keeping well clear of Cape Sable, for they knew about the strong tides, numerous shoals, and rocks off the "Cape," until they felt sure they were "by the Cape"; then they would swing off and run east-no'th-east down the "Cape Shore." When they had run their "distance up" (in their best judgment) if it were still thick weather, they would "heave to" with jib to windward, "jogging" until the weather cleared up, then make their way in, and run across Chedabucto Bay, then through the Straits of Canso, and anchor at Port Mulgrave. There they would get a supply of wood and water, make sail again and run across to Prince Edward Island, then on up into Chaleur Bay.

The spring my father was nineteen, he went to Western Bank, hand-line dory fishing for cod, in the schooner *Archer*, with his brother Wesley, who was skipper. They caught a fine trip of fish (cod, dressed and salted), brought them home, unloaded them and then "fitted out" the *Archer* for the hand-line mackerel fishery to the Bay Chaleur. Just before they were ready to sail the skipper was taken ill, and his doctor told him that he must not go fishing that trip. So the owners of the *Archer* had to find a new skipper for their vessel. They talked the matter over and then asked father to go skipper. He was young, only nineteen, so he hesitated about assuming the responsibility. The crew and cook all urged him to take the vessel; said they would stand by and help him in any way they could, and the owners urged him to take her, so he finally consented. The vessel was nearly ready to sail, except putting on board stores and some water in barrels, so in a short time they had the *Archer* ready, and decided to sail the next morning, July 5, 1864.

A week later the *Archer* was sailing along on the port tack, with a light wind, in Chaleur Bay. Part of her crew were grinding "toll-bait" in the "bait-mill," some of them were chopping clams with the "bait-chopper" in a "salt-keeler" and others were polishing up their "mack'rel jigs" and coiling up their lines getting ready to fish. Then came the command from the skipper: "Take in th' stays'l, boys, an' clew up th' gaff-tops'l." When the crew had finished the skipper said: "Hard-a-lee! Let th' jib run down, we'll heave to, an' try for fish." As the skipper rolled the wheel down, the *Archer* shot up into the wind, and swung off on the starboard tack. "Ease off th' fore an' main-sheets, boys, an' hook on th' main-boom-tackle," said the skipper. When the vessel had lost her headway, he rolled her wheel hard down and made it fast with the becket. The crew then lined up along the starboard rail, each man having been previously allotted three feet at the rail, in which to stand and fish, with an empty barrel behind him in which to slat his mack'rel, called by the fishermen, "a strike barrel."

The skipper's "berth"* at the rail when fishing, was

---

* The skipper's "berth," in this case, means the three feet of space at the rail in which he stands to fish. He also has a berth in the cabin where he may "turn in" to sleep.

always just forward of the main rigging, near the end of the vessel's break. The skipper threw the "toll-bait," which was made from menhaden (porgy slivers pronounced "slyvers"), ground up in the "bait-mill." This, with a few chopped-clams added to it, made the very best mack'rel "toll-bait." This "toll" was put in the "bait-box," which hung over the side of the vessel, having previously been made fast to the main rigging; a draw-bucket of salt water was put into it; then it was ready for use and was called "chum." With the long-handled mack'rel bait-dipper the skipper threw the "chum" for'ard and aft alongside, every few minutes; it brought the mack'rel "up," and kept them around the vessel while they were "jigging" fish in over the rail. In a few minutes the skipper had a bite; zip went his line through the water as the mackerel sheared about while he hauled in the line hand over hand quickly and skilfully, and then deftly flipped a handsome large fish over the rail into his "strike-barrel" behind him. Instantly there was excitement among the crew all along the *Archer's* rail.

"Hurrah for the skipper; he's caught the first fish!" shouted several of the crew.

Then Joe caught one, also Ben and Tom and the fun began. Soon the young skipper filled his "strike-barrel" cut it away and then got an empty. A "strike-barrel" is one of freshly caught mackerel and a "wash-barrel" is one full of dressed fish put to soak in salt water.

The mackerel bit lively for about three hours and they caught thirty "wash-barrels" which were dressed and salted that evening.

The next morning they tried again for fish but failed to raise any although it was a fine day with a light sou'-west wind.

SCHOONER "ARCHER" HOVE TO IN CHALEUR BAY IN 1864,
THE CREW JIGGIN' MACKEREL

Mackerel are a freakish fish, often changing from one locality to another very suddenly, and where they are plentiful one day, on the next there are none to be found. The skipper thought perhaps there might be more fish farther northward so he told the "boys" to set the stays'l and gaff-tops'l, and then rolled the wheel up and the *Archer* swung off heading for Point Miscou up the "Bay."

In the afternoon the crew "headed up and stowed down" their fish, about twenty-five "salt-barrels." The next morning at sunrise they were off the "Point," and the skipper hauled her up by the wind to stand across the "Bay" over towards the west shore.

About seven o'clock, they sighted a fleet ahead and in two hours' sailing were up among them and found they had good fishing, so they hove the *Archer* to and "lined the rail." They had a fine "spurt" for a while and fished until about three in the afternoon, when they had caught thirty-five "wash-barrels." The fish then slacked off and stopped biting. During the night the wind breezed up fresh from the sou'sou'west and the whole fleet jogged over towards Point Miscou. By morning they were off the "Point," with the wind blowing strong, about all the vessels could stand up under with their three lower sails, so the whole fleet beat up to Shippegan and anchored under the lee of the island. After supper, about four o'clock, nearly all the men from the vessels in the fleet manned their yawl-boats and rowed ashore. The hand-line mackerel vessels always carried a yawl-boat on their davits at the stern. Most yawl-boats were eighteen feet long, well and strongly made and would hold all the crew in case of accident if they had to leave the vessel. No dories were carried on these vessels.

Two baseball teams were formed from among the younger men and they played ball until darkness set in. They all had a fine time and a lot of fun. The next morning at daylight the whole fleet got underway, and ran down around the "Point," and then headed up into Chaleur Bay, close hauled on the port tack, for the wind was still from the southwest.

This point of sailing was just to the liking of the crew on the *Archer*, for she was a smart sailer "by the wind" and in an hour's time she was leading the whole fleet.

At eight o'clock father hove 'er to and tried for fish, and in a few minutes raised some mackerel, but they didn't bite very well and the crew had "pickin' fishin'" all day and caught only seven barrels.

After supper they hoisted the jib, swung off, jibed over, then set the stays'l and gaff-tops'l and the skipper turned the wheel over to the watch saying: "Keep her no'no'theast!"

"No'no'theast, Sir," replied the man at the wheel.

When the skipper turned in at nine o'clock that night he said to the man on watch, "Pass the word along to give me a call at twelve o'clock!"

"Aye, aye, Sir!" replied the man.

When the skipper was called at midnight, he went on deck, and looked around and satisfying himself they were off Bonaventura Island, the light bearing west by north, and the distance about six miles, he took the wheel and sent the man for'ard to tend the jib sheet, saying, "We'll tack ship!"

When the *Archer* came about, he said: "Make the tail-rope fast to wind'ard, we'll jog until morning!"

He then went below and turned in again.

The next morning after breakfast, the skipper said: "We'll heave to an' try for fish! Ben, throw some toll-bait!"

Ben did as he was told, and also threw out one of the skipper's lines which had an old bait on the jig. As he was clearing the second line from the cleat under the rail he heard the line which was out "snap and sing," and instantly knew the reason for there was a large mackerel on it. Quickly grabbing the line, he hauled the fish in and flipped him over the rail on deck, saying as he did so: "Skipper, they're here. Gosh! he bit savage as a meat-axe!"

The skipper and crew quickly lined the rail and such fishing as they had for several hours, for the mackerel were hungry and bit so good and fast that they caught seventy-five "wash-barrels." The crew on the *Archer* were all very happy about their "good luck" and proud of their young skipper for going north to find the fish. The *Archer* was the only vessel there that day, for the rest of the fleet were somewhere far to the south'ard.

After dressing their fish and getting them all "under salt," it was two o'clock in the morning, and by that time the wind had backed into the southeast and was breezing up fast so that it was quite rough. The skipper knew a storm was coming on and he didn't want to stay out with a deck-load of salted mackerel, so he said, "Hoist the jib, boys, Cape Gaspe is under our lee a few miles and we'll make harbor."

He rolled the wheel up and the little schooner swung off before the wind and was soon racing along very fast. The storm increased. They had rain squalls frequently about daylight and the *Archer* was going like a racehorse under her three lower sails, when the weather cleared up a bit after a severe squall, and the lookout sighted Gaspe Head on the starboard bow. Soon they were passing in to the Gaspe Basin where they came to anchor, lowered and furled sails, and made all snug, glad to be safe in a harbor.

Here is an incident that happened on this trip aboard the *Archer*, while she was in the "Bay." I have heard my father tell about it a number of times. Here is his story:

"The first trip that I was skipper in the *Archer*, one day we was fishin' off to the west'ard of the Magdalen Islands, and the wind was from the no'theast. It was blowin' a good breeze, and breezin' up fast all the time. We had caught a few barrels of mack'rel, but they was only pickin' around, so I told the boys to coil in their lines, and we would dress what fish we had. That night, about dark, we hove-'er-to under a balance-reefed mains'l, instead of beatin' her up under the lee of the islands. It was rough and blowed hard all night. The next mornin', at daylight, the cook blowed his whistle for breakfast and I went on deck and as I was goin' for'ard to the fo'cas'le, I noticed one of the crew's lines snarled up, washin' around in the lee-scuppers. I throwed the jig overboard, to clear the line, intendin' to coil it up on the cleat under the rail. When I started to haul it in, there was a fine large mack'rel on it, so I flipped him in over the rail on deck and throwed the line out again. It no sooner struck the water than I caught another fine, big fellow, an extra No. 1. Then I sang out loudly: 'All hands on deck! They're here, boys. Plenty of mack'rel. Line the rail!' The crew all rushed on deck, went to the rail, put out their lines, and started fishin'. Man alive! What fishin' we had. For they was hungry and bit right savage all day long. They would even bite the hook when it was almost bare of bait. The bait used when starting to fish, was part of a clam's head. After a few mackerel had been caught, a slice was cut from the belly of a fish, and then cut up in small pieces about half an inch square. These were put on the hook until it was full, and made a nice white bait, that would last for an hour or two.

"It was rough, for the wind was blowin' a gale and the vessel was rollin' and pitchin' bad. It was hard work to make an empty barrel set still on its bottom for it would fall over and roll down across deck into the lee-scuppers and we was chasin' after our empty barrels all day long; but after we had put a few mack'rel in it, the barrel would set still on its bottom. We had 'em fast as we could haul 'em, for they bit lively all day long. We fished 'til dark when they stopped bitin'. Then we started to dress down our deck load of fish. We rigged up in gangs of three men, a splitter and two gibbers to each gang. We split 'em, gibbed 'em, washed 'em and salted 'em into barrels. We worked on 'em all night by lantern light and by daylight in the mornin' we had 'em all dressed and salted. We had about a hundred and ten barrels of fine, large No. 1, mackerel.

"It was still rough and blowin' hard and as we had our deck full of fish we didn't try to catch any more right then. So I said to the boys we'll try and make a harbor somewhere. 'Hoist the jib!' Then I rolled the wheel up and when she swung off and gathered head-way, we hauled aft our main sheet, then tacked 'er to port, and under her whole jib and a balance-reefed mains'l, we run across to Margaree Harbor, over on the Cape Breton shore. In a few hours time she was across the 'Bay' and under the lee of the land. Then we set her fores'l and when off the mouth of the harbor we could see that it was full of vessels.

"The *Archer* handled like a play-boat, for she was quick in stays and a fine sailer, so I felt pretty sure that we could beat her up thro' the fleet and anchor her in smooth water. As we beat up the harbor all the men on them vessels was up in their riggin', a watchin' us come in with our deck full of fish. No sooner was our anchor down on bottom, then several of the skippers come aboard (most of them was friends of ours from home) and then they begun to ask me questions.

" 'Where'd you git your fish, skipper?' asked skipper Sam.

" 'Got 'em off the Magdalen Islands, 'tween there and East Pint,' says I.

" 'When'd you git 'em?' asked skipper Joe.

" 'Got 'em yesterday,' says I.

" 'Yisterd'y! Why man erlive, it was er gale o' wind, th'r 'hole fleet was 'ere in th' harbor!' exclaimed skipper Bill.

" 'Well, I know it blowed hard; and t'was pretty rough and nasty out there; but that was when we got our fish, for we fished all day long, from daylight 'til dark.'

" 'Well I snum!' said skipper Sam.

" 'Well I'll be jiggered!' said skipper Joe.

" 'Well I'll be blowed!' said skipper Bill.

"They could hardly believe it possible that we'd caught a deck load of mack'rel in a gale o' wind. But there was our fish, freshly salted in barrels on deck. That was proof positive," concluded father.

After staying on board the *Archer* for about an hour, the visiting skippers returned on board their own vessels and shortly after supper that night the *Archer's* own crew all "turned in" for a much needed rest and sleep. The next morning they "headed up and stowed down" their 110 barrels of mackerel in the vessel's hold and went ashore in the afternoon and filled several barrels with fresh water at a spring near the beach and brought them aboard the vessel in their yawl-boat. It had been blowing hard all day, so the fleet still lay at anchor in the harbor. During the evening some of the crew were spinning yarns; finally some one said, "Henry, tell us about the trip you was in the *Harvest Home* when she was lost on Malpeque Bar, Prince Edward Island, during the great September gale of 1851." After some coaxing on the part of the crew, Henry Bray told his story as follows:—

"We had ben jiggin' mack'rel fer several days in th'

Bend o' th' Island, an' 'long 'bout th' fust o' September, we had caught 150 bar'els that wuz stowed in 'er hold below, when one night, just at dark, er leetle air o' wind cum out o' th' east'ard. It wuz thick er dungeon o' fog, an' ca'm es er mill-pond, an' had ben thick es mud fer two or three days, sort o' mullin' an' fixin' up fer sumthin'. Sum o' th' boys said 'twuz. Th' barometer wuz er risin' fast fer an easterly blow, an' th' Old Man wuz sort o' oneasy like, fust down below to have er look at th' glass, then up on deck ag'in er trampin' 'round th' quarter.

"It soon begun to breeze up, an' pretty soon it wuz er blowin' er good stiff breeze, an' we wuz headin' 'er off to th' south'ard. I knowed well 'nough th' Old Man wuz plannin' to git 'er out by East Pint, afore we had to heave 'er to under 'er two-reefed fores'l. 'Long 'bout ten o'clock that night she had all she could carry under 'er three lowers, an' it er breezin' on all th' time. Pretty soon she rolled down 'til 'er shear-poles wuz under water, an' then th' Old Man says: 'Boys, stand by to take in th' mains'l, an' we'll tuck two reefs in it.' By th' time we had it reefed an' set ag'in, we had to scratch th' fores'l down an' put two reefs in that; an' by th' time we had it swayed up, th' Old Man told us to haul th' jib down. Sumbudy cast off th' halyards an' she fetched er slat an' parted th' jib-sheet, an' that sail ripped open an' slat to pieces afore we could git it down. It wuz er screechin' rite out loud by that time, I tell yer, an' er haulin' out to th' southeast all th' time, an' er headin' o' us off an' drivin' us inshore. It wuz er pipin' on harder all th' time an' th' old gal wuz er makin' bad weather o' it. Sumtimes she would fetch er dive an' go under chock to 'er fore m'st an' everythin' loose on deck wuz washed overboard.

"By an' by th' Old Man says: 'Boys, we'll have to take th' mains'l offen 'er. She can't stan' it no longer.' So we hauled it down an' arter erwhile we got sum stops eround it an' tied it up, but it wuz sum job, I tell yer. It wuz 'long 'bout midnight by that time, es fer's I can reco'lect, an' all th' sail we had on 'er wuz 'er two-reefed fores'l. Hove-to, we wuz, th' wheel wuz hard down an' fastened with th' becket. 'Long towards mornin' it wuz er blowin' like er man, an' when she would rise on er sea she would lay over on 'er side, 'til th' water wuz up eround 'er hatches on deck. Her whole lee-side wuz under water, an' we wuz er hangin' onto er life-line, what wuz made fast to wind'ard 'long 'er weather-rail, an' we wondered if she wuz ever goin' to cum up ag'in a' tall.

"By an' by, 'way went th' fores'l, th' fore-gaff snapped off like er pipe-stem, an' that sail slat to pieces quicker'n you could say Jack Robinson. When she fell off in th' trough o' th' sea, er comber broke onto 'er weather-quarter, washed two men overboard, smashed our yawl-boat to pieces, hangin' to th' davits, an' broke th' main-boom short off in th' slings. Arter erwhile we got th' storm-trys'l bent on to try an' hold 'er up, but in erbout ten minutes arter we had 'er set, she busted clean open an' slat to pieces. Then she fell off ag'in, an' th' Old Man scud 'er under bare-poles, 'bout all we could do now enyway. In erbout an hour it wuz daylight, an' we wuz watchin' fer er chanct to beach 'er. Pretty soon we could make out land on th' starboard bow down to loo'ard, then sum one seed land on 'er port bow; then we made th' breakers dead erhead, an' we guessed we wuz on Malpeque Bar.

"We knowed, well 'nough, that we had but one chanct in er thousand fer 'er to go over th' bar on er sea.

When she reached th' shoal, she fell in th' trough o' er heavy sea an' struck th' bar, an' both 'er masts went over th' bow broken off short. She then swung eround side to, an' th' next heavy comber rolled 'er over on 'er beam-ends, in th' breakers, on th' beach.

"Arter all hands wuz washed overboard, I found er hatch-cover floating near me in th' water (when I got my senses), so I grabbed it an' held on to it fer quite er spell. Arter erwhile I washed up onto th' beach, in th' breakers, an' er man on shore pulled me out o' th' water up onto th' land, more dead than erlive. I wuz th' only one saved o' all our crew. All th' rest o' my poor ship-mates wuz lost. They wuz drownded in th' great September gale o' 1851," said Henry Bray, in conclusion.

After ten days good fishing, the *Archer* was full, a fine trip of 300 barrels, and ready to start for home.

This first trip made by father as skipper, in the smart little schooner *Archer*, was a record one, the quickest trip in the hand-line mackerel fishery, ever made to Chaleur Bay, from the island of Southport, Maine. They sailed on July 5, 1864, and in just one month, to a day, were back home. This record trip was made possible by a strong nor'wester, that took them clear to the "Bay" in four days time, and when they had caught their trip of mackerel, and were ready to start for home, they were fortunate in having a clear easterly that lasted all the way home to Southport.

During the fifties, sixties, and seventies, when our American fishing vessels went to Chaleur Bay "jiggin' mack'rel" and their crews fished on shares, every man had his own private mark on each barrel of his fish. Some of the more industrious men "messed" their salt mackerel, when they had opportunity, for it sold for as much as ten dollars a barrel extra. "Messed mackerel" were treated as follows: first the heads were cut off, then all the settled blood around the napes, throat, and backbone was scraped off with a mackerel knife, and the fish washed very clean and white. Many men in father's boyhood days "messed" part of their mackerel when "hooking in the Bay," and his crew often "messed" their mackerel when they had the chance, while he was skipper in the schooner *Archer*.

Skipper Alvan Mallock (Al Miller) once told me that on a trip seining in the "Bay," after they had got a fine school and while at anchor in Port Hood harbor, they had "a deck" of salt mackerel, and he and his crew worked all day "messing" part of their fish that sold for $35.00 per barrel when they arrived home in Gloucester.

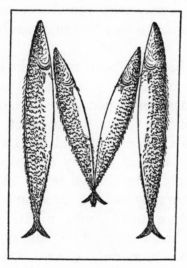

Mackerel

Chapter III

The Western Bank Hand-Line Dory Fishery
Salt Fishing, 1858-1880

THE reel and cod-line, with three and one-half pound lead, "snoods, gangings,"* and two hooks bent on, make up the "gear" used by the hand-line dory cod fishermen. For more than two hundred and thirty years, the New England fishermen caught all their fish by hand-line from the deck of their fishing vessels.

In 1858 the first fishing vessel from Maine, to go hand-line dory fishing, was the schooner *American Eagle* of Southport. Michael Read was her skipper. I have heard old men say that a year or two previous to this date, some vessels went from Massachusetts, hand-line dory fishing, but only a few, and mostly from Marblehead.

There have been many changes in the life on board a fishing vessel during the past hundred years. As time went on the men demanded more variety and better food. In the old days (1830-1850) when Yankee fishermen went to Chaleur Bay and the Labrador coast after cod and mackerel (mostly in pinkys), the men lived very simply, and their diet was chiefly fish of some kind. Often they had fish three times a day, and a lunch of it before turning in at night. They carried hardtack for a bread supply (they did not bake bread for they had no stove, only a small open fireplace), some salt pork, potatoes, Indian cornmeal, table salt and molasses. They had no meat, sugar, or butter. Later on, in the sixties, the owners put on board their vessels

* Pronounced *ganjings*.

plenty of plate beef (salt horse), flour, beans, peas, butter, brown sugar and some vegetables. By this time vessels carried a cook to prepare the "grub" for their crews. In the eighties, a barrel of granulated sugar came aboard with evaporated apples, raisins, some canned goods, condensed milk and eggs. The case of milk and case of eggs, were extras, paid for by the crew.

Most of the "Down East" vessels went salt fishing, and so had no ice with which to keep fresh meats, but sometimes when in port at the wharf of the fish firm, the men had fresh meat. Boston and Gloucester vessels, that went fresh fishing during the eighties, began to have more or less fresh meats for their crews, as they carried ice in pens, and the cook could keep his meats fresh; but the crew had to pay the difference in price between salt and fresh meat.

As time went on and the men wanted better food, they had to pay for other extras, such as fresh eggs, evaporated milk, canned goods and fresh fruit of various kinds. These extras would be deducted from the crew's half of the stock and would range from three to five dollars per man at the end of the trip, when they "settled up."

It was the custom in Maine fishing ports for crews to help get their vessels ready in the spring to go on fishing trips. They would work for a week or more without pay, but always got their dinners and suppers on board the vessels, going to their homes for the night. It was not the custom in Boston and Gloucester for crews to get their vessels ready for fishing trips. There the skippers hired "lumpers" to do the work, the crews preferring to have their time ashore and pay their part of the expense at the end of the trip, not going aboard until about ready to sail.

Southport, Maine, vessels for many years were fitted with Swampscott-built dories, which were of fine model, and well built of good materials. Many Maine fishermen, however, used Amesbury-built dories, which also were well made.

There have been many kinds, shapes and weights of cod-leads used by the New England fishermen during the past three hundred years. I do not recall the exact year, but sometime in the late seventies, Eben L. Decker, of Southport, Maine, invented a cod-lead which was called "Decker's Patent Lead." He made them in three sizes, 3½, 4, and 5 pounds. Most of the hand-line dory fishermen in Maine preferred the 3½ pound lead. The top end had a brass staple set in the lead and on this was a brass swivel. The end of the cod-line was fastened to the swivel with an eye-splice. On the lower end of the lead was a "brass horse," about four inches long, set into the lead at an angle of 45 degrees upward, in the outer end of which was a hole, into which was fitted a swivel. These swivels were a great help in keeping the line free from kinks, especially a new line. "Decker's Patent Lead," once tried, was always used by a fisherman.

The *American Eagle* sailed on her first trip from Southport, during the first week in April, for Western Bank, fitted out with eight dories, each thirteen feet long. The schooner *Ceylon* sailed about the same time also from Southport, but without dories. Her crew were to fish with hand-lines from the deck of their vessel. By June 10th, the *American Eagle* had a full trip of 900 quintals of salted cod, and the *Ceylon* had only 160. When about to start for home the skipper of the *American Eagle* lent his set of dories to the *Ceylon*, and her crew soon began to fill her up and she arrived home on July 1st with 600 quintals. The fishermen pronounce this word *kentle*. I never heard a fisherman call it quintal. The word means 112 pounds of dry salt fish. All fresh and pickled fish are sold by the cwt. or, hundred pounds.

The fishermen soon found that they could catch a trip of cod much quicker by hand-line fishing in dories, on the Bank, than they could by the old method of hand-line fishing from the deck of their vessel and this new method was adopted by most of the vessel owners at Southport, and by others along the coast. During the sixties, seventies, and eighties, there were many vessels engaged in this fishery from nearly all the seaports of Maine and Massachusetts and especially from Portland and Provincetown. The fleet was a large one that went to Western Bank and Banquereau, each spring and summer after cod,—perhaps 500 sail.

In 1875, father went skipper of the *Mountain Laurel*, from Bristol, hand-line dory fishing. They sailed on April 10th, went to Western Bank, where they caught a fine, full trip of salted cod, and on May 26th they were back home at Bristol, the first vessel home in Maine, that year. It was one of the quickest trips ever made in the hand-line dory cod fishery for they were gone from home only six weeks and four days. The usual time was about ten weeks for the trip.

On April 8, 1880, father sailed as skipper of the schooner *Astoria*, bound for Western Bank, hand-line dory fishing for cod on a salt trip. Previous to that date, the fishermen of Southport, during the fifties, sixties, and seventies, manned all their own vessels, but at that time there were not enough good fishermen available to make up a full crew for all their own vessels, for many of the young men had left Southport to find employment in Massachusetts cities, where they would have a better position in life, not wishing to go fishing for a living. So many of the Southport skippers sought fishermen from Nova Scotia as part of their crews. When father was ready to leave home in the *Astoria*, he sailed her out by Monhegan Island, shaping his course east-south-east for the run across the Bay of Fundy to Cape Sable and then went into Clark's Harbor, Nova Scotia, to get six men to make up the crew.

The *Astoria* carried ten dories, each thirteen feet long, one man in each. The skipper and cook made twelve. She was a vessel of 62 tons and would hold 800 quintals of cod. They stayed in Clark's Harbor that night and the next morning got under way and sailed for the Bank. In a few days time, with a fair wind, they were on soundings, near the edge of the Bank (by the skipper's dead reckoning), so he gave the command:

"Let th' jib run down, boys, we'll see if we can find bottom." One of the men on watch rolled the wheel down and luffed the *Astoria* up into the wind.

When she had lost some of her headway, the skipper threw his lead and cod-line with two well baited hooks, far up for'ard alongside the vessel to make a sounding, and had 35 fathoms of water. In a minute or two he was hauling in a fine pair of large cod, and when the fish were up alongside the vessel, one of the crew with a long-handled gaff, hauled them in over the rail on deck. The skipper then looked them over critically to see if they were the right kind of "school fish."* First, he took note of their body color; then saw that they were good plump, brisk and lively fish; also, that their

---

* The term "school fish," as applied to cod (which are "ground fish"), means a large body of cod which have recently arrived on the Bank, for cod are a migratory fish.

SCHOONER "ASTORIA" UNDER BANK SAIL, 1880

fins stood up well. He noted that they had bright, clear eyes of good color, that they closed their jaws together tightly, and finally being quite satisfied that they were "good school fish," he turned to his crew and gave the command:

"Let go th' anchor, boys, an' pay out on th' cable!" When the anchor fluke took hold on bottom, the vessel swung around and came up head to the wind. Then the skipper said:

"Let th' fores'l run down, an' furl it up!" When that work had been done, again came the order:

"Take in th' mains'l, now hook on th' crotch-tackles, lower away on your throat an' peak halyards; easy now, swing th' main-boom over into th' crotch; that's it; now boys, lower away!"

The crew unbent the mains'l, tied it up, and then put it down in the lazaret where it would keep dry. They got the "riding-sail" up, bent it, and set it. This sail is triangular in shape and is made fast with lugs around the main mast, being hauled out taut with tackles, and made fast aft, to both the main-boom and stern of the vessel. The "riding-sail," also called a "try-sail," helps to keep a vessel head to the wind when at anchor on the Bank, and it prevents her somewhat from rolling so badly when the sea is rough in windy weather.

The *Astoria's* crew were now ready "to go to house-keeping." This means, in fishermen's language, that they were anchored on the Bank and ready to catch fish. The next morning, at sunrise, the crew hoisted out their dories, then rowed out in all directions from the vessel and started fishing.

A dory fully equipped for fishing is fitted with the following articles: an anchor and anchor line or "rode"; one pair of 8-foot ash oars; one or two pairs of woolen "nippers"; two hand-lines fifty fathoms each, on reels, with a 3 ½ pound lead, "snoods," "gang-ings (ganjings)" and two hooks attached; bait bucket (wooden water-pail); bait-board; lunch-box; spare hooks (ganged); a gaff; bait-knife; water-jug; bail-ing-scoop; and a "gob-stick." Some men also carry a dory compass. The dory has a painter, stern-becket, thole-pins (or rowlocks), a thwart (or seat), and two kid-boards.

The bait-board is a very necessary part of the dory's equipment, for it enables the fisherman to put the bait (salted clams) on his hooks quickly and three or four clams are used on each hook to fill the shank full.

The bait-board is six inches wide and in length the width of the dory, for the two ends fit into a slot in each gunwale and when in place it is across the center of the dory in front of the man who is facing aft to-ward the stern. It has small strips of wood, half an inch square, tacked on the top side to keep the bait from sliding off, and a half-round hole, two inches deep and three wide, cut out on the after side, to keep the fish from sliding around while being unhooked.

When a cod is hauled into the dory and has been caught by the mouth, it is easily unhooked, but some-times it has swallowed the baited hook and it is difficult to unhook quickly; then the gob-stick is used. The gob-stick for cod is usually made from some old broken fork, or gaff-handle, and is about two feet long, one end cut flat with a small notch made in it. By holding the "ganging (ganjing)" taut with the left hand (fish on the hook), the gob-stick is run down the throat of the fish until it fills the shank of hook, and then with the right hand a quick push and haul is made and the hook usually comes out clear.

The fisherman stands up in his dory with a cod-line in each hand, moving them up and down, with the baited hooks just clear of the bottom and when he gets a bite, he drops one line which is made fast to the opposite rising behind him and hauls in the other line. It is very difficult for a "green-horn" to stand up in his dory when it is rough, with the dory tossing around, but the experienced fisherman knows how to keep his balance without falling down even in rough, choppy seas and in windy weather.

When cod are plentiful and biting well they are caught "pair an' pair" (two hooks on a line), as fast as the fisherman can "haul 'em." When they are up alongside the dory, a dory-gaff is used on the large fish to flip them into the dory, for they are heavy and liable to tear out the hook. All fish are buoyant in the water, but when taken out their weight is apparent.

The fisherman unhooks quickly, baits the hooks, then grabs the lead in his left hand and throws out the "gear," clear of the dory, with both hands. He then turns and hauls in the other line on which is likely to be a pair of fine large cod and so he works, fast and hard, until he has a dory load of fish, perhaps 1700 or 1800 pounds. A fifteen-foot dory will carry 2000 pounds of fish. Sometimes a fisherman has to "make a berth" when fish are scarce, and so hauls in his "rode" (anchor rope), pulls in his anchor, and rows the dory a quarter or half a mile to "new grounds" where he anchors again, hoping for better luck.

Each thirteen-foot, hand-line dory has two kid-boards, that are cut to a slant on both ends to conform to the sides of the dory. The forward one is about a foot wide; its length is the width of the dory, and when in use it is fitted under the thwart (dory seat) in an upright position to keep the fish in the bow of the dory from sliding into the standing room while the man is fishing. The after kid-board is about two feet wide and is fitted under the bait-board in an upright position and is held in place by having notches cut out on both ends to fit snugly on over the dory-rising. The dory-timbers also help to keep both kid-boards in place.

The *Astoria's* crew very soon found plenty of cod, and caught about twenty-five quintal-and-a-half tubs, the first day. They fished in that "berth"* four or five days, getting twenty to thirty tubs each day, and when the fish grew scarce, hove in their cable and got their anchor; then made sail and shifted to a "new berth," seven or eight miles to the east'ard, farther down the Bank. In this way, by moving along with the fish (which also were on the move to the east'ard), every few days, to "new grounds," they found good fishing and at the end of three weeks time had about half a trip. One of the crew from Clark's Harbor was a man that the others called "little Josh." During the first part of the trip his Nova Scotia friends were often heard bragging about "little Josh," as a very fast split-ter. The way in which they spoke about him was rather amusing to the Yankee part of her crew, for this is what they said: " 'Little Josh' is very fast and splits a good fish." What they really meant was this: they thought "little Josh" was a very fast and good splitter. Father was a splitter himself, and he heard more or less of their talk about "little Josh." He paid little atten-tion to it but occasionally, out of the corner of his eye, he watched him at his work. One day when they were dressing down a deck of fish, father walked across to

* The word "berth," in this case, means where the vessel is at an-chor on the Bank.

where "little Josh" was at work, and spoke to him, saying:

"'Josh,' I understand you and your friends think you are a very fast splitter?"

"Josh" looked up, rather surprised, and replied: "Well, skipper, I can split a few fish!"

The skipper then said: "All right, 'Josh,' I'll race you on the next tub o' fish."

"All right, skipper, it's a go!" replied "Josh," smiling and very confident of his ability to beat the skipper, for he was called the "champion splitter" of Cape Island, Clark's Harbor.

Father then told the crew to fill both their tubs with an equal number of fish, of about the same size. Each man sharpened his splitting-knife and stood by his table ready to start when the word should be given: "Ready, go!" How those two men made the bones fly! It was a sight worth seeing! When the skipper had split his last fish and dropped it into his splitting-tub, he walked across deck and saw that "little Josh" had six more fish left in his tub to split. Father stood watching him, and when he had finished, said:

"We all know now, 'Josh,' who is the fastest splitter; but I am not yet satisfied, so now we'll have the crew pitch out on deck both tubs o' fish, and let them say which man is the better splitter o' the two."

The crew examined the skipper's fish first, and all of them agreed that every one of his fish were well split, A No. 1, market cod. Then they examined "little Josh's" fish and found three that were slashed open at the tail, what fishermen call "swallow-tails," not A No. 1, market cod; also, two of his fish were not split open enough so that they would lay out flat. "Little Josh" knew he was badly beaten, but he was man enough to say: "Skipper, you are the *fastest*, an' also the *best splitter* I ever saw in my life!"

Most fast splitters are not good splitters. A man who is a good splitter usually is not a fast splitter. And here I want to repeat a story that father used to tell.

"One summer, when I was skipper of the *Archer*, hookin' in the 'Bay,' one day we was at anchor under the lee of Entry Island. Several of us went on shore in our yawl-boat and found the women folks dressin' cod near the beach, for all the men was out in their boats fishin'. I stood in amazement watchin' a young woman split-tin' codfish. She was about twenty-five years old, a large, strongly-built woman, nearly six feet tall. She stood in an empty flour-barrel to keep her dress clean from the blood and gurry of the fish. How that woman could split fish! I never saw a man who could split fish equal to that girl! I considered myself a fast splitter, but I honestly believe that girl could split two fish to my one. I talked with some of the other women about that girl bein' a fast splitter, and they told me that no man on the island could split fish as fast as that girl could, and that all the men called her the 'champion splitter' o' the Magdalen Islands. I asked them why the women folks was dressin' fish instead of the men, and one of them spoke up and said: 'Th' season fer codfish is so short here at th' islands, that th' men have to work frum 'arly mornin' 'til late at night catchin' fish, an' have no time to dress 'em, so us women folks dress an' cure all o' th' codfish.' Those people had to earn enough durin' the short summer season to last them through the long, hard, cold winter," concluded father.

As he worked the *Astoria* down over the Bank, they found fairly good fishing and finally were pretty well down to Sable Island, and then they lost track of them for the fish had disappeared somewhere. So they hove in their cable, got their anchor, made sail, and ran to the north'ard working around the Nor'west Bar and into the "Bend of the Island." They anchored in about twenty fathoms of water that evening and the next day found plenty of fish and got thirty-two tubs, a good day's work. They had pleasant weather, with good fishing of large size cod, were filling up fast and would soon have a fine, full trip. The following Sunday some of the crew went ashore, in a dory, on Sable Island. It is smooth water on the beach on the north side, in fine weather, but no landing is possible on the south side at any time. While the men were ashore they picked some cranberries and when they came aboard gave them to the skipper who brought them home, for I remember (although only a small boy) that he had them in a new water-bucket.

It is a dangerous place to fish in the "Bend of Sable Island," for if you are caught there in a heavy northeast gale, your vessel may drag her anchor (for it is sandy bottom and not good holding ground) and go ashore and most likely be a total loss.

Sable Island is composed entirely of sand, and is a bleak, dreary place for any one to live, especially so in winter-time. The island is twenty miles long, east and west, and is in the form of a crescent, only about a mile wide at its widest part along the center of the island. At each end there is a long bar that extends out for several miles, over which the water is shallow and breaks furiously in a gale. These are called the "Northeast Bar," and the "Northwest Bar," and they are very dangerous to all shipping, owing to the shallow water so far out from the island. Many hundreds of vessels of all kinds have been cast away on these Bars and thou-

sands of lives lost during the past centuries. The fishermen speak of Sable Island as the graveyard of the Atlantic. There are two lighthouses there, one on each
end of the island, with dwellings for the light-keepers
and their families; also, a fog-whistle station near each
lighthouse and several life saving stations.

Within a few days the *Astoria* had a fine, full trip,
her "salt all wet," and she was deep in the water, for
her hold was full of salted codfish. Then they were
ready to start for home and so the crew washed out
their dories, hoisted them in on the main-deck, stowed
them bottom up, and lashed them securely. The skipper hoisted her colors to the main-truck, the crew
hauled the riding-sail down, got the mains'l up from
the lazaret, bent it and set it, hoisted the fores'l and
then hove in her cable. When her anchor was on the
bow, "cat-headed," they hoisted her jib and she swung
off and filled away, bound home to Southport, where
she arrived on June 3, 1880.

The spring when I was seventeen, I went to Western
Bank hand-line dory fishing for cod, with father who
was skipper of a fine new vessel, the schooner *Lady
Elgin*, seventy-two tons (new measure), built in 1883
by Irving Adams and Son, at East Boothbay, Maine.
She was owned by William T. Maddocks who had a
fish-firm at Ebenecook Harbor, Southport, Maine. She
was built for my father who was to be her skipper and
part owner. I went as "hand," caught an average share
of fish, and did my portion of the work as one of her
crew. It was the custom of the fishermen at Southport,
in those days, to start getting the vessel ready for the
"Bank fishery," about March 25th. The first thing we
did was to take out all her ballast (beach rocks), load
it on scows and dump it at high tide on the beach. The

vessel lay at anchor out in the "stream," during the winter, so we hove in her chain and anchor, hauled her in alongside the wharf, and "bent her sails," while the carpenters were at work putting up salt-pens in her after hold. Then we put on board 180 hogsheads of salt, in her pens, stowed 75 casks of fresh water down in her fore hold and on top we stowed 60 barrels of shucked and salted clams for fish bait. William T. Maddocks, who owned five "Bankers," in the eighties, bought the bait (salted clams) for his vessels in Portland. The five vessels required about 250 barrels and the price paid was $5.50 per barrel. The "clammers" were men who lived around Harpswell Bay and they sold their clams to Portland dealers. These clammers had to dig their bait, for the most part, in March, for during January and February, the flats were often covered with ice. The men were able by hard work to dig several bushels (in the shell) each low tide (two each day), as the clams were very plentiful in that locality. It was a smart man who could dig enough clams in one day to shuck out a barrel of meats. Shucking was done at high water, and also during the evening. About all the Down East vessels bought their bait in Portland, the industry giving employment to several hundred men, for there must have been about a hundred sail of vessels requiring an average of fifty barrels each or a total of 5000 barrels. That industry is now a thing of the past for there are practically no "Banker's" today that go hand-line dory salt cod fishing. Our stores came next: 10 barrels of flour, 5 barrels of plate-beef ("salt horse"), a barrel of salt pork, a barrel of sugar, vegetables, canned goods, and small stores in proportion,— "grub" enough to last sixteen men on a three months' trip. In those days the "Bankers" carried only salt meats, plate beef, hams, bacon, salt spareribs, and salt pork. We had no ice to keep fresh meats, such as all fishing vessels have today (1930). On Sunday we usually had "plum duff" for dinner. The fisherman of today live much better and have more fresh food than the men did in the eighties and nineties.

The *Elgin* carried fourteen dories and these we stowed bottom up on the main deck and lashed securely. We sailed for the Bank on April 8th, and as we passed out by Monhegan Island, the skipper called all hands aft to "thumb the bucket, and set the watch."* Two men were in the watch, one at the wheel, the other for'ard, on the lookout.

As the watch relieved the wheel, the skipper said to him: "Keep her east-south-east, Joe."

"Keep her east-south-east, sir," repeated Joe, as he took his trick at the wheel.

The skipper then got his patent log and log-line from the cabin, came on deck and put it out over the stern and made the line fast to the lee-davit. The patent log gave the distance in knots sailed by the vessel, and was an aid to help the skipper to keep run of his vessel, should it shut in "thick o' fog" on the run across the Bay of Fundy. We had a fresh nor'wester, which was a fair wind, and it gave us a fine run across to the

---

* This custom was followed by most fishermen as the fairest way to set the watch when starting out on a new trip. The crew would stand in a circle holding a bucket so their thumbs were on top. The skipper then turned away his head, and reaching over, touched one of the thumbs, and then counting around from left to right (with the sun) any number previously decided upon. Usually the number chosen was the number of men in the crew. The first man the count reached had the first watch. The counting then began at the next thumb with "one," and so on until each man knew his watch, with the injunction from the skipper, "Remember now, whom you call." The circle then broke up, and the one having the first watch took the wheel.

"Cape," and the next day, at noon, we passed it and that night, at dark, went into Shelburne Harbor, and anchored off Sandy Point.

The next morning two men shipped with us and when they brought their clothes-bags aboard, we got under way and left the harbor. Down the coast a few miles, the north wind hauled out into the no'theast and began to breeze up fresh, so we beat up to wind'ard and went into Liverpool Harbor, and anchored, instead of running off to the Bank, as we had intended doing when we left Shelburne. The skipper said his "glass" (barometer) was rising for an easterly blow and sure enough it blew hard that night and all the next day.

The following day we sailed from Liverpool, and two days later were nearing the Bank, when the wind began to breeze up from the southeast, a head wind for us. It was in the morning and we beat to wind'ard all that forenoon with the wind breezing up all the time. At twelve o'clock noon she had about all she could stagger under with her four lower sails, so the skipper luffed her up into the wind and made a sounding. He had 35 fathoms, on the northern edge of Western Bank, and decided to anchor and ride it out where we were.

The wind increased and blew a gale that afternoon, so we had to "pay out" all our cable of 180 fathoms, to hold on and ride out the heavy southeaster. Southeasters are generally short lived, only about six or eight hours long, and at dark the wind hauled more to the south'ard, still blowing a heavy breeze. The wind kept on hauling, and by eight o'clock that evening it was sou'west and blowing hard. It was very rough at that time, for the *Elgin* lay broadside to the old sea still heaving in from the southeast, and it would slop in

Schooner "Lady Elgin" Hove to under Two-Reefed
Fores'l on the Western Bank, 1886

over her port rail and fill her deck full. The wind kept
on hauling and by ten o'clock that night it was blowing a gale from the nor'west. We had bent on our "riding-sail," and with a good scope of 180 fathoms of
cable out, she was making good weather of it, riding
it out in good shape, for she was a fine sea-boat at
anchor.

At twelve o'clock that night I was called and went
up on deck to stand my anchor-watch of an hour. It
was blowing heavy with a bad sea running. I had been
on deck only a few minutes when I heard a crashing
sound above the gale blowing in my ears, and made my
way up for'ard and soon found out what the trouble
was. Our flying-jib-boom was broken off short in the
cap and this is the way it must have happened. When
the vessel fell in the trough of a heavy sea and smashed

her jib-boom under water, the cable must have caught over the end, and when she arose on the next sea the great strain broke it off short. I hurried aft, went into the cabin, called the skipper and reported the loss of the jib-boom. Father roused up quickly and he and I called "all hands"; then for the next hour we struggled with that wreckage under her bow, to get it clear before it should punch a hole in her hull. By that time my watch was out so I went into the fo'cas'le to call the next man and found him moaning, groaning, and praying and half scared to death. "We'll never live through this awful gale, we'll all be lost! Oh dear! Oh dear!" said he. I couldn't get him to turn out and stand his watch, so had to go on deck and stand it for him, disgusted with his fear of being lost, for I was not afraid, although only seventeen, and he a man twice my age.

Before my second watch was out the *Elgin* broke adrift, and when she fell off broadside to the wind with her riding-sail set, the heavy gale hove her down on her starboard side. Making my way aft along her port side to the cabin, I called the skipper the second time that night. He and I called "all hands" again, and we hauled the riding-sail down; then put a two-reefed fores'l on her, and she drifted for more than three hours, with her anchor dragging over the bottom, and 180 fathoms of cable out. Finally, the anchor fluke took hold and held her. She then swung quickly up head to the wind, and buried her bow under water, chock to her fore-mast, in a smother of sea; so then we had to haul the two-reefed fores'l down and set the riding-sail once more. The wind blew a gale from the nor'west all the next day, which was Sunday, but during the night it moderated somewhat.

Of course riding out a gale on the Bank is disagreeable to the fishermen while it lasts, but the strong winds and heavy seas are not a real danger to them if they are in a good seaworthy vessel. For most likely, she will ride out the gale, if rightly handled and is sound and strong and does not spring a leak. If they keep her hatches well battened down and her companion-slides closed, even if the heavy seas break over her and fill her deck full, she will free herself and ride out the gale in safety.

The night I was born (Jan. 17th) my father was in a Gloucester vessel on George's Bank, where they were riding out a heavy no'theast gale, during a blinding snowstorm. The great anxiety on the part of her skipper and his crew that night, was that some vessel in the large fleet anchored on the Bank to wind'ard of them, would part her cable or drag her anchor, and drift down afoul of them, when both vessels would be quickly smashed to pieces and all hands lost. Their skipper gave orders for the "watch" on deck to keep a sharp lookout to wind'ard for any drifting vessels and to have an axe ready at hand for instant use to "cut" the cable (one blow would be enough for the cable was then under a terrific strain) should they see anything coming. It was almost impossible for a man to look up to wind'ard that night, for the blinding snow and hail, and frozen spray, cut like knives against his face and eyes. It was pitch-black darkness and a howling storm. All that anyone could possibly see would be the flash of a riding-light a few yards away, if a vessel was adrift and coming down fast under their vessel's bow. No vessel fouled them, however, and they rode out the gale in safety. Those men did not fear the heavy gale and angry seas that night, but they did fear collision. That was the real danger for them. When a fishing vessel is bound to market with a trip of fresh fish, her skipper driving her hard, should a storm overtake them, with the wind blowing a gale, and it shuts in thick o' snow or fog, before they make the light which they are running for, and the skipper has run his distance *out*, and his time is *up*, the safe thing to do then is to luff his vessel into the wind and make a sounding. If he has less than twenty fathoms of water he should tack ship and stand off shore, clear of the rocks, out into the open sea where there is comparative safety.

On Monday morning, at 4 A.M. the cook of the *Elgin* blew his whistle and called out loudly: "Starboard gang turn out for breakfast!" Our vessel carried fourteen dories so we had seven on each side, called the "starboard-gang" and the "port-gang." While the starboard-gang were eating their breakfast, the port-gang turned out, put on their boots and oil-clothes, went on deck and hoisted out their dories. By the time they had this work done the starboard-gang had eaten and come on deck, and while we were hoisting out our dories the port-gang went to breakfast. When they had eaten they came on deck and all fourteen men got into their dories and left the vessel. We all rowed out in different directions and when a short distance away anchored our dories and each man threw out his two lines and started fishing. We fished until 9.30 A.M. when the skipper set the signal for the crew to come aboard the vessel for dinner. In clear weather the signal calling the dories was a bushel basket hoisted up on the foretopping-lift, fifteen feet above deck.

In foggy weather a small cannon about twenty inches long (set in a block of wood) was fired. The fishermen spoke of this small cannon as a swivel. When father loaded the cannon, he tipped it up on end and poured in the charge of powder, using a small wad of oakum to keep it in. Then he set it on the heel of the bowsprit, just forward of the windlass and going below into the fo'cas'le, got a red-hot stove-poker, and coming quickly on deck applied it to the touch-hole and so the cannon was discharged. He always protected himself by standing behind the windlass.

For several years, during the sixties, seventies, and early eighties, he used a conch (konk) shell about the size of a cocoanut to call his dories. I remember it well and have blown it many times. On one trip in the schooner *Astoria*, on a very foggy day, the dories were a long time (two to three hours) in coming aboard the vessel, and father blew his conch so often and for so long, that his lips were badly swollen and turned black and it was several hours before he could speak above a whisper. Later on he bought a tin "horn" about three feet long.

When the *Elgin* was built her owners bought a patent fog-horn. The case was of wood about three feet long, a foot wide and fifteen inches high; it had a bellows inside connected with the horn which was on the outside of the box. There was a handle on the other side and we could blow the horn by cranking it. All the modern fishing vessels now carry one.

When the first dory came alongside, the skipper took the dory-painter and passed the man a fork; then held the dory alongside while the man pitched his fish out on deck, he counting the number of his fish out loud, and when all the fish were out, the skipper put the amount down on *his board*, under the man's name, for all hand-line fishermen, fish on shares. The cook held the dory-painters on the port side, and when each man had finished his count of fish, the cook would report the amount to the skipper. After eating a hasty dinner we went out again and fished until 3 P.M., when the signal called us aboard for supper. When alongside we pitched our fish out on deck, then hoisted our dories in, nesting them on top of the cabin-house where they were out of the way, for the deck was full of fish, sometimes 50 or 60 tubs.

The hand-line dory cod fishermen used a method entirely different from other fishermen, when hoisting in their dories. The forward tackle was made fast to the after main shroud and the after tackle was made fast to a ring on the main-boom topping-lift. This method allowed for nesting the dories right side up, one inside of another, on top of the cabin-house. When making the passage to or from the Bank, we hoisted our dories in on the main deck, with the regular fore and main topping-lifts, stowing the dories bottom up and securely lashed. The fore-topping-lift is also used to "cat-head" the anchor and hoist in or out cargo. The main topping-lift is also used on the fore-boom to hoist it out, or set it into the fore-boom crotch and to hoist cargo.

We ate our supper and then started "dressing down" our fish caught that day. On the *Elgin*, we had four "dressing gangs" of three men each, and three salters in the hold. The cook had enough to do without dressing any fish. The three men in each gang are called the "throater," "gutter," and "splitter." We had a large hogshead-tub for each gang which held a quintal-and-a-half of round fish; and a smaller one, called the splitting-tub; also a splitting-table for the use of the splitter. First, the throater and gutter filled the large tub with fish, using two-tine pitchforks. The throater grabbed a fish by the nose with his left hand holding it belly up with the neck across the edge of the tub. With a sharp pointed knife, called a "throating-knife," in his right hand, he drew it across the throat, cutting down on each side of the head; then ripped it down the belly, and with a quick motion of both hands broke the head off and threw it overboard. The gutter grabbed the fish by the nape, placed it on the splitting-table, removed the liver, dropped it into a basket, then pulled out the viscera, and threw it overboard, pushing the fish across the table to the splitter. The splitter took hold of the nape with his left hand holding the fish against a cleat on the table, then, with the splitting-knife in his right hand, starting at the neck, drawing it along near the backbone to the tail, he laid the fish open, and cutting under the backbone near the vent, he siezed it with his left hand, still cutting with the knife, and with a quick motion of both hands he removed the sound-bone; this he threw overboard, and let the fish drop into the splitting-tub. All three of these operations are done much quicker than one can tell about it. Sometimes the large sound-bones were thrown into a barrel for the cook, or anyone who wanted to save sounds. When the split-fish were soaked clean in the tub which had been partly filled with salt water, they were pitched into the hold. The salters placed the fish in "kenches," back down, flat open, napes and tails alternating and then covered them with a scoop full of salt. Salting a trip of fish is an important operation and requires good judgment on the part of the salter, for on him depends the successful completion of a good salt trip. He must know how much salt the large fish require so that they will come out right and not be "slack" or "strong," if he uses too little. If too much, they will come out of the kench "dry-as-a-chip"; also, if he uses too much it is wasted and there will not be enough to complete a full trip.

On my first trip hand-line fishing for cod, in the *Elgin*, at the age of fifteen years, I was "salter's devil." While the crew were dressing fish, I worked in the vessel's hold and it was my job to fill up bushel baskets with salt for the salters. I was then too young to go out in a dory, so I fished with two hand-lines from the vessel's deck and caught 1600 cod during the trip.

The Maine hand-line dory cod fisherman carried on its deck four "liver-butts," which were ordinary molasses hogsheads, each one holding about 160 gallons. Two were set on each side of the quarter deck abreast of the main starboard and port shrouds where they were held in place with "chocks" nailed to the deck around the bottom outside edge, and also lashed securely with rope. The "butts" set upright, with a "scuttle" cut in the head through which the "gutter" could dump the bushel-basket of cod-livers he had removed while "dressing down." At the end of the trip the "butts" would be "full up" with cod-liver oil. During the trip the skipper would bore an inch hole in a stave, near the bottom of each "butt," to let the water off, that had settled at the bottom with the oil on top and when the water was all drawn off and the oil began to run out, he drove in a wooden plug. This oil was not used for medicinal purposes, but sold to the commercial trade, mostly as "tanner's oil." It was worth about fifty cents per gallon in 1885. Massachusetts vessels, especially the hand-line dory fishermen from Marblehead and Provincetown, carried their "liver butts" just forward of the cabin house. Some skippers had them upright, and others stowed them in a cradle.

When our fish were all dressed, we washed down decks and pumped out the vessel, for the salted fish settling in the hold had made a lot of pickle since the night before. Then all went below into the fo'cas'le (except the "anchor watch,"—one man who must stay on deck for an hour), and "mugged up," lighted our pipes for a smoke and "turned in" calling it a day's work for it was then 9 P.M. and we had been up working hard since 4 A.M. The term "mug up" means that we take a mug and fill it with hot coffee or tea, for large pots of coffee and tea are always kept full and hot on the range, made ready by the cook. Then we go to the "shack-cupboard" which is kept well filled with bread, butter, milk, sugar, meat, doughnuts, cake, and pieces of pies left over from the table, where we can get what we want to eat. The shack-cupboard is for the use of "all hands." The cook has another cupboard where he keeps his whole loaves of bread, cake, pies, etc., and the crew all understand they are not to use his cupboard. The terms "turn in" and "turn out," mean going to bed and getting up (from the bunk).

We fished every week day, except when the wind blew too hard and it was too "rough" to go out in our dories fishing. Most of the skippers on the "Down East" hand-line dory "salt trips," observed Sunday and were called "Sunday keepers." I have often heard father say that he believed a crew of men on a "salt trip," would do more and better work and catch a trip of fish much quicker, by observing Sunday as a day of rest.

Foggy weather did not prevent us from fishing; if it had we would have made a long trip sometimes. I recall one trip in the *Elgin* when we were on the sou'-west prong of Banquereau, and had a "fog mull" that lasted for three solid weeks (for we never saw the sun once in all that time), but we fished nearly every day. Thick, foggy weather is dreaded by most fishermen, more especially so by all skippers, for then it is a time of great anxiety, for fear some of their dories may go astray and the men become lost. Many such cases are on record where men have been lost in their dories for days and suffered greatly from cold, hunger and thirst, before they were picked up by some other vessel or steamer. Fog is the greatest menace of the sea. When we were out in our dories fishing in foggy weather, we generally could keep run of our vessel and knew in what direction she lay, when it was time for us to go aboard. But sometimes, in moderate weather, the wind died out and it was calm for awhile, and when it breezed up again it would be from another quarter and we perhaps had not noticed the change which had taken place. On this same trip, one day we were out in the fog and just such a change of wind took place. I thought I knew the direction in which the vessel lay, and when it was time to go aboard I hauled in my dory-anchor and started rowing. Pretty soon I met another dory going in the opposite direction, and the man hailed me and said: "Where yer goin', George?"

"Going aboard," I replied.

"Yer rowin' erway frum th' vessel!" he said.

"Are you sure, Joe, that you are right?" I asked him.

"Sure? Yes!" he replied. "Didn't yer know th' wind shifted 'bout an hour ago, George?"

"No," I replied. I had not noticed that the wind had shifted as I was busy fishing, for it was my first trip in a dory, and without much experience in fog on the Bank, it was easy to lose my sense of direction.

One day when we were all out in our dories fishing, the skipper set the signal at one o'clock P.M. for us to come aboard the vessel. I was fishing down to leeward about half a mile, and as the fish were biting well I was pretty busy trying to get a dory-load of them, so did not see the signal when it was set. Then I heard a gun fired and looking toward the vessel I saw the signal, and could see father up in the main rigging swinging his hat. Then I noticed for the first time that it was black and threatening to wind'ard, with a bad squall coming down on us fast, so I jumped into the bow of my dory, quickly hauled my anchor in, and started rowing as hard as I could toward the vessel; but before I got half way aboard, the squall struck. I rowed as hard as I could for perhaps half an hour, then realized that I was making no headway at all, and had about made up my mind to throw out my anchor and try to hold on, when I looked around toward the vessel and saw two men in a dory coming down after me. As they got down alongside, I threw them my dory-painter, and the three of us rowed hard for more than an hour, before we got up alongside the vessel. When we finally got there I was very tired from my long, hard row, and father must have realized it for he said to me:

"Climb in on deck, son. I'll pitch out your fish!" Father jumped into my dory and pitched the fish out on deck and when he had finished, he climbed out on deck and said:

"Young man, the next time I set the signal for the dories, you get your anchor and start at once for the vessel. I hope you have learned your lesson well today and don't you ever forget it." I never have forgotten, for I am telling you about it now.

We had good fishing for the first two weeks on the Bank, getting from 35 to 40 tubs every day when we could go out, but there were three windy, rough days when we could not fish. We worked down along the Bank to the east'ard, and at the end of the third week found the fish very scarce, so one day we hove in our cable, got our anchor, and with the *Elgin* under "bank-sail," with a fair wind from the sou'west, we ran away to the east'ard, intending to go down to the south'ard of Sable Island. About ten o'clock we sighted a vessel getting under way and when near enough we saw that it was the *Gatherer* of Gloucester. Father knew her skipper, Reuben Cameron, so we went up and "spoke her." We found out from him that he was bound to "Middle Bank" (which lays to the north of Western Bank), for a trawler had spoken the skipper that morning and told him there were plenty of fish there. Father decided to go along too, so both vessels sailed in company. We had a fine run across and made the fleet about dark, gave them a "berth" and anchored on Middle Bank. The next morning the skipper said: "Boys, we'll wait awhile until the dories in the fleet go out, for most likely they are fishing on a 'Bank-clam-spot!'" Sure enough, our skipper was right, for in a few minutes all the dories in the fleet (about 150 of them) rowed out and anchored; all of them huddled together in one great bunch "on the spot." So we all rowed out and anchored our dories close by them. My, what fishing we had! Fish enough to haul a man overboard! All large fish too, 60, 70, and 80 pound cod. They were feeding on what we fishermen call a "Bank-clam-spot."

The Bank-clam is a member of the mussel family. It is about five inches long, two inches in diameter, nearly round in shape, and the color of the shell is a brownish blue-black. These mussels grow in large beds on the bottom in certain places, and are secured by a marine growth so that they will not wash away by the action of the sea. Cod are very fond of them and will hardly ever bite at any other kind of bait when they are feeding on these Bank-clams. The large cod break them off the beds and swallow them whole, and in a short time, when digestion takes place, they throw up the empty shells, retaining their rich yellow meats for food. Our bait, of course, was salted clams, so we had to use it at first, until we caught two or three fish which we cut open and removed the freshly swallowed Bank-clams, which we shucked out and used for bait.

The fish were very plentiful and we all caught them "pair an' pair," as fast as we could "haul 'em." Some of us would have a dory-load by eight o'clock, haul our anchor and row aboard, pitch them out on deck, drop down below in the fo-cas'le for a bite to eat and then go for another dory-load. Some of our smart fishermen would get three dory-loads a day and any of the others would get two. Nate Monroe, our "high-line," would get his three dory-loads and be the first man aboard every day, for he was a marvel, the fastest man to handle his lines and the smartest hand-line dory fisherman I ever saw.

The skipper would call us aboard at two o'clock P.M. each day, for by that time we would have 50 to 60 tubs of fish caught, all we could dress before dark, for father did not believe in making his crew work after dark when "Bank fishing." We fished there only eight days, when the *Elgin's* hold was "chock a block" full of fish. The last day we fished until one o'clock only, and had 56 tubs, most of which we salted on deck, making a "kench" between the cabin-house and the after hatch. The skipper had told the salters to go easy on the salt during the last few days, so that we would have enough for this extra "kench" on deck, which we covered over with a "tarpaulin" and made fast with lashings.

It was the custom in those days to set the colors when a vessel hand-line dory fishing had a full trip, so on the last day father called his dories by hoisting the Stars and Stripes to the *Elgin's* main-truck. When from our dories we saw Old Glory fluttering in the wind, it made us all feel a little proud that *our vessel* was the *one* that was *bound home*. It also told those in the fleet: "That fellow has a trip and is bound home today." After "dressing down and washing up," we hoisted our dories in on the main deck, turned them over and lashed them securely, then got under way and started for home. While on the way I will tell you some incidents of the trip, also some others as they come to my mind.

By way of diversion, in our spare time, we quite often had some music, both vocal and instrumental, for Jim Tom played the fiddle, and Howard Smith the accordion, and this entertainment was the means of much enjoyment for the rest of the crew. The two men would play together, such tunes as: "The Fisher's Hornpipe," "The Devil's Dream," "Catching Hake in Frenchmen's Bay," "Little Nell of Narragansett Bay," and others called for by some member of the crew. Joe Stoddard was a pretty good baritone singer and he could sometimes be persuaded to sing for us, and when he was in the right mood would sing for an hour at a time, such songs as: "Rolling Down to Rio," "Sailing the Dark Blue Sea," "The Wreck of the Hungarian," "Her Last Sleigh Ride," and several others. Here is an incident that happened on one of our Southport vessels.

In the spring of 1885, the fishing schooner *Willie*

G. was hand-line dory fishing on Western Bank. One day when her crew were hoisting in their dories, the man who "broke them down," passed out a water-jug that slipped and fell, striking the rail and breaking the handle off which went overboard, the jug falling on deck. It did not break, however, and was used by the man during the rest of the trip. They secured a full fare, came home, landed their fish, fitted out, and went back on their second trip to Western Bank, and anchored about one hundred miles eastward of where they had fished on their first trip. One day when they were dressing down their deck of fish, the knife of one of the throaters struck something hard, so he ripped open the poke of the fish and great was his surprise (also all of the crew) to find the missing jug-handle which, when tried, fitted the jug perfectly. They brought the jug and its handle home, and put them on exhibition in a glass show-case holding curios, in the Boothbay Harbor Custom House, where I suppose they are today. This incident goes to show how far cod will and do swim on the Bank, while in search of food.

Cod are a very voracious fish and will often grab at almost anything that is falling to bottom, for many curious things have been found in their pokes, and when hungry they will eat most any kind of food. Sometimes we would catch a large cod with a small one in its mouth that was on the hook when the larger cod grabbed it. Then again, sometimes cod are very particular about the kind of bait that they will bite at, when they are after certain kinds of food, for when they are feeding on Bank-clams they don't want anything else; when they are after squid they want no other kind of bait; and when cod are chasing capelin they want them, and nothing else will do. Most all

large fish, especially cod, are cannibalistic, the larger
fish living on and devouring the smaller.

There is usually great rivalry among several mem-
bers of the crew on a hand-line dory cod trip, as to who
among them shall be "high-line." Most of us fished
and worked very hard the whole trip, for we considered it a great honor to be called a "high-line" fisherman, and he, of course, would make the most money,
and the "low-line" the least. On the *Elgin*, that trip,
two of our crew were men we had shipped at Shelburne.
They were brothers and both were "high-line" fishermen, but this was the first trip they had ever been shipmates. During the first half of the trip, Bill fished very
hard and was some 300 fish ahead of his brother Nate.
One day Nate told Bill that he was very foolish to fish
and work so hard while we were fishing in deep water
(35 fathoms). "Wait 'til we get down in shoaler water an' I'll show yer who'll be high-line this trip," I
heard him say. Sure enough, he did show Bill, and all
the rest of us, how he could catch fish on the latter part
of our trip, for when we had the *Elgin* full and left for
home, Nate was "high-line" with 6,600 fish, and Bill
had just about an even 6,000. Nathan Monroe was a
fine fellow, one of the best men I ever met in my life,
and he was the smartest hand-line dory fisherman that
I ever went shipmates with. I was 7th line with 4,500
fish (an average share) and the youngest on board the
vessel. The low-line had about 3,000 fish. The total
number in count for the *Elgin's* trip, was about 64,000,
over half of them large fish. When she arrived home
on June 7th, she was very deep, and when she lay
alongside the wharf, her scuppers were in the water,
for she had brought in the largest trip of salt cod (840
tubs, 1260 quintals), landed at Southport for many
years.

CHAPTER IV

THE FIRST COD TRAWLERS OF NEW ENGLAND

SALT FISHING, 1860-1882

TRAWL-TUBS are used in which to coil the trawl so that it can be more easily handled, and also to prevent the trawl-line from fouling or snarling. Most trawl-tubs are made by sawing a barrel in halves making two tubs. Each "tub-o'-trawl" is rigged in the following manner: ground-line, 300 fathoms, 300 No. 14 cod-hooks, 300 gangings, each three feet long and six feet apart (one end of the ganging is bent on the ground-line, and the hook is made fast to the other end); two buoys, two buoy-lines and two 16-pound anchors (one at each end) to hold the trawl fast when it is set on bottom. One end of the buoy-line is made fast to the anchor before it is thrown out, the other end reaches up to the surface and is bent onto the buoy. Vessels using trawls for cod, haddock and halibut off shore use dories 15 feet long on their bottom, two men going in each dory. The trawlers carry all the way from six to twelve dories, according to the size of the vessel. Each dory sets from four to six "tubs-o'-trawl" when fishing out on the Banks. The fishermen bait their trawls aboard the vessel, using fresh bait (iced or frozen) of menhaden (porgy slyvers), mackerel, herring, squid, clams, or capelin. These fish are slivered (slyvered), and cut up in small pieces about an inch square. One piece is put on each hook.

The first trawling done in New England waters, as far as I have been able to find out, was in 1843 when a man by the name of Atwood fished in Massachusetts Bay for halibut. The first vessel to go trawling for cod was the schooner *Oneco* (skipper Charles Aspley). She went to the Grand Banks in 1845. This first trip was really a failure for they caught only 150 quintals. It is claimed that French vessels fished on the Grand Banks, previous to 1843, using trawls for cod, haddock and halibut. Gloucester fishermen were using trawls in 1854, for we have the account of one, "Peter Sinclair in the *Anna*, who went to the Grand Banks after cod and halibut, and was very successful getting a full trip."

The first "Down East" trawler, was in 1858, when Boothbay sent the *Albatross* (a large pinky of 72 tons) to the Bay of Saint Lawrence where she fished on "Bank Bradley," also around the Magdalen Islands, and brought home 900 quintals of very large cod. In 1860, Southport sent her first trawler, the *Island Queen*. She carried two "Hampton boats," 18 feet long, two men going in each and three "tubs-o'-trawl" for each boat. They also carried hand-lines, for part of her crew to fish in the usual way, catching cod from deck. The two "sets-o'-trawls" were each 1000 fathoms long, and they found large cod so plentiful that they caught them very fast and the crew, who were to fish with hand-lines, found no time to fish, for they were kept busy dressing and catching bait for their trawls. She brought home a full trip of 750 quintals of very large cod. That trip was so successful that other vessel owners at Southport sent some of their vessels trawling to the "Bay." In 1860, there were forty-two sail of Bankers and mackerel vessels owned there, and all the able-bodied men and boys on the island were employed on their own vessels. Southport at that time was called the most prosperous and the wealthiest town in Lincoln County, Maine.

SCHOONER "ISLAND QUEEN," OF SOUTHPORT, MAINE
SAILING "WING AND WING" IN 1862

On June 20, 1862, the schooner *Prima Donna* sailed on a trawling trip with Joseph Spofford as her skipper. My father, then seventeen, went as one of her crew and has often told me much about that trip, when he was in a reminiscent mood. The *Prima Donna* was a fine new vessel of about 62 tons and carried 800 quintals of salted codfish when she had a full trip. She was owned by Thomas and Naham Marr, at Marr's Harbor, Southport. At that time Southport trawlers were using dories instead of the large "Hampton boats," as at first, and the *Prima Donna* had five dories, with ten men in her crew, the skipper and cook making twelve.

The reason for the changing over from the use of "Hampton boats," to dories was because the crew could "break down" (knock down the thwarts and kidboards where they would lay flat in the bottom of the dory) the dories when hoisting them in to nest them, one inside of another, thus taking up very little room on deck. The "Hampton boats" could not be nested, and took up a lot of room on a vessel's deck.

They took with them a string of herring nets, about a dozen in all, each one 20 fathoms long. These were to catch bait for their trawls. They were nearly a week making the run from Southport to the Gulf of Saint Lawrence and at first fished well to the north'ard, but found fish rather scarce and small in size.

One day they worked over toward the Magdalen Islands and made a set of their trawls but got very few fish on them, so they got under way again and ran away to the sou'west and that evening the wind died out and the vessel lay becalmed. One of her crew found a codline, baited it with fresh herring and threw it overboard, more in a spirit of fun than anything else, for he had nothing to do. As soon as his lead reached bottom, he sprang into action for he felt strong tugging and twitching on his line, as large cod were biting and soon he was slowly and laboriously hauling them in.

"Git th' gaff ready, skipper! I must have a couple o' whales on this here line by th' way she hauls," he said. When he had his fish up alongside the vessel, the skipper, with his long-handled gaff, hauled them in on deck, a pair of as fine, handsome, large cod as a man could wish to see.

"Let go th' anchor! Let your sails run down, an' furl 'em up. I guess there's fish 'nough here," said skipper Joe.

They had anchored on "Bank Bradley," and that night set their herring-nets by making them fast to the stern of the vessel and let them swing with the tide. The next morning, when they hauled them in, they found plenty of herring for bait, so they "baited up" and then went out to set their trawls. When the crew went out in their dories they each rowed in a different direction; one dory went from the starboard quarter, another from the port quarter, one from the port bow, one up ahead, and the other from the starboard bow. When out clear of the vessel, with one man rowing, the other threw out the inner trawl-buoy which had been made fast to the buoy-line. The buoy had a pole four feet long on the end of which was a small canvas flag. When the buoy-line was all out he threw out the anchor, which was made fast to the ground-line, on which were the baited hooks. When one tub of line was all out he grabbed another, made the end fast and continued throwing until the trawl was all out. He then made the end fast to the outside anchor, which he threw out, then the buoy-line and lastly the buoy. The outside buoy had a pole four feet long on the top of which was a "black ball" flag, and the outer end of the trawl was nearly two miles from the vessel. When the trawl was all out, the ground-line, with its baited hooks, laid along on the bottom and the fish swallowed the bait, the hook catching in the throat holding them fast.

Trawls are set at different times in the day, often in the morning, and hauled once or twice during the day. Sometimes they are set in the evening, for night fishing, and are hauled, or sometimes "under-run" in the morning. When fishermen "under-run" their trawl, the anchors are left out, the ground-line is hauled up and across the dory, for as they haul along they remove the fish, and let the line run out over the other side of the dory, until at the inner end of the trawl. This method of fishing is called "under-running."

When the *Prima Donna's* crew went out to haul their trawl they rowed out to the outer buoy, if it were clear weather so they could find it (if it was "thick" they started at the inner buoy) and hauled in the buoy-line and anchor, then the ground-line, hauling toward the vessel so that when the trawl was in and they had a dory-load of fish, they would be nearer the vessel. When they started to haul, the bow-man hauled the trawl in over a "trawl-roller," on the starboard bow of the dory and the man behind him unhooked the fish and coiled the trawl-line in the trawl-tub.

Sometimes, when fish are very plentiful, the fishermen get a dory-load by the time the trawl is half hauled. They then make the buoy fast to the trawl and let it swing free while they are gone to the vessel with their load and then return and finish hauling. This was the case on that trip of the *Prima Donna*, for fish were so plentiful and of such large size, that they often had a dory-load by the time the trawl was one quarter hauled. They never were able to haul *all* their trawl in the usual way. All they could do was to "under-run" it a few hundred fathoms at either end, when they would have a dory-load of large cod. These fish were there after herring. Finally the four younger men of the crew, fishing in two dories, told the skipper they could bring aboard the vessel all the fish the older men could dress. So the skipper had the older men stay aboard and dress, while the youngsters hauled their trawls and brought the fish aboard. The fish were all very large cod weighing (whole), from 60 to 70 pounds each, and ten of them would fill a quintal-and-a-half tub. When a dory came alongside the vessel, deep as she could swim, the crew were obliged to haul the large fish out on deck with long-handled gaffs, for they were unable to fork them out in the usual way. In about three weeks they filled the hold of the *Prima Donna* solid full, and then set sail for home.

The average price of dry salt cod in those days was about $2.50 per quintal, with large fish $3.00, but the owners sold that trip to parties in New York City for a special price of $4.00 per quintal.

Since about 1853, when the New England fishermen first began trawling for cod (salt fishing), there have been many vessels engaged each year in this fishery, even up to the year 1920. I should say the trawl salt cod fishery reached its height during the ten years from 1880 to 1890. Previous to 1890 most of the trawl fishermen dressed and salted all their cod. Of late years many of them have changed over and carried ice in pens, to bring part or the whole of their trips in as fresh fish.

Gloucester, for many years, sent more trawlers salt fishing than any other New England fishing port. In

1880 she sent a fleet of about 200 sail. For several years she also sent a large fleet of George'smen hand-line fishing from deck, but she never has sent a large fleet hand-line dory fishing for cod.

Provincetown, during the years from 1870 to 1890, sent a large fleet, most of them vessels of 150 tons, some up to 250 tons, that brought home large trips of 2,000 quintals, on up to 3,500 quintals, from Western Bank, Banquereau and the Grand Banks, where they had secured trips of salt cod by the hand-line dory method of fishing. The Portland fleet, in those days, that went fishing for cod, were for the most part hand-line dory fishermen that went off shore, on the Banks. Some small vessels went trawling on the nearby inner Banks along the coast. Most of the "Down East" vessels in those years, that went salt fishing, were hand-line dory fishermen. Only a few went trawling off shore, Bank fishing.

Most of the trawlers that went on salt trips for cod, were Gloucester vessels, and they were for the most part larger vessels than the average hand-line dory fishermen. They carried a flying-jib-boom and a fore-top-mast, so they could carry more sail. They used fresh bait for their trawls, and as a baiting would last them only about ten days, they would have to go in after more, two or three times, before they had secured a trip. These trawlers on salt trips lost much time going in to land after a baiting, for many times when bait was scarce and hard to find, they often spent a week or more going from one harbor to another at Newfoundland, before they could find any bait.

During the eighties and nineties, Gloucester trawlers on salt trips after cod bought fresh herring (*Clupea harengus*, Linn.), from the local fishermen at Newfoundland (during the spring and also late in the fall), mostly caught in gill-nets; some of the local fishermen, however, used a small purse-seine.

In June, the capelin, a small boreal fish (*Mallotus villosus*, Cuv.), was used for bait. During the summer season the bait used was squid (*Ommastrephes illecebrosa*), and these were caught in the harbors, by local "liviers," from punts, skiffs, and wherries, with a squid-jig and line. The squid-jig is a little larger than a mackerel-jig (three inches long). The lower end has eight pins set in the lead and these are bent up U-shaped. A little tallow is sometimes pushed in around the lower end to make a more attractive bait. When the fishermen pull the squid out of the water they squirt a stream of ink, and so the men hold them out a few seconds, for the ink might strike them in the face and fill their eyes, causing great pain. When squid are first caught they are about the color of a brick, but in a short time turn to a pale yellow color.

That bait condition existed until the advent of cold storage plants, where bait is now sold to the fishermen. Of late years our New England fishermen have been able to buy their bait at Boston, Provincetown, Gloucester, Portland and Boothbay Harbor, at the large local freezers.

The trawlers that went salt fishing, "dressed and salted" all their fish, as did the hand-line dory fishermen, and usually by the time the third or fourth baiting was used up they would have a hold full of salted cod. These trawlers, like the hand-line dory vessels, did not carry any ballast, for the large amount of salt, ice for bait, water in barrels, and stores, put them in trim until they caught some fish. They usually fished in deeper water than the hand-line dory-fishermen, often fishing in 50 to 70 fathoms. I have seen many Gloucester trawlers on Western Bank, and Banquereau, fishing off on the edge of the Bank.

The crew on "trawlers" go on a different "lay" than the "hand-liners," and perhaps it will be well for me to explain here the different "lays." The crews on trawlers for either cod, haddock or halibut, also the crews on all mackerel seiners, the gill-net mackerelnetters, also cod-netters, and swordfishermen, the flounder-draggers and herring-netters, "all share and share alike." The gross stock is divided: one half goes to the owners of the vessel, the other half is divided among the crew. The owners furnish the vessel, dories and trawl-gear, salt, bait and stores and pay the skipper his percentage, which is usually from 5 to 7 per cent, out of their half. The crew pay the cook his wages, which is usually from thirty-five to forty-five dollars per month; this is first deducted from their half. The remainder is divided equally among all the crew, including the skipper and cook, for they receive a share, as well as their per cent and wages.

All hand-line fishermen for cod, halibut, mackerel, and pollock, have half the money their fish bring, each man sharing in proportion to his own catch. The other half goes to the owner of the vessel. The "high-line" earns the most money and the "low-line" the least; all the rest share in between. The skipper has half the money his fish brings, and his percentage extra. The cook has half the money his fish brings, and his cook's wages extra. This method is called by the fishermen "fishing on halves." When a fishing vessel brings in a large trip of fish that sells for a fair price, she will make a good stock, which means the gross earnings for her trip.

Chapter V

The Mackerel Purse-Seine Fishery
Salt Fishing, 1864-1881

MACKEREL are caught with the purse-seine when they are schooling on or near the surface of the sea. The first purse-seine known to Southport fishermen was in the early sixties. It was a very crude affair about one hundred fathoms long and ten fathoms deep, knit of rather coarse twine which made it very bulky, heavy and hard to handle. The first one I know anything about was brought there from Boston in 1864 by Amherst Spofford. It was bought by ten fishermen at Cape Newagen, who formed a stock company and secured a small fishing vessel named *Niagara*. They also purchased a large, square-sterned boat. A purse-seine in those days cost quite a sum of money ($2,400.00), for it was in wartime and cotton twine was very high in price. But so were mackerel, for they brought about $30.00 per barrel. That purse-seine had only about one fourth the amount of twine, but it cost three times as much as a seine did during the eighties, when we were fishing with a purse-seine that was two hundred and twenty-five fathoms long and twenty-two fathoms deep and was made of fine cotton twine steam-tarred. These men at Cape Newagen caught a lot of mackerel with their seine, in the nearby waters, and did well, making some money. Soon after that date (1864), other vessel owners, all along the coasts of Maine and Massachusetts, bought purse-seines for their vessels and in a few years' time there was quite a large fleet of seiners, perhaps 250 sail.

73

During the season of 1875, Skipper Hanson B. Joyce of Swan's Island, Maine, in his fine fishing schooner *Alice*, was "high-line" of the New England mackerel purse-seine fleet; he was "high-line" each year up to and including 1881. During the season (April to November) of 1881, the last year that he was "high," he landed in his schooner the most mackerel (4,900 barrels) ever brought in by any one skipper of the mackerel fleet. Most of them were dressed and salted but some 1,000 barrels were landed fresh. His vessel stocked $28,000.00, the largest stock ever made in the mackerel fleet up to that time. However, his stock was not large but rather small for the vast amount of fish landed, for mackerel brought only five to six dollars per barrel that season, as a very large amount (392,000 barrels) was landed by the fleet. The 4,900 barrels landed by skipper Joyce would bring a small fortune today for the owner, the skipper, and his crew.

In the month of July, 1881, in one week, he landed two full trips of 500 barrels each, a total of 1,000 barrels. During the summer of 1880, he went to Chaleur Bay, caught and brought home a trip of 700 barrels of salt mackerel. Skipper Joyce was the greatest mackerel purse-seine fisherman that Maine ever produced and during the six years that he was "high-line" ('75 to '81), he landed an enormous amount of fish. For several years after this date he was up among the best fishermen and brought in each season a very large amount of fish, his vessel making a large stock and he and his crew shared well each year, earning from $1,000.00 to $1,200.00 each, for the season of eight months. The "high-line" skippers had their pick of the best men and always had a fine crew, for the fishermen were anxious to "ship" with the best skippers (as

Schooner "Niagara" at Anchor in Newagen Harbor,
Southport, Maine, 1864

they were more likely to make a good season's work) and many of them had the same crew for several years.

In those days, during the seventies and eighties, many times very large schools of mackerel were caught at one haul of the purse-seine, all the way from 300 to 700 barrels. Most of the mackerel were then dressed and salted at sea, where they were caught, and when they got a large haul the fishermen had to bail them on deck, filling her full from rail to rail, from windlass to wheel-box, for they dare not leave the fish in the seine very long, as the dogfish and mackerel-sharks would gnaw holes in it and let the fish out, for the seine was made of fine twine. The holes made by the dogfish and mackerel-sharks had to be mended before the seine could be used again and this was a great loss of time as well as loss of money to the men, for often it prevented them from getting another catch while the fish were yet schooling, as frequently they stayed up only a short time. In the summer time, on hot days when the vessel's deck was full of fish, they grew soft very quickly, and before the crew could get the mackerel all dressed and under salt, some of them would spoil and were not fit to dress. So the fishermen felt there was a great need of devising some way by which they could keep mackerel alive and fresh, alongside their vessel, when they had secured a large school.

Skipper Joyce felt this great need keenly and being a progressive and resourceful man he devised a "bag-net," in the summer of 1877, and had one made of haddock ganging-line to keep mackerel in, alongside his vessel, when they got a large school at one set of the seine. This "bag-net" was called by the fishermen a "mackerel pocket"; sometimes it was called a "spill-er." In 1878, H. E. Willard, of Portland, invented and used a "mackerel pocket" that was fairly successful and he had it patented. In 1880, George Merchant, Jr., of Gloucester, invented and put into practical use, an improved "mackerel pocket," and soon all seiners were fitted out with one. This "pocket" was knit of very coarse twine, with small meshes and was heavily tarred and the fishermen were happy to find that it would resist the ravages of the dogfish, when it held a school of fish, for dogfish are a real menace and a curse to all mackerel purse-seine fishermen. When the "pocket" was not in use it was rolled up on the starboard rail of the vessel. They were made in different sizes according to the size of the vessel, but most of them were about thirty-six feet long, fifteen feet wide and forty feet deep. There were two "bag-booms," fifteen feet long, fastened to the vessel's rail, one just aft the fore rigging, the other just forward of the main rigging; with guys on the outer ends to hold them. These booms were swung up alongside the rigging when not in use.

When the fishermen had caught a large school of mackerel in the purse-seine, and wished to trip them out of the seine into the "mackerel pocket," the crew lowered the bag-booms down near the surface of the sea, then hauled the "pocket" out to the ends, near which lay the seine-boat. With the fish in the seine the corks were then laced on to the outside edge of the "pocket," and the purse-weight (80 pounds) was made fast to the center, which sunk it down under water. The crew in the boat then dried in on the twine and spilled the mackerel out of the seine into the "pocket." These "mackerel pockets" would hold three hundred barrels or more. When the fishermen had made a large haul with their purse-seine, they would spill the fish out of their seine into the "pocket"; then bail out on deck about fifty barrels at a time and dress them and in this way they were enabled to dress a whole trip in good order.

When skipper Joyce and other skippers as well, got a large haul of mackerel in the purse-seine and had spilled them into the "mackerel pocket," with his vessel "hove to," while his crew were at work dressing, he would often haul her fores'l down, furl it up, and lay under her mains'l. A mackerel seiner that lay under her mains'l, out at sea, was often spoken of by a fisherman on some other vessel close by as follows: "That fellow has got a mains'l haul." This saying meant that he saw a vessel (mackerel seiner) which had a large haul of mackerel in the "pocket" alongside, lying under her mains'l, her crew busy at work dressing their fish at sea where they had caught them. Skipper Joyce was not only "high-line" each season for six years, but he was often among the first to land a trip of mackerel in New York, each spring.

During the seventies, only a few vessels went south in the spring, after mackerel, perhaps fifty sail; but during the eighties more vessels went and the fleet soon increased to one hundred and fifty sail. Maine sent fifty sail, Massachusetts, one hundred. Those from the Maine seaports were mostly from Portland, with a few from Southport, Boothbay Harbor, Swan's Island, Deer Island and Vinal Haven. Those that went from Massachusetts were mostly from Gloucester, as she sent the largest fleet of all. Quite a fleet also went from Wellfleet, Dennis, Harwich and Barnstable.

Some of the famous skippers of the seining fleet during the past fifty years, whom I recall, were Sol Jacobs, Hans Joyce, Eben Lewis, John Seavey, Johnnie Vautier, Frank Hall, Joe Smith, Rube Cameron, Joe Swim,

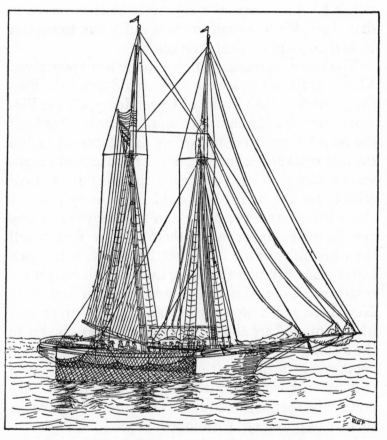

SCHOONER "ALICE," WITH MAINS'L HAUL, DRESSING
MACKEREL FROM A POCKET, 1881

Maurice Whalen, Charlie Harty, Al Miller, Marty Welch, Ambrose Fleet, Lem Firth and John Dahlmer. These skippers all had fine fishing vessels, the best in the fleet in their day, and most of them were very fast sailers for the seiners as a rule were built for speed so that their skippers could make a quick run to market with their trips of fresh mackerel.

The southern mackerel fleet usually left home about March 20th and in a week they would be on the fishing grounds in the vicinity of Cape Henry, off the Virginia coast. Some went as far south as Bodie Island, off the North Carolina shore, where they expected to find the first mackerel schooling. The first mackerel caught were taken to New York, even though only a small school, for the first fish in, sold for a fancy price of about thirty cents per pound. In those days of sailing vessels, their skippers sailed them to New York to sell their first fish at Fulton Market, but today, with much better transportation facilities, the first fish caught are taken into Cape May and shipped, iced in barrels, to New York and Boston. By so doing the fishermen save much time and are able to return much more quickly to the fishing grounds where, perhaps, they may catch another trip during the time that is saved by not going to New York with their fish. Later on, when the mackerel are farther northward, the fishermen of today take their trips into New York to sell.

In the spring, mackerel are moving northward most of the time, and only school occasionally. The rest of the time they are swimming under water, so it is difficult for the fishermen to keep run of the fish. They often "jog" their vessels with jib to wind'ard, heading northward most of the time, trying to keep with the mackerel; then when they "show," they will be "on fish." In those days of sailing vessels, when the fleet had good fishing (many of them making big hauls), the fastest sailers reached market first and got a good price for their fish, of from 10 to 20 cents a pound, making a good stock, their crews sharing well for the trip and often making a hundred dollars. But it was a much different story with the slow sailers, the last vessels in, for they often had to sell for a low price. I remember one spring in the eighties, when there was a large fleet of a hundred sail in New York, all of them with large trips of 200 to 300 barrels. The first vessels in sold their fish, but many of the later arrivals could not sell at all, at any price, for the market was glutted, and they had to dump their whole trips overboard when they got outside again.

The southern mackerel fleet of sailing vessels often were fifty miles or more off shore when looking for fish, and were not able to seek shelter when a storm came on, so had to stay outside and ride out the gale. The fishermen did not dread this for the safety of their vessels, for they would weather the storm all right, but they did fear for the safety of their seine-boats, for the loss of their boats would spoil their trips. During a heavy gale, which may last two or three days, the seine-boat often fills with water from the spray and breaking seas, and when she has become water-logged she tows badly and often capsizes; then, as the vessel surges ahead, the boat is badly strained and the planking at the stern finally opens up and the boat is ruined. A seine-boat, when bottom up, often tows under and dives, and either parts her painter or has to be cut adrift, so that when the storm is over, the vessel has to return home for a new seine-boat. When the mackerel had worked farther northward, off the New Jersey coast, sometimes skippers would run into New York with two or even three trips a week. By May 10th, the fish would be off Fire Island, Montauk Point, Block Island and around Nantucket (South-Shoal) Lightship. Then when they got trips, they often would go into Newport Harbor, and sometimes to Boston. Usually they were away from home, on the spring southern trip, about six weeks, and by May 15th, would return home and "fit out" for the "Cape Shore."

It was in the early eighties when mackerel seiners first went on the "Cape Shore" trip to the southern coast of Nova Scotia. The fishermen soon found out that the fish appeared regularly each spring off Liverpool, about May 20th, and would school part of the time while on their way down the coast, bound to Chaleur Bay, and the Gulf of Saint Lawrence, where they would spawn during June. Most of the time when the fish were schooling they were swimming very fast, going to the eastward about four miles an hour, nearly as fast as a crew of men could row a seine-boat and the skipper must place his seine-boat well ahead of the school before starting to set his seine, so that it would have time to sink down below the fish before they struck the twine, which would turn them back, or else they could swim clear by going out under the bottom of the seine. Most skippers set their seines in the form of an ellipse rather than in a circle, as was the usual way when the fish were not going so fast in a given direction. At that time, 1880-90, most of the vessels went salt fishing and their holds were full of barrels and salt, for they dressed and salted their fish; but a few of the fast sailers carried some ice in pens as well as barrels and salt. The skippers of these vessels would have their crews dress the first two or three hauls of fish and when all their barrels were filled, would ice the last school caught and as soon as they had them bailed out on deck they would set every inch of canvas and drive the vessel hard to Boston market.

Of course, mackerel seining was then, and is today, very uncertain work, the most so perhaps of any New England fishery. Some skippers did not get any mackerel on their "Cape Shore trip," while others got good trips. Some few of the "killers" (the smartest skippers) would get "big trips" quickly and be the first home. Skipper Sol Jacobs was the first home from the "Cape Shore" with a "big trip" for several years, as well as the first skipper into New York with a trip, when out South in the early spring. I recall one skipper who did not get any fish at all on the "Cape Shore" trip, but on his way home he swung his vessel off and went down the South Channel and got a fine, full trip off Sankety Head, in three days time, and when he arrived in Gloucester, surprised the whole water-front with his "good luck."

About July 1st, many of the vessels which had been trawling for cod and haddock during the winter, changed over and went seining during the summer, and the vessels which had been hand-line dory cod fishing, to Western Bank, during the spring (mostly Down East vessels), now changed over and fitted out for seining. All of these vessels, plus those which had been seining out South during the spring, made up a large fleet of 500 sail of mackerel seiners. One day in the summer of 1885, when seining in the *Lady Elgin*, while she was "jogging with jib to wind'ard," off Monhegan Island, I counted from the masthead, a fleet of over 300 sail in sight at one time. I have often seen Boothbay Harbor so full of seiners that you could walk from one to the other, for many were anchored so close to each other that their crews lashed them together.

Forty-five and fifty years ago, during the summer months, mackerel were very plentiful off the Maine coast down into the Bay of Fundy. The best fishing grounds then were off Mt. Desert Rock, Matinicus Rock, Monhegan Island, Seguin Island, Cape Elizabeth, and after September 1st, off Boone Island, Isles of Shoals, in Ipswich Bay, Massachusetts Bay, and late in the fall, off Cape Cod. For the past ten years, 1920 to 1930, mackerel have not gone nearly so far to the eastward as they formerly did, for most of the fish of late years have been caught on George's Bank, down the South Channel, out around No Man's Land, Nantucket Lightship, Block Island, around Cape Cod and off Thatcher's Island.

When out seining, the fishermen seldom try to fish in foggy weather as it is very difficult for them to keep run of either vessel or the seine-boat. Neither do they try to fish when the wind blows fresh and the sea is rough and choppy, for it will fill the seine-boat; so they usually run into some harbor for shelter, if the skipper thinks it is going to breeze up and blow hard with stormy weather. When seiners are outside, cruising for mackerel, they always have a man on the foremasthead on the "lookout," who scans the surface of the sea, far and near, with a practiced eye for any signs of a "school," and when he sees one he sings out lustily: "School O'!" The vessel is then swung off in that direction to sail near it, and their seine-boat is made ready, to set the purse-seine around the school.

Sometimes when they are out cruising and the lookout does not see fish schooling, he may see some vessels, five or six miles away, which he thinks are "on fish," by their actions, for he knows by experience that these vessels are not simply sailing along in the usual way; so he will call out to the skipper: "Skipper, I think them vessels out to the south'ard, are on fish!" The skipper would then say to the wheelsman: "Swing 'er off south!" The skipper would then go up on the mast-head himself, and in a little while, as they sailed nearer, they would be able to see several "boats out," for soon one vessel hauls her jib down, "heaves to," and starts "bailing," as her crew had been out and set their seine and caught a school of mackerel. In a short time every vessel in sight will be on her way, with every sail set, so that they, too, can make a set, and this is one of the reasons why skippers want smart sailing vessels, so they can beat the other fellow and get there first, before the "bunch of fish" is broken up.

When mackerel come up and "school," there are nearly always many schools showing at one time, perhaps from fifty to one hundred, covering an area of a square mile. Some are large schools, while others are small ones, containing only a few barrels of fish. Mackerel often "school" best in the morning and stay up until seven or eight o'clock; then they "settle away" for the day. Sometimes they will "show" again in the late afternoon; at other times, not until just before sunset. Some days they may not "come up" again at all. Some days the fish are very wild and hard to catch, diving under the purse-seine each time it is set; on other days they are easy to catch.

There are many signs that tell the fishermen, when we are out on the fishing grounds, that mackerel are in the nearby waters; such as "gannets," "flocks of sea-geese," many "fin-back whales," and "porpoises" sporting about, with several "calm slicks" showing.

Sometimes one can actually smell mackerel when they are "up schooling" to windward. I have many times. When any of these "signs" are observed we "heave to" and "jog" with the "jib hauled to wind'ard," and wait for the mackerel to "show."

Many fishermen can tell most of the vessels in the fleet by their appearance and name them, if they have ever seen them before and are familiar with their rig, size, shear of hull, and general appearance. When I was seining in the *Elgin,* one of our crew was a man named Thomas Lundy. He was very unusual in this respect, for he had a "faculty" for telling a vessel and could tell you her name right off if he had ever seen her before. Sometimes there would be an argument among the crew about the name of a certain vessel, and often in the end they would ask Tom, and he most always knew and could tell them her name. No two vessels ever built look exactly alike, any more than two persons. The experienced fisherman can tell not only a vessel's name, if he has ever seen her before, but he knows what fishery she is engaged in, for he can tell the trawler from the hand-line dory fisherman, the fresh halibut trawler from the George'sman, and the gill-netter from the swordfisherman, or mackerel seiner. He can tell the yacht from the coaster, and an American vessel from a Nova Scotian vessel, when they are three or four miles distant. Farther than that they are very hard to tell, but can be seen eight to ten miles away on a clear day. From the masthead I have seen, on a very clear day, the tops of vessels' sails on the horizon which were distant twelve or more miles (estimated), when their hulls were not visible due to the curvature of the earth. There are as great differences in vessels as there are in people; some are beautiful, while others are homely.

Some vessels are reliable and dependable and will obey the helm quickly; are sure to come about when the skipper rolls the wheel down, or will swing off smartly when he rolls the wheel up. The skipper knows she will take him off a lee-shore in a gale (for she is able and will carry her sail well, sailing fast in rough water) and he knows she will not fail him in a tight place. A man soon becomes attached to a fine, able, fast-sailing vessel, and often learns to love her as something alive. I have known of several such men. Take the case of Tom McLaughlin who sailed his fine, able, fast-sailing schooner, the *Sarah H. Prior*. He often would walk down to the wharf where she was lying and stop and admire her and say: "What a vessel! What a vessel!" Some vessels are cranky, tricky and unreliable, for they will lay down in a blow, often misstay, and get "in irons" when in a bad place near rocks or bars, and finally cause you no end of trouble.

Mackerel seining in the night was first tried by some fishermen, about 1874, with success. Soon others heard about it and in a few years, night fishing was practiced by all the purse-seine fishermen. Mackerel seldom, if ever, school in the night, but when a body of fish are moving near the surface, a fathom or two under water, they are easily seen from the masthead on a dark night, as a bright glow in the water, owing to the phosphorescence which shows any moving object in the sea. Night fishing on a seiner is called by fishermen, "owling."

The method of seining for mackerel in the night, during the eighties, on sailing vessels was as follows: The vessel was under sail, out on the fishing grounds, on a dark night when the weather was favorable, with her skipper on the fore-masthead usually (some ves-

sels had a masthead-man); the cook was at her wheel
and the crew in the seine-boat, which was towing astern
on a short painter on the starboard quarter, with two
men in the dory towing astern, their painter made fast
to the boat. The crew always dressed warmly in their
oil-clothes and sea-boots, for the nights were cold in
the spring and fall when night fishing was carried on.

When the skipper was on the fore-masthead, in the
night, looking for a school, he usually asked some
member of the crew, the most capable man, to take the
steering-oar in the seine-boat while the seine was being
set. When the skipper saw a school he would call out
loudly to the cook, who was at the vessel's wheel:

"Starboard your wheel! Steady, now! Port a little,
cook! Steady, as you go!"

This manouvering was to bring the vessel up nearer
the school, with the fish off on her starboard side, then,
when she was in the right position, he would sing out
loudly to the crew in the boat: "Let go th' end o' your
seine! Cast off th' painter!"

Under his directions the crew then rowed the boat
and threw out the seine, making a large circle enclosing the school, the steersman guiding the seine-boat
around, then up alongside the dory-man who had been
left at the end of the seine to pass the purse-line. It
was very difficult to make a good set in the night, so
that the seine-boat would meet the dory's end and
bring the two ends of the seine together, so that the
crew could purse it up; otherwise it was quite impossible to do so. For this reason, a lighted lantern was
carried in the dory and it was concealed in a "canvas-
pocket" by the man in the stern. This light the dory-
man showed, once in awhile, as a guide for the steersman in the seine-boat.

No light was shown in the seine-boat while pursing the seine, for it would attract the fish and they would go out under the boat. After the seine was pursed, two torches were lighted and shown so that the crew could see to do their work. The lights would also show those on board the vessel where the boat was, so they could keep run of her. Sometimes when the lights in the seine-boat were extinguished,* those on board the vessel would be unable to find her until daylight, and the whole crew would be obliged to stay out until picked up by the vessel.

One fall when seining in the *Astoria*, we were off Sandwich, one very dark, foggy night, with very little wind during the early evening, but father would not fish that night as he said the barometer was falling fast and we were likely to have a heavy squall. The squall struck very suddenly about ten o'clock that night coming from the northeast, and he beat the *Astoria* up into Provincetown harbor where we anchored with the wind blowing half a gale. A number of skippers were fishing that night (a reckless thing to do with a squall likely to strike at any moment), and their crews had a hard time of it, for seine-boats filled with water, several men were drowned, and several vessels lost their seine-boats, purse-seines, fish and all.

As a rule, mackerel are easily caught in the night, when the purse-seine is set around the school properly, for they very seldom dive the seine, as they often do in the daytime. Mackerel purse-seine fishermen do not fish in the night, during the warm summer months, as the water does not "fire" then. The fishermen speak

---

* Two kerosene torches were used and sometimes were blown out by the wind. If the crew had no dry matches, they had to stay out in the seine-boat in the darkness.

of the phosphorescence in sea-water as: "The water 'fires' well tonight!" or perhaps they will say, at other times: "The water does not 'fire' at all tonight!" Any moving body that disturbs the sea on a dark night (on the dark of the moon), causes a phosphorescent glow in and also on the surface of the water. A body of mackerel moving in the water, a vessel's wake, or waves thrown off by her bow, a rope dragging in the water, or a draw-bucket dipped into the sea, will sparkle with a glow of faint light. One can easily see these sparkles on the hand, the oil-clothing, the boots, the deck, any place where the water strikes.

In my boyhood days, when mackerel fishing in the good old schooner *Astoria* (she was then thirty years old and her hull now lies at the bottom of the sea on the Grand Bank off Newfoundland), we were seining for mackerel in the fall of the year, "up to the westward," a term used by the "Down East," Maine, fishermen. I was only thirteen years old when this incident happened, but I remember it as clearly as if it were only yesterday. It was a beautiful day in late September and we lay becalmed off the Magnolia shore. The skipper was leaning over the rail, aft, looking down into the clear water, when suddenly he gave the command: "Man the boat! Quietly now, boys, don't make any noise!"

The crew, snatching their oil-clothes and sea-boots, climbed quickly, but quietly into the seine-boat, where she lay at the boat-boom alongside the vessel. Pushing the boat astern, they put out their oars and backed her up to a point just off the starboard-quarter and then began to set the seine. They were rowing the boat as fast as they possibly could and with the skipper steering her, they made a complete circle around the vessel, back to the dory, at the end of the seine, and began to "purse 'er up" and "dry 'er in." While the crew were pursing the seine, the cook and I, on board the vessel, were trying to get her out of the seine. With the aid of a little puff of wind, she fanned along and when her bow reached the cork-rope, the cook and I, with a long seine-boat-oar, pushed it down under her fore-foot and it slowly slid along under her bottom as she moved ahead and out of the seine.

A few minutes later one of our crew found a large mackerel caught in the twine and then he asked the question:

"Skipper, how'd you know these 'ere mack'rel was 'ere?" The skipper smiled, then said:

"Boys, dry 'er in and let's see what we've got!"

When we had the fish bailed out on deck, dressed down and salted, we found we had caught sixty barrels of fine, large, No. 1, mackerel.

The skipper told the boys shortly afterward that while leaning over the vessel's rail, he had seen the school passing under her, about three fathoms down in the clear waters.

The same fall, during October when mackerel were not schooling well, we would often "heave to" and throw "toll-bait," to bring the fish up alongside, where we could catch them with "jig and hand-line." When they were biting well and the skipper thought there might be a good "school" of fish under the vessel, he would say: "Haul in your lines, boys! Now get into the boat quickly!" They would go out in the seine-boat and set the seine by making a complete circle around the vessel and "purse 'er up." The cook and I would throw "toll-bait" to keep the fish "up" in the seine; then we would haul aft the fore sheet, hoist the jib, roll the wheel hard up, and sail the vessel out of the seine by pushing the cork-rope down under her fore-foot, when she reached it. This method of catching mackerel was called by the fishermen "pursing up the vessel."

We did this several times that fall and often got all the way from ten to twenty barrels at each set of the seine. One day off Plymouth, we got forty-two barrels at one set, in this manner. We fished until about October 25th, and had a good trip of 280 barrels, about all the *Astoria* would hold, then sailed her down home to Southport, and "hauled her up" for the season. Most of the "Down East" vessels did not go winter fishing, but were anchored in the cove, their sails and running rigging sent ashore and stowed in the loft during the winter.

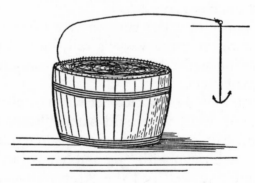

A TRAWL TUB

CHAPTER VI

PURSING THE MACKEREL SEINE
SALT FISHING, 1885

THE purse-davit is a very important part of the equipment of a seine-boat for by its use it is possible for the crew to purse the seine by hand power. One day in the fall of 1885, the *Elgin* was lying at anchor in Gloucester harbor. The wind had been blowing hard from the nor'west for two days. That evening it died away and at twelve o'clock, midnight, the skipper called all hands by saying:

"Turn out, boys, we'll get under way!"

When the crew came on deck, he said:

"Cast off th' stops an' hoist th' mains'l!"

We set the sail, swaying it up good and taut, then hoisted the fores'l, while three of the crew at the same time set the main-gaff-tops'l. Then we manned the windlass and hove in the chain and when the anchor was up to the hawse-pipe, we hoisted her jib and flying-jib as the *Elgin* swung off and filled away, bound out the harbor.

The skipper was at her wheel, for it was then the custom (and is today on all fishing vessels) for the skipper to sail his vessel *out* and *in* all harbors. When she had rounded Eastern Point, the skipper hauled her up along the Cape Ann shore and said:

"Set th' stays'l an' balloon-jib!"

When the sails were set and their sheets trimmed down, he asked the question:

"Who's watch is it?" and someone replied:

"It's George's and Frank's watch now, sir!"

"Yes," I said, "It's my wheel, skipper." I walked aft

93

and took the wheel and as the skipper turned it over to me, he said:

"Keep her as she's heading, with Thatcher's Island Lights open on your weather bow, George!"

"Aye, aye, sir!" I replied, and Frank went up to the fore-masthead on the lookout.

The next morning at ten o'clock we were up in Ipswich Bay a few miles off Plum Island, sailing along by the wind on the port tack, with a light breeze from the nor'west. All at once, the lookout sang out lustily:

"School O'!"

"Where is it?" asked the skipper.

"Two points off th' lee-bow, sir!" he replied.

"Swing 'er off!" said the skipper to the wheelsman.

"Aye, aye, sir!" he said as he rolled her wheel up and the vessel swung off.

The skipper went quickly up the weather-fore rigging and soon had his eyes on the school.

"Steady your wheel!" the skipper said.

"Steady, sir!" replied the wheelsman.

During the few minutes while the vessel was running down to the school, we had put on our sea-boots and oil-clothes ready for action. When the vessel was down to leeward of the school the skipper said:

"Roll your wheel down, an' shoot 'er up in th' wind!"

"Aye, aye, sir!" the wheelsman replied.

When she had lost her headway, again came the command from the skipper:

"Throw th' dory overboard an' haul up th' boat!"

Part of the crew hoisted the dory out, while the rest of us hauled the seine-boat up alongside.

"Man th' boat!" came the command from the skipper, and the crew scrambled pell mell into the boat.

Some jumped in, others slid in, any old way, to get in quickly. The cook came out of the fo'cas'le, rushed aft and took the wheel and the skipper came quickly down from the masthead, ran across the deck up onto the rail, jumped onto the seine, and into the stern of the boat and taking his long steering-oar said:

"Push off, men, an' start 'er up!"

We then rowed out near the school, nine men on the oars (each man rowing with one long oar, four on the starboard side and five on the port side), also three to heave the seine out, the seine-heaver, the bight-passer and the cork-thrower. The skipper was now watching the school intently (where they were schooling off to starboard of the boat), to see how they were acting and in what direction they were moving.

"Start 'er up, lively now, boys, lively!"

When the boat was in the right place, he said:

"Let go th' end o' th' seine, give 'em twine!"

The seine-heaver threw the end over and as the bights were passed to him, he threw them out clear of the boat. The cork-thrower was busy, the men on the oars were rowing hard, and the skipper was steering the boat in a great circle around the school, back to the end of the seine and the dory, in which were two men, ready to pass the purse-line with the end of the seine, when the line was quickly rove through the purse-davit blocks and then we started "pursing 'er up."

When the seine is first set in the water, the corks, 2,000 in number along on the cork-line keep the "head" afloat, and the "foot" of the seine sinks quickly down, for it is leaded with four hundred, three-ounce lead sinkers, strung along the foot-rope, which made a total weight of about eighty pounds. Also there are bridles, six fathoms long, made fast three fathoms apart on the foot-rope, with twenty-five one-inch, gal-vanized iron rings three inches in diameter, weighing two pounds each, on the bridles. Around the bottom of the seine through these large rings runs the purse-line (one and three-fourths inch hemp rope twenty-five fathoms longer than the seine), and when it is all hauled into the boat after it has been pursed up, it closes the bottom of the seine, which we then haul into the boat, and the school of fish is enclosed, as it were, in a great bag. When first set, the seine is similar to a great wall, twenty-two fathoms deep (one hundred and thirty-two feet—a fathom is six feet), two hundred and twenty-five fathoms long (thirteen hundred and fifty feet), in a great circle around the school. The seine at that time is wide open at the bottom, and these fish have fins and tails and they know well how to use them. Many times I have seen a school of fish go out of a seine when we had it nearly "pursed up." They would "rush" and then "dive." Down they'd go, right out under the foot-rope and come up again on the outside and go to schooling, laughing at us, as much as to say: "You didn't get us that time, did you?" Those were the days when the fish were wild, the Old Nick him-self couldn't catch them then, for we would set, time after time, all day long, and never get a fish. Other days they were quiet, tame, and would school in the seine all the time we were pursing up. It was no trouble to catch them at all.

All was now intense excitement on the part of our crew, from the time we had first started to row around this school until we had the seine pursed up, for if we got these fish it meant perhaps a hundred dollars or more to each man; if we didn't get them, it would be a "water haul," and we would have had all our hard

THE CREW OF THE SCHOONER "ELGIN" PURSING THE
MACKEREL SEINE IN IPSWICH BAY IN 1885

work for nothing; for once the seine is set, we have to
purse it up and dry it in, whether we get the fish or not.
Every one was eager and anxious, so we pulled and
hauled for every pound that was in us.

While we were pursing the seine, the skipper was
watching the fish and encouraging us by saying:

"Rouse 'er in, boys, lively now, hand over hand!
Close up th' hole, boys, close up th' hole! Get th' twine
under 'em, men, get th' twine under 'em! All together
now, a long pull, a strong pull, an' pull together!
Weigh th' rings, boys, weigh th' rings; bring 'em in!
Take 'em across th' boat! In with 'er, men! Come up
behind! Make 'er fast!"

In about ten minutes we had the seine pursed up and every man was completely exhausted. We were panting for breath and dripping with sweat, but we had caught a good school, so all were happy.

Then we started to dry in, hauling in the twine and flaking it across the boat, with a man at each end of the boat hauling in the cork-rope, and two men in the center hauling in the foot-rope. When we had the seine pretty well in, and close around the fish with a good strain on the twine, a man held up an oar to let the cook know that we had the fish, so that he should sail the vessel up near us. Then we took the corks on the boat and the skipper, with four men, got into the dory and went aboard the vessel. He then luffed the *Elgin* up alongside the seine-boat and the crew at the same time let the jib and flying-jib run down, casting off the fore and main sheets, and hooked the pennant on the main-boom-tackle. Hauling the sheet out taut, and rolling the wheel hard down, the skipper made it fast with the becket. The vessel was then lying alongside the seine-boat (with the school of mackerel in the seine), hove to, broadside to the wind, on the starboard tack. In the meantime, two men threw out bow and stern lines and these we made fast to each end of the seine-boat.

We had a large school of fish in our seine, so the skipper said we would put them in our "mackerel pocket," which process has already been described in the first part of Chapter V. After having done this work, we bailed (out of the "pocket") on deck, about fifty barrels, and began dressing.

There were sixteen of us on the *Elgin* so we made up five gangs, three men in each, with the cook splitting in one, at such times when he was not busy in the fo'-cas'le getting our meals ready. Two gangs rigged up on the quarter- and three on the main-deck, for'ard. Each gang had one "splitter" and two "gibbers." First, we placed two barrels side by side and on the top of them we put the "splitting-keeler" and the "gibbing-keeler." Each one was three feet square and eight inches deep. We then bailed the mackerel up from the deck, into the splitting-keeler, with "hand dip-nets." The splitter had a "splitting-board," six inches wide, at one end of his keeler and on this he placed a mackerel with its head from him, holding it with his left hand, on which was a woolen mitten. In his right hand he held a splitting-knife, the blade of which was about three inches long, made of the best steel, and very thin and sharp. Beginning at the nose of the fish he drew the knife toward him alongside the backbone (his right thumb guiding it carefully), splitting the fish from head to tail and then quickly slid it into the "gibbing-keeler."

The gibbers wear cotton gloves, when dressing fish, to protect their hands. First, we picked up a fish with our left hand, holding it head toward us, then with the right thumb, pulled out the gibbs on each side of the head, with two quick turns of the wrist, removed the viscera, and threw the fish into the wash-barrel which was partly full of salt water. When the barrel was full of mackerel, a man "cut it away," and took the "draw-bucket" and filled it with water drawn from overside, to soak the fish clean, and then got another empty barrel, doing this while the other gibber was filling up the splitting-keeler again.

A fast splitter can keep two men going, gibbing mackerel. Some splitters become very expert at their work and can split mackerel very fast, as many as fifty a minute, and keep it up for several hours. Some of the fast men are not as good splitters as the slower men, for many of them often cut the gibbs, which makes it hard for the gibbers to do their work quickly. Some fast splitters occasionally cut too deeply at the tail, making swallow-tails of their fish and this makes them a lower grade.

Father was a *very fast*, as well as a *good splitter* of mackerel. When a boy I used to pick up mackerel for him, and he could split them as fast as I could place them on his splitting-board, *sixty a minute*. I once saw him split *sixty-five a minute, for three consecutive minutes*. He was very active and quick motioned, the fastest splitter of both *mackerel* and *cod* that I ever knew.

We continued dressing our fish all that afternoon and during the evening. About ten o'clock at night it began to breeze up from the northeast. It was moderate at first, but soon the wind increased and at eleven o'clock the skipper said:

"This won't do, boys! for we're drifting inshore, so we must scratch out o' here. Cut th' barrels of fish aft as far as you can; also some of them for'ard as far as they'll go; so's we'll have room to bail th' rest of our fish on deck!"

We had already dressed one hundred and fifty barrels and had one hundred barrels still left in our "pocket," alongside the vessel; so we started bailing and filled her main-deck full; then hoisted her fores'l, jib and flying-jib, hauled aft her sheets, and stood along on the starboard tack, only long enough for her to get good headway, then tacked to port. The wind kept breezing on all the time until it was blowing a good, stiff breeze, but the *Elgin* was carrying her sail pretty well, although she had a very heavy deck-load of fish (two hundred and fifty barrels), that made her rather top-heavy, so she was unable to carry her sail spread quite as well as usual.

It was dark as pitch, for a storm was coming on, and all we could possibly see were the lights; but father was at her wheel and he drove her hard, so that we could get out by the "Salvages" and other ledges north of Thatcher's Island, before it breezed on any harder. This we finally did and then he swung her off for Eastern Point Light. When she reached it he luffed her up quickly, close around it, then stood up the harbor and anchored near Ten Pound Island. We then started dressing again on our hundred barrels of mackerel on deck and finished about eight o'clock the next morning.

Our wash-barrels were then drained by holding a dip-net in the head of the barrel, and tipping it down on deck to let the bloody water drain off. It was then filled up again so that the fish would soak clean and white. We then "broke out" some of our barrels of salt in the hold, hoisted them on deck and started salting the fish. The salting lasted during the day and up to about dark that evening.

She then had on her deck, two hundred and fifty barrels of fine, fat mackerel, all dressed and salted. Every foot of deck space on the *Lady Elgin* was taken up with barrels of fish, packed full, so that we had to climb over the top of them, to get for'ard and aft, when we went into the fo'cas'le and cabin, to "turn in" after having been hard at work for more than thirty-six hours.

After a good night's sleep we "turned out" the next morning, had a good breakfast, put on our sea-boots and oil-skins and went on deck and "headed up" and "stowed down" our deck-load of fish. Since the mackerel had been salted the first time they had settled down in the barrels several inches over night, as they shrunk, so we packed in some more fish before we headed them up. It was our first work in the morning and this was done mostly by the younger men in our crew, while the older, and more experienced men "headed up the fish," that is, put the head in the barrel. They used a cooper's adze and driver, to drive the barrel-hoops down firmly, so that the barrel of fish would be tight and not leak, for if the pickle should leak out, the mackerel will soon "rust" and become spoiled. After the barrel was coopered, we laid it down on its side, bored an inch hole in the stave, inserted a tunnel and filled it up with strong salt pickle, all it would hold, and drove the plug in and it was ready to go below for we "stowed down" our fish in the vessel's hold. These fish are called "sea-barrels" and sometimes are sold in "fishermen's order," as they do not contain two hundred pounds of fish. When salt mackerel are landed they have to be first "sorted," then "culled" into "tinkers," "threes," "twos," "ones," and "extras," then "inspected." Two hundred pounds of fish are packed into each barrel, which is then ready for the market.

MACKEREL TOLL-BAIT DIPPER
AND COD GAFF

Chapter VII

Our Largest Haul of Mackerel
Salt Fishing, 1886

THE purse-weight is used after the purse-seine has been set, to make it purse deeper under the school of mackerel in the seine. The purse-weight blocks are hooked on to the purse-line and it is allowed to run down to the purse-rings on the bridles where, by its weight of eighty pounds, it has a tendency to keep the bottom of the seine down. It is especially useful when the tide is running strongly. The summer I was seventeen years old I was seining in the schooner *Lady Elgin*. One day in the latter part of September, early in the morning, we got under way and left Portsmouth harbor, bound out to the fishing grounds, with a light sou'west wind. We sailed along by the wind on the starboard tack over toward the Isles of Shoals and about ten o'clock that forenoon the wind died away and we lay becalmed about two miles west of the islands. It was a beautiful day with the sun shining brightly. The sea sparkled and shimmered like burnished silver and it was very quiet and smooth. Father was on the fore-masthead with the lookout, when all at once he sang out loudly:

"Haul th' boat up!"

We hauled the boat up alongside; again came the command:

"Man th' boat!"

If ever you saw scrambling on the part of the crew we did it, for we rushed into the fo'cas'le and cabin to get our sea-boots and oil-skins and then piled into the seine-boat. The skipper sent the watch down, staying on the masthead himself, and told William Alley to take the steering-oar in the seine-boat.

The vessel lay very quiet and still heading west. Father had first seen this school as it crossed her bow, only about sixty yards away from the vessel, swimming under water and heading northward. When we were ready to start out in our seine-boat she was up alongside heading west. The skipper told us to row up ahead of the vessel and then swing to starboard, as the school by this time was off northwest of the vessel. When we were off the starboard bow, in the right place, the skipper called out loudly:

"Let go th' end o' th' seine!"

We rowed in a great circle around the school on the north side of the vessel with the skipper directing the steersman and as we came together and started pursing, father could still see the fish in our seine, when he left the masthead. While we were rowing around, setting our seine, we in the seine-boat couldn't see any mackerel schooling on the surface, as we usually did. About all that could be seen was an occasional one breaking the water. We had confidence, however, in our skipper and felt sure he had seen what fishermen call a "red school," meaning, a school of mackerel under water a fathom or two, that had not yet come to the surface, which once in a great while is seen as a dark red, purplish shadow under water, by a man on the masthead looking for fish who has very keen vision. These "red schools" are generally very large schools of mackerel, for they are very compact, and this is the reason why they show as a dark red color under water. They are seen only on a day when the sun is shining brightly and casts shadows. It is quite impossible to see them when looking towards the southeast, south, and the south-

THE SCHOONER "ELGIN" BECALMED SEPT. 10, 1886
A RED SCHOOL; MAN THE BOAT

west toward the sun, for it glistens on the water and
dazzles the eyes, but it is possible to see them when
looking towards the northwest, north, and the northeast away from the sun.

The two men in the dory rowed to the vessel, got the
skipper and brought him aboard the seine-boat. When
we had the seine pursed up and began to dry in on the
twine and cork-rope, the skipper soon realized that we
had a very, very large school of mackerel in our seine,
probably more than we could possibly handle ourselves,
so he swung his hat back and forth, as a signal to skipper Mark Rand, in the schooner *Uncle Joe*, which lay
becalmed only a short distance away, to come and help
us. He came with his crew, in their seine-boat and their
two dories. We put his two dories on our corks to help

hold them up, for part of them were under water, due to the great heft of the large body of fish in our seine. We then lashed his seine-boat to the back side of ours, to help hold her up, for the gunwale of our boat was down almost to the water's edge. It was calm and the sea very smooth, fortunately so for us, for if there had been any wind, with a choppy sea, it would have filled our seine-boat and we never could have saved this large school of fish.

When a school of mackerel finds itself entrapped in a purse-seine, the fish try to get out, and all of these thousands upon thousands of mackerel, in this large school in our seine, with their noses up against the twine, swimming ahead trying their best to get out, made a great strain, a great heft, and several tons weight was drawing our seine down. These two crews combined, over thirty men, worked hard for more than two hours trying to dry our seine in, but we could not get it in, try as we would. Finally, we found out what was the trouble. There was "a turn in our seine." So we swung the seine-boat around by using an oar at the bow and stern of the boat (the dory also towing hard at one end) and soon we had our seine clear and were able to get it in enough to take the corks on to our boat.

By this time there was a little wind so the *Elgin* was luffed up alongside the seine-boat and we bailed one hundred barrels on deck, and "spilled" out into our "mackerel pocket" something over three hundred barrels,—all we thought we could dress. We then gave skipper Mark Rand the rest of the fish, just as they were in the seine. After hoisting the jib and dragging ahead a little, out of the way, he luffed the *Uncle Joe* up alongside the seine-boat, made fast, and his crew bailed some mackerel on deck and started dressing, getting three hundred barrels. Our crew on the *Lady Elgin*, dressed four hundred and twenty barrels; making a total of seven hundred and twenty barrels in this one school of mackerel. This may seem like quite a "*fish yarn*," but it is the truth, just the same, for schools of mackerel range in size all the way from a few barrels, up to a thousand barrels, or more, in one school. Many schools have been lost by the fishermen, because they were so large the crews were not able to handle them. Often, when the fish started to take the seine down, the men had to cut and let them go or the seine-boat would be capsized, the crew thrown into the water and perhaps drowned, for not all fishermen can swim; and even if they could, they would be greatly hampered with their rubber-boots full of water and their oil-skins on.

In those days it was the custom, on most seiners, to dress and salt all their mackerel. When they got a large school, the crew must work on them day and night, without any sleep, until their fish were all under salt, perhaps for twenty-four, thirty-six or forty-eight hours at a time. During the time we had been catching and dressing this large haul, we had worked on our fish for three days and two nights, sixty hours, without any sleep at all. I well remember how tired and sleepy I was that second night while salting fish, for along about two o'clock in the morning I found myself nodding and falling asleep several times, and very nearly fell into the "salt-keeler" while at work; but I would not give up for I wanted to do my share with the rest of the crew.

When we began to salt the fish, we hoisted our jibs and swung her off and with the skipper at the wheel, and a good fair sou'west wind blowing and the *Elgin* on a no'theast course, by the time we had our fish all under salt we were down home at Southport. When she lay alongside the wharf, her scuppers were in the water and it was clear across her deck in front of the break at the waist, for she was the deepest in the water of any vessel I ever saw in my life. The skipper had told the crew to salt the mackerel very lightly, so that we would have enough salt for the extra forty barrels. We could do this with safety to the fish, for father planned to have them sorted, re-salted and packed, by the men at the firm in a few day's time. Mackerel that are dressed and salted at sea, and are likely to be kept in barrels in the vessel's hold for two or three weeks and perhaps longer, need to have plenty of salt on the fish, and the barrel is also well filled with good strong pickle to make the fish keep, otherwise they will "rust" and spoil.

The *Lady Elgin* carried three hundred and eighty barrels, and we had them all full of salted mackerel. The two dories we had put on top of the cabin-house, and there were twenty barrels in each dory, making four hundred and twenty barrels, the largest trip of mackerel ever landed at Southport, by any vessel. We put out her lines and made her fast to the wharf, hauled her sails down and furled them up and then "turned in" for a well-earned rest. The next morning we "turned to" and "headed up" our barrels of fish, and rigged up a tackle, hoisting them out with a horse, on to the wharf during the day.

The next morning we put on board more barrels (380), about one third of them filled with salt, and a few more stores for the use of the cook and started out again that afternoon on another trip. We beat down the Sheepscot River, then out by Seguin Island, and that evening when we were off to the south'ard of the island a few miles (about an hour before sunset) sailing along with a light sou'west wind, the mackerel came up schooling. I was on the fore-masthead, for it was my lookout, and I have never seen such a sight before, or since, in my life, as I looked at that evening when those fish came up. In every direction there were rafts, and rafts, and rafts of mackerel schooling, as far as the eye could see, and one can see a long way from a vessel's masthead. By rafts, I mean this. Sometimes, schools of mackerel are broken up into small bunches of three or four barrels, called "dory pods." On other days, the fish are in schools of fifty, one hundred, one hundred and fifty, two hundred, or three hundred barrels. Once in a great while a number of these schools go together and make very large ones of a thousand barrels or more in one great school. These we call rafts. One could hardly imagine there were so many mackerel in the whole ocean as were in sight that evening from our masthead off Seguin Island. Some of these rafts were so long that a purse-seine would not reach half way around them. Fish are very hard to catch when in such a large raft, for if you row through the school to cut it off, they are frightened and will dive the seine before you can purse it up.

When I first sighted the fish, and had called out lustily, "School O'!" the skipper had come up quickly to the masthead. Father knew it was folly for us to set our seine and try to stop any of these fish when in such a long raft, so he waited a few minutes until we should see a smaller one. He also had another reason for waiting, as dusk is the best time of day to catch a school with the purse-seine, for then the fish cannot see the twine and are not so likely to dive and go out of the seine. We had time for only one set before dark and he wanted to make sure of getting some fish so waited until he saw a school that our seine would reach around. It was a pretty good-sized school,—very likely five hundred barrels or more.

We could wait no longer, so went out and set our seine around the head of the school and held up on our oars a few minutes until they filled her full, then rowed around behind them, back to the dory and the end of the seine. We worked fast and "pursed 'er up" as quickly as possible, but the seine was so full of mackerel that those nearest the seine-boat went out. However, we got the seine pursed under them quickly enough to save two hundred barrels in the bunt. After bailing them all on deck we started dressing about nine o'clock that night. We were the only vessel there when these fish came up schooling that evening. The fleet of mackerel seiners were all to the west'ard and ahead of this large body of mackerel, for we had seen many vessels off Cape Elizabeth, Boone Island and in Ipswich Bay, where we had caught our large school of fish when we were up that way. It was then about September 20th and time for the mackerel to be "up to the west'ard."

Plenty of fish were being caught by the fleet on some days, but they were fishing on the advance guard, for the great body of mackerel were behind them off Seguin, and were working along shore sou'west. These fish, no doubt, had come from the Bay of Fundy where they had been all that summer. We had already caught three good trips there, in July and August, away to the southeast of Mt. Desert Rock. In those days, during the eighties, many large trips of mackerel were caught off the Maine coast, and it was no unusual sight to see a vessel lying "hove to" with a "mains'l haul." Our

crew on the *Lady Elgin* had experienced this pleasure
four times during that summer, when we had caught
large hauls of mackerel. Fishermen consider those who
have been so fortunate as to secure a "mains'l haul," as
"lucky dogs."

The evening we got the two hundred barrels off
Seguin, we lay there dressing our fish all night, and the
next morning it breezed up, blowing fresh from the
sou'west, so we hoisted our head-sails, swung off and
ran into Boothbay Harbor and anchored under the lee
of Mouse Island. We worked on our fish all day, salting, and finished up late that evening. The next morning after we had "turned out" and eaten our breakfast,
ten of our crew started packing their clothes-bags, saying they were going home to go gunning the rest of the
fall. These ten men lived at Clark's Harbor, near Cape
Sable, where there was fine gunning for sea-birds flying by in the fall of the year. They had been in the
Elgin since early spring, when they made the trip
hand-line dory fishing to Western Bank, and had made
four trips seining. They had earned from four hundred to five hundred dollars apiece and had *money
enough* so they were going home and have a good time.
Father tried to persuade them to stay for one more trip,
but they wouldn't listen to him, for they had made up
their minds to go home. Finally the skipper said:

"Hoist the fores'l, then we'll heave ahead and get
our anchor."

When the anchor was on the bow we hoisted our
head-sails, swung off and ran up through Townsend
Gut, then beat down the Ebenecook and shot her up
alongside the wharf, put out our lines and made them
fast, hauled her sails down and furled them up. We
then headed up our two hundred barrels of mackerel

and hoisted them out on the wharf. A total of six hundred and twenty barrels landed in six days,—the most mackerel ever landed at Southport by any skipper in so short a time.

Masters of fishing vessels were often called "skipper Sam," "skipper Joe," or "skipper Bill," as the case might be. Father was called "skipper George William," and was considered a very successful skipper, a smart fisherman and a capable man to handle a vessel, for he had good judgment and was a fine pilot along the coast. During the twenty-six years he sailed as skipper he never lost a man, never lost a vessel, or ran one ashore. One fine day that summer, we lay "jogging" with our "jib to weather," off to the south'ard of Monhegan, waiting for the fish "to show," for we had seen them schooling in that vicinity the evening before. The skipper took three empty mackerel barrels and placed them side by side in a row on the quarterdeck, and just as he was dressed, with his heavy leather sea-boots on, without even removing his coat, he jumped into the first barrel, sprang out and into the second, out and into the third, out of the third, landing on deck without moving or upsetting any of the barrels. Very quietly he said:

"You young fellows try and do it!"

Of course, we all had a try at it. Some of us could jump into one, some into two, and then fall headlong knocking down the barrels, but none of us were able to jump into all three, as neatly as father did it. We were all having a fine time and making a great racket, when up came the cook on deck to see what was going on.

"Come on, cook, you try it," some one of the crew said.

"Not one of us can do it like the skipper did," the man said.

"Well, if the skipper did it, I guess I can," said the cook.

The skipper was forty-one years old and the oldest man aboard the vessel. The cook was thirty-five, was lightly dressed and in his shirt sleeves; had on light-weight leather slippers and had his cooking-apron rolled up in front. The cook jumped into the first barrel and when he sprang out he caught his toe on the edge of the second one and fell sprawling, knocking all three barrels down which rolled about over the deck. He got up quickly and ran to the for'ard companionway and down into the fo'cas'le, without once looking behind or saying a word.

TRAWL BUOY AND BLACK BALL

Chapter VIII

The Wooden Model and Rule O' Thumb

THE early shipbuilders of New England built most of their vessels from a model that had been whittled out of wood by some man who was a genius with his jackknife. In 1870, there was a man by the name of George Willard who lived in Portland. He was skipper of a fishing vessel and during his spare time whittled out models of fishing vessels with his jackknife. One day he made a fine model that he was much pleased with, and he decided, then and there, that he would have a vessel built from it for a mackerel seiner, a small vessel of about sixty tons. When she was ready to be launched she was christened for his daughter, the *Georgia Willard*. She was a handsome vessel and many of her admirers predicted that very likely she would be a great sailer. In about a month she was rigged and ready to sail and soon proved that she was a very smart sailing vessel—"by the wind." During the ten years that George Willard sailed her, before he died, she was never beaten in a race, for she was especially fast "by the wind," close hauled, as she would lay half a point nearer up into the wind's eye than most any other vessel; yet she would foot ahead faster at the same time. When racing with another vessel and both of them held a long tack of four or five miles, she would be one eighth of a mile right dead to windward of the other vessel, for the *Willard* would work right out to windward of most any vessel in the fleet. My, how that vessel would sail with George Willard at her wheel!

Now let us for a moment consider just what it is that

SCHOONER "GEORGIA WILLARD," BY THE WIND, LEADING
THE MACKEREL FLEET IN 1870

goes to make up a fast sailing vessel. In the first place
she must have a finely modeled, well-built hull. She
must have easy lines and be rather sharp forward at the
water-line, so that she will slip through the water easily without much fuss under her bow. She must have a
good clean run aft so that she will not drag any dead
water, she must have a good floor under her body to
sail on, easy bilges, and width enough to make her able
to carry her sail well. Then when she is launched and
her spars are stepped, they must be of the right length,
stepped in the right place (not too far, either forward
or aft), so that she will balance up well and have the
right sail spread for her size, and water-line length, to

make her handle well and steer easily. Most vessels that are fast sailers steer very easily and mind their helm quickly, for they are *hung up right* and *balance well*. Most vessels that steer hard are off balance and as a result are very poor sailers. A vessel also must have the right amount of ballast, not over ballasted for she will be loggy and slow, but not too little, for she will be cranky, and not able to carry her sail spread well. Then her ballast must be in the right place in her hold, to bring her down on her best sailing lines, when in her right trim. Some vessels trim a little by the head, others a little by the stern, when in their best trim.

The *Georgia Willard* was very sensitive as to her right trim, for ten barrels of mackerel (one ton) too far for'ard or too far aft, would throw her out of trim. Her skipper made a long, careful study of trimming his vessel, sailing her against many other fast sailers, until he found out her right trim where she would do her best sailing. Then he rigged a plumb-line and bob aft near the wheel-box, so that when he wanted to sail her in a race, he could put her in her right trim. A vessel must also have a fine suit of sails, properly cut and well made, sewed so that they will set right and draw well. This is very essential if you expect her to do her best sailing, for her sails are her driving power. Many a fine vessel has made a poor showing in a race because of poorly fitting sails. Most of the sails on a fishing vessel are cut right, well made, and set well when new, but are often hauled out too hard and taut when first bent, on both the boom and gaff, quickly ruining the set of the sail. A sail must be roped right so that it will not be too flat, for then it will not hold the wind as well as a sail that has a little fullness all over, by reason of being roped a little tighter than the canvas. Many times I have seen a sail, especially the mains'l, with its leech-rope continually flapping when the vessel was close hauled, for it was a poor setting sail and would not hold the wind well. Often the set of a fine suit of sails is ruined by the fishermen themselves, for the sails are swayed up too hard and taut when dry and are not slacked down in wet weather, with the result they are stretched too hard when swollen by rain or fog and never set well afterward. On several occasions I have seen my father slack the halyards down, on both the throat and peak, when it was wet weather.

When a vessel is ready for sea she then must have a man at her wheel who knows how to sail her. To become a great sailing-master a man must first of all be a fine wheelsman. He must have natural ability, use excellent judgment and have a great love for his work. If he has all of these qualities he will be a genius. Such a man was George Willard, acknowledged by all fishermen as the greatest sailing-master in his day.

When a young man I went seining in the *Georgia Willard*, out of Portland. Her skipper at that time was Gene Stanley. She was then sixteen years old and still a pretty good sailer, for very few vessels could beat her, even then, when she was "close hauled by the wind." But she was nothing like the vessel that she was when George Willard held her wheel, for he loved to sail her and he knew how as no other man ever did. I have been shipmate with a man who was cook of the *Georgia Willard* the spring she was new. He told me that when they were fitting her out in Portland, to go out south seining for mackerel, that some of the men who had shipped in her as part of her crew, backed out and would not go, for she was so sharp they were afraid of her and called her a "diving-bell." Some of them predicted that she would be lost in the first heavy gale that she was out in. The cook told me they did have a heavy gale that spring, while they were out south, and that they had to "heave-to" under her two-reefed fores'l. He said: "She rode out the gale like a gull," then added to it by saying: "She was one of the finest sea-boats that I ever sailed in, George." He told me that the skipper soon found that she was a smart sailer, especially "close hauled by the wind," for she could beat any of the other vessels that they fell in with while out south.

"Tell me about some of the races you had that spring, cook, while you were in the *Georgia*," I said to him. So the cook told me this little story.

"One day we was in th' seinin' fleet when we had er fine 'spurt o' fish,' er lot o' fish was caught that day; some big hauls made by th' 'killers,' an' we was 'lucky 'nough' to git er good haul of er hundred an' fifty barrels. Some o' th' big fellers got their fish long 'fore we got ours, an' as soon as they had 'em bailed on deck they started fer market. We was way to th' sou'east o' th' Highlands, 'bout er hundred miles from New York.

"There was only er light air o' wind from th' nor'-west, right dead erhead it was, er long hard beat to wind'ard. Some o' th' first vessels to git fish, had ben gone fer more 'n an hour when we was ready to start, so they was 'most out o' sight to wind'ard o' us. When we had our fish bailed on deck, we set sail an' started after 'em, with th' 'Old Man' himself at th' wheel o' th' *Georgia*. In er few hours' time we begun to overhaul 'em, fer th' *Georgia* was then sailin' fast 'by the wind,' eatin' right out to wind'ard she was, an' crawlin' up on 'em all th' time. Durin' th' night we passed vessel after vessel, an' th' next mornin' when off Sandy Hook, we was right close up with th' leaders, them as was th' best sailers in th' fleet, but they was no match fer th' *Georgia* in beatin' up through th' Narrers, fer this kind o' sailin' was just to 'er likin' an' we soon passed 'em. Fer she was quick in stays, an' lively like, fillin' er way quick on t'other tack, makin' good time, an' so we was th' first vessel into Fulton Market that mornin' with our fish, an' got er good price fer 'em, makin' er good stock, an' we shared well over er hundred dollars on that trip.

"A great little vessel, was th' *Georgia*," concluded the cook.

Another genius with his jackknife was the famous whittler, Mel McLain. He was born at Friendship, Maine, where he grew up, and when he was twenty years old, left home and went to Gloucester where he shipped as one of the crew on a mackerel seiner. He was a smart young man, learning the business quickly, so in a few years he was given command of the *Lucy E. Friend*. He sailed in this vessel several years, doing well for the owners, his crew, and himself, seining for mackerel, for he was a smart young skipper and a fine fisherman.

Skipper Mel always carried several pieces of dry pine wood with him and whenever the chance offered, as they lay at anchor in some harbor storm-bound, he would be busy at work with his jackknife whittling away making models of fishing vessels. One day he made a particularly fine, beautiful model with which he was much pleased, so he showed it to his crew. They were all carried away with it and one of the older men said to him:

"Skipper, you'd ought to have a vessel built from this model, for she'd be a beauty, an' a fine sailer."

The skipper replied by saying: "Well, I was thinking that I might ask the owners this fall to build me
one, for I could build a piece of her myself, as I have
a few hundred dollars saved up."*

So that fall, when they'd finished the mackerel season, they "hauled the vessel up," alongside the wharf
and the skipper put the model in his coat pocket and
went up to the office of the firm, to "settle up." After
this business had been transacted, he said to the owners:

"I would like to have a new vessel built this winter.
I could build a piece of her myself."

"All right, skipper, we'll have one built and we're
glàd that you want an interest in her for we like to
have our skippers part owners of their vessels," replied
the senior member. Then he asked this question:

"What kind of a vessel do you want, skipper Mel?"

Mel McLain pulled the model out of his coat pocket
and replied by saying:

"I'd like a vessel of about eighty tons built from this
model," which he handed to the senior member of the
firm.

The two men were highly pleased with his model
and told him so, the elder member saying:

"Tomorrow morning, skipper, we'll go up to Essex
and see Mr. Story, and have him build us a new vessel."

So the next morning the three men drove up to Essex,
found Mr. Story, and told him they wanted a new vessel built. When they showed him the skipper's model
he, too, was highly pleased with the looks of it and said:

* When the owners of a fish firm have a new fishing vessel built
for one of their skippers, it is customary for him to own a part of the
vessel, a sixteenth, an eighth or perhaps a quarter. In the eighties, when
the *Haskins* was built for skipper McLain, she cost about $10,000.00.
The *Elgin* was built in 1883 and cost $9,000.00 as she was ten tons
smaller than the *Haskins*.

Schooner "Lottie M. Haskins" Beating into Gloucester Harbor, under Her Staysail

"This is the handsomest model of a fishing vessel that I ever saw, gentlemen," and as an afterthought he added:

"She will not only be a beauty, but a fast sailer as well."

When the contract was drawn up and the papers signed, the owner said to the skipper:

"Mel, you are not planning on going fishing this winter, are you?"

Skipper Mel replied: "No, I was not planning to do so." Then the owner said to Mel:

"Why not spend part of your time up here in Essex, and watch the building of your vessel? I feel sure Mr. Story will be glad of any suggestions you might care to make, so that she will be built just as you want her."

"I shall be glad of any suggestions from the skipper," said Mr. Story, so skipper Mel McLain spent part of his time at Essex that winter, watching the construction of his new vessel. She was finished early in March, and at the launching was christened the *Lottie M. Haskins*. She was one of the handsomest vessels ever built for a fisherman and when brought to Gloucester, hundreds of people from far and near, both men and women, boys and girls, came down to the wharf to see the new beauty. Here her masts were made and stepped, her rigging set up, her running-rigging of sheets and halyards rove off, spliced and whipped and her sails bent and furled. Then came the ballast to put in her hold, also salt and mackerel barrels to be stowed and fishing gear, keelers, dip-nets, draw-buckets and a "mackerel pocket"; her water-butts were filled and then her stores were put on board and she was about ready to sail.

Early in April she sailed for the southern mackerel grounds and her young skipper soon found out he had a fine-working, handy, fast-sailing vessel. They did well, out south, and returned to Gloucester. One day that summer, while sailing along by the wind in a light breeze, the skipper said to one of the crew up for'ard:

"Haul th' jib over to wind'ard an' make it fast with th' tail-rope," and then turned to the wheelsman and said:

"Roll your wheel down an' let 'er lay."

The wheelsman obeyed by rolling the wheel hard down and the *Haskins* came up into the wind and then filled away on the other tack.

"Well, what kind of a vessel is this, that tacks with 'er jib to wind'ard!" remarked the skipper, as he walked aft, and took the wheel himself.

"I'm going to find out just what this vessel will do," he said, as he rolled her wheel down and made it fast with the becket-rope. The *Haskins* came up into the wind, tacked, filled away, swung off, jibed over, came up into the wind again, filled away, and kept on going around and around in a small circle with her wheel hard down.

"Well, I'll be blowed!" exclaimed the astonished skipper. Then turning to his crew, he asked:

"Boys, did you ever see a vessel act like this one?"

Several of them made reply:

"No, skipper, we never saw a vessel act like this one, before in our lives!"

"I wonder if she'll do th' reverse!" said skipper Mel, as he rolled her wheel hard up and made it fast. The *Haskins* swung off, jibed over, came up into the wind, tacked, filled away again, swung off, and kept on going around and around in a circle the other way.

"Well, this does beat all! I never saw a vessel perform like this one, before in all my life!" remarked the skipper. Then as she came up he untied the becket-rope and rolled her wheel amidships and sailing along by the wind a few minutes he tacked her and with her jib made fast to wind'ard, he kept her up in the wind until she lost her headway, then he slowly rolled her wheel down part way and she lay "jogging" with her jib "to weather."

The *Lottie M. Haskins* was a wonderful vessel in many ways and would do many things which no other vessel could do. She was "hung up right" with nearly a perfect balance, responded to her wheel instantly, and was a very easy vessel to handle. She would "tack ship" with very little headway and you could beat her up a narrow channel, as she was sure to come about. She steered very easily at all times, even in heavy weather. No other vessel, to my knowledge, was ever sailed and handled by her own skipper, as was the fishing schooner *Lottie M. Haskins* by Mel McLain.

One day as they were bound into Gloucester with a trip of mackerel, with the wind blowing a good little breeze from the no'-no'theast (directly out of the harbor), as they neared Eastern Point the skipper said:

"Boys, I'm going to try this vessel today an' see just what she will do!" So the skipper gave his orders and his crew carried them out as follows:

"Clew up th' tops'ls! Take in th' balloon-jib, an' furl 'er up! Let th' flying-jib run down! Take in th' mains'l, an' furl 'er up, boys! Let your jib run down! Take in th' fores'l!"

After these orders had been given and carried out, the *Haskins* was luffed up close around the "Point," and all the *sail* she then had *set* was her fisherman's *stays'l*. Under this one small sail alone, Mel McLain beat the *Lottie M. Haskins* up into Gloucester harbor and put her alongside the wharf, a most remarkable performance, and the *only vessel* ever able to do it, so far as I know.

The fishing schooner *Arthur Binney*, was another fine, handy vessel and a very fast sailer. The famous fishing skipper, Maurice Whalen, sailed the *Binney* for several years, fresh fishing out of Boston, "trawling" for cod and haddock on George's Bank, and many a quick trip he made in her during the time he was her skipper, for the *Binney* was a very able vessel and could carry whole-sail when many other vessels were under single-reefs. She was an excellent sea-boat and in rough water, when it was blowing a gale, she would behave well and make good weather of it, going right along about her business, reeling off mile after mile and doing her twelve knots an hour.

I went seining in her one summer and found her to be one of the finest vessels I ever sailed in. She was very fast, especially so "by the wind," and one of the easiest vessels to steer, on which I ever held the spokes of a wheel. Many a time when I sat on her wheel-box, during "my trick" at the wheel, when she was "by the wind," I would not have to move her wheel for five minutes at a time and then only a spoke or two, up or down.

Another fine sailer was the fishing schooner *Red Jacket*, of Gloucester. She went mackerel seining, to the "North Bay," the first summer she was new. The first time I saw her she lay at anchor in a fleet of about thirty sail, under the lee of West Cape, Prince Edward Island, during an easterly blow. The next day the wind hauled out around to the sou'west and began to breeze up fresh, so all the vessels got under way and ran down around North Point and then had a long, hard beat up to Tignish, where we anchored under the land close inshore. I was in the *Lady Elgin* with father and recall how we all admired the fine showing made by the *Red Jacket* that day. By the time the fleet had run down by the "Point" and hauled up by the wind, it had freshened still more and was blowing a good, stiff breeze about all we could carry under our four lower sails. Our rail was down under water and some of the vessels had a single-reef tucked in their mains'ls. The *Red Jacket*, however, "walked to wind'ard" right up through the fleet in a wonderful manner, passing vessel after vessel and was soon away ahead leading them all. She was the first to anchor off Tignish and had been there for more than two hours before the last vessel got up and anchored near her, under the lee of the land.

CHAPTER IX

FRESH HALIBUT TRAWLING ON THE GRAND BANKS

HALIBUT are of two kinds, the white-bellied, and gray. The white-bellied are considered the finer fish and bring a higher price in the market. Halibut are among the very largest of our New England food-fishes and sometimes they attain a size of four hundred pounds. They are caught in three ways: by hand-line, on trawls, and in the beam-trawl bag-net. In the early days they were very plentiful on George's Bank where they were caught by hand-line fishermen from the deck of the vessel, who were after large cod as well, so that both kinds made up their trips. Halibut have sometimes been caught in very shallow water, of five or six fathoms, in certain places about Newfoundland, and Greenland, but the greater portion of them have been and are today, caught on the Grand Banks in seventy-five to one hundred fathoms, and at times off the edge of the Bank, in the "Gully," at a depth of two hundred and fifty fathoms.

Halibut were caught on trawl-line hooks as early as 1843, but not to any great extent by the trawling fleet until about 1865. From that time on, during the next eleven years, many vessels fitted out, so that by 1876 there was a fleet of about forty sail, most of them from Gloucester. The schooner *Centennial* was one of this fleet, a new vessel and a very fine, able schooner of 116 tons. She made a remarkable record during her first year in the fresh halibut fishery, trawling on the Grand Banks, under the command of her first skipper, D. C. Murphy.

SCHOONER "CENTENNIAL" OF GLOUCESTER, OUTWARD
BOUND TO THE GRAND BANKS IN 1876

Most of the vessels that went trawling to the Grand
Banks, for fresh halibut, were the best, largest and ablest in the fleet, and for the most part were fast sailers,
as it was a long way to go, some eight hundred miles,
and they had to be staunch and seaworthy to make the
long passage in severe winter weather. They were vessels of 80 to 120 tons and carried six to eight dories,
with crews of fourteen to eighteen men. Unlike the
hand-line dory fishermen and cod trawlers that went
salt fishing without ballast, these vessels carried ballast,
that was floored over and stanchioned down firmly so
that it could not shift if the vessels were "hove down,"
which they were, at times, when making the passage in
severe windy weather. Good, strong, ice-pens were
built in the vessel's hold, for the halibut were brought
to market fresh, and they carried from twenty-five to

forty tons of cake ice. These vessels were often anchored in deep water when fishing on the Bank, so they carried plenty of cable, eight and one-half or nine inch rope, and in length from three hundred and fifty, to four hundred fathoms, the greater part of it coiled on the port side, for they used the port anchor. About one-fourth of it was coiled on the starboard side, made fast to the spare anchor, and they all carried a third anchor which was lashed securely under the windlass. These three anchors weighed from five hundred to six hundred and eighty pounds each. It was very essential that these vessels should have good, heavy, "ground-tackle" and plenty of cable, enough for a good "long scope," when riding out the severe winter gales on the Bank, so they could hold on and not break adrift.

Many times when riding out a heavy gale, they would have all their cable out and as soon as it moderated somewhat, they would heave in part of it, for if it was all left out and allowed to settle on the bottom, even for only a short time, it would be likely to chafe off on some sharp rock and part and they would then lose their anchor and some of their cable. In one instance the cable was allowed to settle on the bottom for only half an hour, when the wind had suddenly moderated, and it caught under a sharp rock and parted, the vessel losing her anchor and one hundred and twenty fathoms of cable. It was a long, tedious job of three or four hours, for a crew of men on a halibut trawler, to "heave in" three hundred and fifty or four hundred fathoms of cable, when getting under way to make a berth or start for home.

The dories used on halibut trawlers are sixteen feet long on their bottom, made with extra heavy gunwales and very strongly constructed so that they can withstand the heavy work required of them. Halibut trawls are made up of much heavier gear than cod trawls, for their anchors, buoy-lines, ground-lines, gangings and hooks are all larger. Each "tub-o'-trawl," also called a "skate-o'-trawl," used for halibut gear, has seven and one-half lines, of fifty fathoms each, which makes the ground-line three hundred and seventy-five fathoms in length, on which are gangings five feet long, one end made fast to the ground-line. On the other end large hooks are bent on, one hundred and fifty in number, to each tub, six hundred in all, for each dory usually carries four "tubs-o'-trawl." The total length of the ground-line of the four tubs is fifteen hundred fathoms or nine thousand feet, nearly one and three-fourths of a mile in length, when the trawl is set, ready to catch fish on the bottom. The buoy-line must be a few fathoms longer than the depth of the water (to allow for the current), for it must reach from the buoy on the surface down to the anchor on bottom, when the trawl is set ready to fish. The length also varies with the different depths of water on the Bank. The first baiting for halibut trawls is usually taken from home, or procured elsewhere before reaching the Bank, and is either fresh menhaden, herring or tinker mackerel.

When the crew are ready to "bait-up," they bring up the bait and sliver ("slyver") the fish by cutting strips from the head to the tail, on each side close to the backbone. These strips are used entire, making a bait about two inches wide and six to eight inches in length. When the vessel is anchored on the Bank, fishing, and the crew have been out and set and hauled in their trawls once, they usually catch some cod, haddock and hake and these fish are cut up into strips of the size before stated and are used for halibut bait and called by the fishermen "shack," or "gurry bait." Halibut usually prefer it to any other kind, when fishing on the Bank, but sometimes, when fishing in shallow water, about Newfoundland or Greenland, they prefer fresh herring and will not bite at any other kind of bait at that particular time.

The fishing grounds for halibut have been, from the early days and so on up to the present time, as follows: George's Bank, Cashe's Ledge, Seal Island Grounds, La Have Bank, Western Bank, Banquereau, and the "Gully," between the Bank and Sable Island; Saint Peter's Bank, Green Bank, and off Scatari Island; Magdalen Islands, Anticosti Island, Greenland, Iceland and on the Grand Banks.

In January and February of each year, a large body of "school fish" (cod) "strike on" George's Bank. I do not mean that they school on the surface as do mackerel, herring and menhaden, but cod, haddock, and halibut (ground fish) migrate in large bodies at certain times of the year on the different Banks. During the last of April and the first of May, fishermen look for cod in vast numbers, to "strike on" Western Bank, and speak of them as "school fish." They are usually on the move and do not stay long in one place, so in order to have good fishing, it is necessary to get under way and move along with the fish, after finding the direction they are going.

Pebbles are sometimes found in the pokes of cod, and older men in the crew will say, "These are 'school fish,' and they swallowed the pebbles for ballast when about to start on a long journey."

In July and August, cod are found in large bodies (school fish) around the Magdalen Islands and on the Labrador Coast, chasing "lant" and "capelin," and often rising to the surface in pursuit of them.

During August, cod are sometimes very plentiful on the "Rocky Bottom" of Banquereau (often called by the fishermen Bank Quereau). This large body of "school fish" appears on the Bank when the "squid strike," for cod are very fond of them. The hand-line dory cod fishermen frequently were able to catch all the squid they wanted for bait, on the Bank and after dressing down their deck of fish in the evening they would catch their bait supply for the next day's fishing. The Grand Bank hand-line dory cod fishermen often found good fishing about the "Virgin Rocks," when a large body of "school fish, struck on" in August. Good fishing also was to be found at the "Eastern Shoal Water."

In the early fishery (about 1835) on George's Bank, halibut were so plentiful they were often seen on the surface and could be caught by fishermen anywhere in the water, from the surface clear down to the bottom. Some vessels were able to make a round trip from Gloucester in two or three days, their crews catching a trip of 15,000 to 20,000 pounds of halibut in one day's fishing between sunrise to sunset. Sometimes there would be plenty of fish on the northern part of the Bank, for a few weeks and then the halibut would suddenly disappear. At other times, a large school would "strike on" the southeastern part of the Bank, and there would be fine fishing for a short time until the fish moved along on their way to other feeding grounds.

In March, 1870, a fresh halibut trawler, the schooner *John Corlis*, skipper George Brown, anchored on the western part of the Grand Banks, in sixty fathoms of water. In the first set of the trawls they got about 4,000 pounds of halibut, in the second set, 40,000 pounds, in the third set, 35,000 pounds, and on the fourth day only about 1,000 pounds of fish, for the school of halibut had moved along to other grounds. Skipper Brown had thought of getting underway after making his first set, and working to the eastward, but as the wind was ahead (northeast) he decided to make one more set. They got their large catch of 40,000 pounds that day, for a school of halibut had "struck" on the Bank. They had only two days good fishing, but got a fare of 80,000 pounds of fine white halibut, and sailed for home, making a quick trip that stocked $4,000. This trip shows that halibut move very quickly over the Bank at times, evidently in search of either better feeding, or spawning grounds.

There are "small spots" (one or two miles in area) on the different Banks, where halibut have been found very plentiful and several good trips have been caught before the fishing grounds played out; either by being all caught up, or driven away by so many trawls set close together. Halibut were very plentiful on Green Bank when it was first discovered in 1882, and many vessels caught big trips, but in a few months' time the fishing there played out entirely. St. Peter's Bank was another great halibut ground, where many large fares were caught by the Gloucester trawlers over a period of several months. On both of these Banks there were many "spots," where halibut gathered and stayed, feeding and breeding, not moving along at that time.

When fresh halibut trawlers first began fishing on the different Banks using the trawl-line and hook method, they fished in water from fifty to sixty fathoms deep. Later they found good fishing at one hundred fathoms, and still later, halibut were accidentally discovered to be very plentiful in two hundred to two hundred and fifty fathoms of water, especially in the Gully between Green Bank and the Grand Banks, and also in deep water off the southern part of the Grand Banks. Many halibut were caught in the Gully between Sable Island (eastward) and Banquereau, and also on the southwest prong of Banquereau.

The best fishing for halibut is usually had during the spring months and the poorest fishing is found late in the fall of the year. The fresh halibut fishermen usually start their vessels about the 15th of January, and follow the fishery for eight or nine months, then "lay up" for three months, about the 15th of October.

When the *Centennial* arrived on the western part of the Grand Bank, after a good run from Gloucester, she was anchored in about one hundred fathoms of water. Her crew furled her sails and set the riding-sail, then made ready to hoist out their dories to set their trawls in the late afternoon, so they could haul in the morning, weather permitting. When the crew left the vessel in their dories, they each rowed out in a different direction (on this first setting) to try out the "grounds." After the halibut had been located, they all set on the side of the vessel where one dory had found the best fishing.

Trawling for halibut on the Grand Banks, especially during the winter season, is perhaps the most exposed, dangerous, and laborious of all our New England fisheries. These fishermen are called upon, at times, to go through some very harrowing experiences, exposed as they are to icebergs, floating ice with ice fields, severe winter gales, angry, heavy seas breaking, stormy, rough weather with snow squalls, hail and cold raw winds. During the winter months they are obliged to fish in rather windy, rough weather, or not at all, for it is seldom calm, fine weather then, so they must be ever on the alert, watching out for heavy seas which may trip or fill their dory when they break upon them.

When out hauling their trawls in deep water, of one hundred and fifty up to two hundred and fifty fathoms, by hand, over a "roller" on the bow of their dories, fishermen found it to be very hard work. Then someone invented the "hurdy-gurdy," which made it easier, so now all the halibut fishermen use it when hauling, rather than by the older method over a roller. When the men went out in their dory to haul their trawl, the bow-man took a turn around the "hurdy-gurdy," then

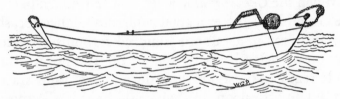

HURDY-GURDY FITTED TO A HALIBUT TRAWL DORY

passed it to the other man who held the turn, and coiled the line on a "skate," while the bow-man worked a crank and hauled the line in. While they were hauling, both men were always watching out carefully for breaking seas, as there was a heavy strain on the line, for when they first started to haul, before they got any fish, the dory was light and rather cranky, so was easily capsized. After the buoy-line had been hauled in, next came the anchor which was unbent, then they began hauling in the ground-line, and when there was good fishing, there would be many halibut on it, all the way down to bottom, which made it very heavy and hard to haul in.

When a halibut was up alongside their dory, the first thing they did was to hit the fish two or three good blows on the nose with their "halibut killer" (a stout oak club, four feet long, also known as a "gob-stick"), to stun and partly kill the fish, so that it could be gaffed with the "halibut-gaff" and hauled into the dory with safety. A large halibut will sometimes put up a great fight when alongside the dory and much care was used to gaff it in, for it would swim wildly about, surging hard on the line, at times even tearing out the hook or breaking the ganging, so that fish were lost. This was more likely to happen when fishing in shoal water, for the halibut were lively and fresh then and not tired out by the long haul as when caught in very deep water.

When fishing in deep water and the fish have been on the trawl for several hours (perhaps two or three days during a gale) they are not so hard to handle for then they are nearly drowned. Strange as it may seem, a fish is easily drowned when caught on a hook, and its mouth held open for some time by a strain on the line. When fishing for cod on Western Bank, hand-lining in a dory, I have sometimes caught halibut and had to "play it" for fifteen or twenty minutes before I could bring the fish up alongside my dory. It would come up quite easily for a few fathoms, then get its head down and start swiftly for bottom and I had to let the line run out until it slacked up somewhat, for if I had snubbed it too much with my cod gear, it would have broken the hook or parted the ganging and I would have lost the fish. After playing the fish for several minutes until it was partly drowned, I would be able to get it up close where I could reach it with my "gob-stick" and rap it on the nose to stun it, then, with my dory-gaff, I could flip it in with a dexterous movement when the gunwale of my dory was down level with the water. A man must know just how to do this, by experience, or he will fill his dory half full of water, especially if it is rough weather with heavy, breaking seas. When a large halibut, of two hundred pounds or more, is hauled into a dory, by the time it is unhooked, most likely it will come to and begin to pound with both its head and tail. Then it must be killed with the "gob-stick" or it will damage the dory. A few smart blows on the nose will silence it.

When the crew of the *Centennial* came alongside the vessel, with their dories deep in the water loaded with halibut, and it was rough, with the vessel rolling badly, they had to watch their chance to get their fish on deck. Most of the halibut were hauled out with long-handled gaffs, for they were too heavy to pitch out with a fork. When all the dories had been unloaded, dressing began by ripping the fish open and removing the gills and entrails. Then the fish was scrubbed and washed clean inside and dropped into the vessel's hold where they were packed with ice in the pens.

Halibut were plentiful and after several days fishing, they had caught a fine trip of one hundred thousand pounds and were ready to start for home. When about to start heaving in on their cable, the skipper went to the fo'cas'le companion-way and said to the cook: "Lash your pots an' kettles, cook, for th' *Centennial* is bound to th' west'ard!"

This command has been famous among the fishermen for many years and has often been spoken of by them. This order given to the cook, by the skipper, meant that he intended to drive his vessel hard on the passage home and it was intended as a warning of what might happen to the pots and kettles. I know of an instance when one of the crew who lay in a leeward bunk, was badly scalded by the contents of a large coffee-pot thrown off the range when the vessel was "hove-down on her beam-ends," during a very heavy squall, while on her way home from the Grand Banks with a trip of fresh halibut. It is necessary for the skipper to drive his vessel hard, when on a passage home, so that his fish will be in good order when they reach market. When several vessels leave the Bank about the same time, the first one in, of course, will get the best price for her fish.

Many of Gloucester's famous skippers have been men who sailed on the fresh halibut trawlers, and known as great sail-carriers and hard-drivers. Such men as D. C. Murphy, Jerome McDonald, Nat Greenleaf, J. W. Collins, Tommy Bohlin, Clayt Morrissey and Archie McLeod. These men were not reckless and careless, although hard-drivers and great sail-carriers, for they used good judgment and common sense at all times and knew how much their vessels could stand with safety.

Making the winter trip was often very hard on both the skipper and his crew, for they had many things to contend with. Large cakes of floating ice were very dangerous to the safety of their vessel, especially at night, for if the vessel should strike one, she would sink very quickly. Often they had cold winds blowing a gale with snow, sleet, hail, rain or fog; frozen sails to reef and frozen ropes to handle, and many times the vessel herself was badly iced up. In the winter time they often met with severe westerly gales that blew hard for many days; a head wind making their trip home a long and hard one.

"A Beverly vessel was forty-two days making the passage home from the Grand Banks in the winter 1879." Compare this passage with some of the fastest ones, made in four to five days, during the same year. Some quick trips were made in those days by the sailing vessels, for in "1874 the schooner *Lizzie K. Clark*, made the round trip in 17 days, bringing in 88,800 pounds of halibut and her stock was $4,676.00." This trip was the quickest one on record for many years and her stock was high for those days, as she got five and a quarter cents per pound for her fish, while many times during the seventies and eighties, halibut only brought from three to three and one-half cents per pound. To-day, they often bring from twenty-five to thirty cents per pound.

"The schooner *Centennial* made a remarkable record the first six months of 1876. Starting out on February 15th, she made six round trips to the Grand Banks, by August 20th, when she had landed 600,000 pounds of halibut, averaging 100,000 pounds each trip. Her skipper at that time was D. C. Murphy. The next year, in 1877, she brought home one of the largest trips on record, 137,000 pounds of fine halibut. The same year the schooner *G. P. Whitman*, skipper Jerome McDonald, made a record trip of 137,500 pounds. One of the highest stocks made in those days was the trip of the schooner *N. H. Phillips*, skipper Wm. McDonald, who landed a fare of 47,600 pounds, and stocked $5,300.00 her crew sharing $213.00 each."

That was a very large stock for an average trip, but they got a good price for their fish. Many times when halibut were at a very low price, a fare of 100,000 pounds would not bring nearly as much money. The fresh halibut fishery was at its height in 1880, when some fifty sail of fine schooners were engaged. Then it fell off gradually and of late years only about twenty sail are regularly engaged in this fishery.

One of the most famous fishing vessels, of recent years, was the schooner *Henry Ford*, in command of her equally famous skipper and owner, Clayton Morrissey of Gloucester. The schooner was a very fine, able vessel of 152 tons and a fast sailer. Her skipper drove her hard and made some quick runs, both to and from the Grand Banks, trawling for fresh halibut, making many fine trips during the seven years he sailed her, before she was lost in the spring of 1928. While on a halibut trip in the Straits of Belle Isle, during a thick fog, she struck a sunken ledge that punched a hole in her bottom. She filled and quickly sunk and her crew, including the skipper and cook, took to the dories, rowed in to land and were sent home to Gloucester by the American consul. When they arrived home I met skipper "Clayt" on the street and talked with him about the loss of his vessel. He felt very badly indeed to lose his fine schooner, the famous, fast-sailing *Henry Ford*.

The halibut fleet, during the past fifteen years, has undergone a great change, for most of the schooners have had crude oil engines installed, changing from sail to power. These auxiliary vessels are able to make quick runs, of three and one-half to four days, to and from the Grand Banks. On the fishing grounds the crew set their trawls while the vessel is cruising under power, instead of anchoring on the Bank as was the old custom when under sail alone. One of the most successful of these modern halibut trawlers is the fine, large, able, fishing schooner *Catherine*, commanded by Archie McLeod, who has been the "high-liner" of the halibut fleet for several years past and still holds the record. The *Catherine* has a large, crude-oil-burning engine of 250 h.p. that will drive her at a speed of ten knots per hour. She is a seaworthy vessel of 160 tons, and when under sail was a fast sailer. She had the longest main-boom and the largest mains'l of any fishing vessel out of Gloucester, a few years ago. Today, she has no top-masts, for they have been sent down, and only her two spars, foremast and mainmast, and sail enough only to keep her steady in rough water when under power cruising.

Skipper Archie McLeod has made the most remarkable record, of all time, in the fresh halibut fishery, not alone in the amount of fish landed, but he has made the largest stock each year, for several years past. This has been due partly to the fact that he was able to get higher prices of late years for his fish. In the seventies and eighties, halibut prices were often very low, and a vessel with a large trip of 100,000 pounds that got only four or five cents a pound for her fish, would stock only $4,000.00 or $5,000.00 for her trip. During the past few years halibut are not so plentiful and the prices are much higher, so a vessel landing a trip of 60,000 pounds, at twenty-five cents a pound, will stock $15,000.00 for her trip. Skipper McLeod has landed many trips of 60,000 and 80,000 pounds and made large stocks of $15,000.00 or $18,000.00 and during the year stock $100,000.00. One year he stocked $110,000.00 and his crew shared over $3,400.00 for their season's work,—the most money ever made by any crew in the Gloucester fishery.

The schooner *Catherine* carries twelve dories, a crew of twenty-four, which with skipper, cook and engineer makes a total of twenty-seven men. The halibut fishermen usually start out about January 15th each year and fish until about October 15th, making a season of nine months for this fishery.

CHAPTER X

THE COD AND MACKEREL GILL-NET FISHERY

BOTH cod and mackerel (other fish as well) are caught in the gill-net when it is set in an upright position in the water. The fish strikes the net and its head goes through the mesh, which closes behind the gills holding them fast. I will first describe the cod gill-net fishery in Ipswich Bay.

"During the year 1878, Prof. Spencer F. Baird, United States Commissioner of Fisheries, brought to this country some gill-nets he had secured in Norway, where the fishery had been carried on for some years. The first trials in Ipswich Bay were not a success, chiefly owing to the lightness of the twine used."

I have heard old men say that in 1880-81, skipper Martin used, successfully, gill-nets made of twelve-thread, Scotch flax twine which proved to be very strong and satisfactory. The nets were one hundred fathoms long and three fathoms deep. The head-line was one-inch rope and the foot-line a little larger. Along the head-line glass globes were made fast, two fathoms apart, to keep the net in an upright position when set. On the foot-line were sinkers weighing two pounds each, also spaced two fathoms apart, to keep the foot-line down on the bottom. Cod gill-nets were set on the bottom (for cod, being ground-fish, swim near the bottom of the sea) and were fastened at each end, by twenty-five pound anchors. Sometimes "killicks" were used in place of anchors.*

* A "killick" was used by the early fishermen in place of a small anchor. Killicks ranged in size from twenty-five to sixty pounds, and were used to anchor a punt, skiff, dory, rowboat, or sail-boat. They

At first, corks were used on the head-line, but being constantly under water, soon became water-soaked and useless, so glass globes were used instead. These were covered with netting to prevent them from breaking. On each end of the gill-net were quarter-barrel buoys, floating on the surface, with a buoy-line running to the anchor-line, made fast at a point about half-way from the anchor on the bottom to the end of the net. The gill-nets were "hung" with twine a little larger in size than that of which they were made and the size of the mesh was nine inches four and one-half inches square. At first, I believe, a smaller mesh was used, but the fishermen soon found out that the nine-inch mesh was the best size to catch the large cod found in Ipswich Bay during the winter. It is believed by the fishermen that the presence of large cod, found in Ipswich Bay during January and February, is because these fish go there to spawn on the sandy bottom. The fishermen used dories to set their gill-nets. At first two men went out, one man rowing the dory in a straight line, while

were also used to anchor the trawls, cod gill-nets, mackerel, herring, alewive, and shad gill-nets. The early fishermen had very little money to spare and as an iron anchor cost money, they used a homemade killick, which cost them only their labor. During the seventies (when a small boy), I often helped father make a killick in the following manner: first, he found a thin, flat rock (around the shore) about sixteen inches long and weighing about twenty-five or thirty pounds, and with cold chisel and hammer cut a shallow groove on each side across the center on the flat side of the rock. Then he went into the woods and found a hardwood limb that had a branch on it that would form a crotch. Next he took a good hardwood barrel-stave three inches wide, sawed it off the right length, sixteen inches long, sharpened the ends, and then bored two one-inch holes in the stave the thickness of the rock apart. By placing the rock at right angles on top of the stave he fitted the crotched limb down over the rock, with the two ends through the holes in the stave, and fastened them securely underneath by boring a small hole through the ends and driving in a wooden pin.

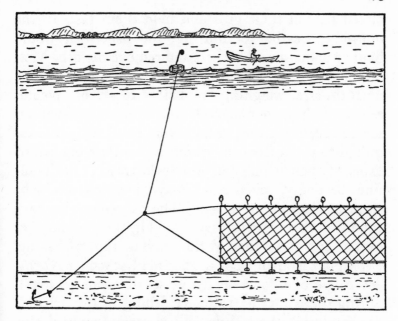

A COD GILL-NET AS SET ON THE BOTTOM OF THE SEA

the other threw out, first the anchor, then the buoy and its line; next, the gill-net was carefully paid out, and lastly, the buoy-line, buoy and outside anchor. Later on only one man went in a dory. When the cod gill-net was set right, it extended in a straight line along near the bottom in an upright position ready to catch fish. They were usually set in the evening and allowed to remain out all night, as this was the time when the fish were caught for cod could see the net in the daytime and would not enter it. Very few fish were caught on dark nights for then the water "fired," and the net was all ablaze with the sparkle of phosphorescence in sea-water, and the fish would not go near it.

The best fishing was found on moonlight nights when the water did not "fire," for then the fish could not see the net and when they struck into it, the mesh closed behind their gills and held them fast. In the morning, weather permitting, the fishermen would haul or under-run their nets and remove the fish. Most of the cod caught by the gill-nets were large fish of uniform size, weighing from sixty to seventy pounds each, which made fine steak cod. The cod gill-net has several good qualities in its favor. First, no bait is required to catch the fish, which is usually a big bill of expense when fishing with either the trawl or the hand-line. Secondly, much time is saved which would be spent in "baiting up trawls." The fishermen also have found out that more fish are caught by the same number of men and dories than by the trawl method of fishing.

Skipper Martin went in the small schooner *Northern Eagle* of Gloucester (a vessel of about 40 tons), during the winter of 1880-81 fishing in Ipswich Bay for cod, using the gill-net. They carried eight dories, only one man in each, with three nets, which they often fastened end to end and set in one string anchored at both ends. Skipper Martin and his crew did well and caught a lot of fish, more than twice as many as other vessels with the same number of men who were fishing with trawls. It was soon found they could under-run their gill-nets to advantage, without hauling in the anchors at all and done in this manner. Starting at the windward end, they would haul up the end of the gill-net, pull their dory under it, and haul it on the lee-side, removing the cod, and letting the gill-net run out, over the windward side of the dory, as they hauled along. The men used their dory-gaff to haul the fish into their dory, otherwise the large, heavy cod would tear the net badly. For many years small sailing vessels were used exclusively in this fishery, as the fishing grounds were only a few hours sailing from Gloucester, where they

A DORY-MAN UNDER-RUNNING COD GILL-NETS
IN IPSWICH BAY, 1880

marketed their catch. It was possible, many times, to
run in daily, or at most, every few days, and sell their
fish. There was always a good market for these fish, for
they were splendid, large cod and brought a good price,
selling for steak-cod in the fish markets, that had the
best hotel and restaurant trade. This fishery was carried
on for years during the winter months by sailing vessels, but recently new methods have been employed.
With the advent of the gasoline engine and later on,
the crude oil engine, many power-boats entered this
fishery and the small sailing vessels have passed out
entirely.

The surface gill-net was used in Europe by the English, Scotch, Irish, Norwegian and Swedish fishermen,
for many years before it was introduced into the New
England fishery. It is said that the first mackerel gill-
nets in New England were used off Provincetown in

1841-42 by a man named Atwood. After this they were used all along the coasts of Massachusetts and Maine. For many years they were called "drag-gill-nets," and small fishing vessels of twenty or twenty-five tons using them in this fishery were called "drag-boats." It was the custom of these gill-net fishermen, at that time, to fasten several nets, end to end, when set. A long rope was then made fast to the leeward end of the string of nets, called a "net-swing" and the other end was made fast to the bow of the vessel, which would be drifting slowly to leeward, stern first, under her mains'l, during the night. Later, these fishermen set their mackerel gill-nets stationary, near the surface, by using an anchor at each end. Today most mackerel gill-nets are thirty fathoms long and two and one-half deep, with a mesh of three inches. Mackerel gill-nets are not steam-tarred, as are the purse-seines, but are dipped in a solution made of "catechu" boiled in water, and are "tanned" a brown color. This protects the twine from the action of the sea-water, and a set of gill-nets, with proper care, if kept dry when not in use, will last several years. The nets are "hung" to the cork-rope which runs the length of the net on top, and the corks are spaced one foot apart to make the net float on the surface. The net is also "hung" to the foot-rope on which are small lead sinkers, one foot apart, to make the foot-rope sink in the water. On each end of the net are quarter-barrel buoys and the anchor-line, with an anchor, to hold the net out straight. This also secures it and prevents it from drifting away.

Mackerel gill-nets are set near the surface in an upright position, the cork-rope on the surface and the foot-rope hanging down in the water, two and one-half fathoms below the surface. They are set in the late afternoon and hauled early (daylight) the next morning. The best time to fish is on "moonlight nights" when the mackerel cannot see the net. The fish are caught when they strike it and try to pass through, the mesh closing behind their gills and holding them fast. On the "dark of the moon" the water "fires" so brightly that mackerel can easily see the net and will not go near it. The mackerel purse-seine fishermen do *their* fishing on the "dark of the moon" when they can see the schools of mackerel as a luminous body moving in the sea, while the mackerel gill-net fishermen do *their* fishing on "moonlight nights" when the nets are not luminous.

For many years past, even up to the present time, there has been quite a large fleet of "netters," mostly out of Gloucester. These vessels are smaller than the seiners, for the most part composed of "draggers" and "swordfishermen," and are auxiliary powered with crude-oil-burning engines. They go out south, every spring, with the seiners, to meet the mackerel coming northward in April. The netters set their gill-nets in strings east and west, off shore, where the great body of fish are coming along, and often make big hauls on moonlight nights, getting all the way from five thousand pounds up to twenty thousand pounds to each vessel. They carry about eight dories (one man in each), and set five nets to each dory, making a total of forty for each vessel. They follow the fish up the coast during April and May, and fish around Block Island, No Man's Land and Nantucket until about June 1st, then they go home to Gloucester and "fit out" for swordfishing. Very few of them follow the gill-net fishery during the summer season, but along about October 1st, several enter it again for the fall fishing, and some of

them do well, following the fishery up into December.
In 1931, the last trip of the mackerel gill-net fishermen was made by an Italian boat from Gloucester.
They got three thousand pounds off Cape Cod, and
landed their trip in Boston on December 17th, getting
seventeen cents a pound for their fish. This was a small
trip, but a good price for the fish.

In the spring, during May and June, the Nova
Scotian and Cape Breton fishermen do well and get a
lot of mackerel in their gill-nets, while the fish are
moving down the Cape Shore and up into Chaleur Bay
and the Gulf of Saint Lawrence. Most of the mackerel
caught there are shipped, iced in barrels, on board the
Halifax and Yarmouth steamers, to Boston markets.
While mackerel seining on the "Cape Shore," in May
and June, 1926, I saw several hundred of these gill-
nets set north and south, off the coast a few miles, in
the track or course of the great body of mackerel,
which were bound down the Nova Scotia coast in an
easterly direction, finally going around Cape Breton.
We had to keep a sharp lookout on board our vessel, to
steer clear of these hundreds of nets, so that we would
not foul and tear them.

Think of the great distance these "Gulf" mackerel
swim each spring and fall! In the early spring
(March), they start from somewhere south of Cape
Hatteras (off the North Carolina coast) and swim to
the Gulf of Saint Lawrence, where they spawn in June.
In the fall they leave the Canadian coast, bound south,
and again swim this long distance of several hundred
miles. Is it not a marvel that these small mackerel
"tacks, blinks, or spikes," hatched in June, know
how, when, and where to go. How do they find the
way? It is one of the many mysteries of the Great
Deep.

Chapter XI

Fresh Haddock Trawling on George's Bank

FOR many years, haddock were thought to be a much inferior fish to the cod, and were considered not worth catching and salting as they made a very poor dry salt fish. The hand-line dory cod fishermen would not save them when caught and threw them away. Previous to 1860, most of the New England fishermen dressed and salted their fish (cod) on the Bank and brought them home as fares of salt fish. Later on, a few vessels (trawlers) began to take some ice in pans so as to bring in part of their trips as fresh fish. At first, there was very little sale for fresh fish as the general public had not then learned to call for them. In those days there were no refrigerator cars, or other means by which fish dealers and shippers could send fresh fish in good condition to inland cities and towns.

When the fishing vessels first began to bring in fresh haddock, it was difficult to dispose of them. About this time (1870) some bright man conceived the idea of smoking fresh haddock and putting them on the market as "finnan haddie."* So treated these fine fish met with instant approval and soon there was a great demand for this delicious table food. During the seventies, more and more people learned that fresh haddock were fine eating and soon there were thousands of thrifty housewives calling for them.

Many small vessels out of Portland, Maine, went trawling for haddock during the winter season, in the seventies, eighties and nineties, most of them fishing on "shore-soundings" and the nearby Banks, a few miles

* Finnan haddie" were first cured in Scotland, many years ago.

off shore. Many of these "shore-haddock" (the best fish) went to the several "smoke-houses" in Portland, where they were converted into fine "finnan haddies" for the best trade. Most of these small vessels went single-dory fishing; each man in a dory thirteen feet long. The dory was dropped off while the vessel was sailing along, the skipper casting off her dory-painter at the right time. The man would then let go his windward anchor and set his trawl to leeward as the dory drifted down. When all the crew had left the vessel, the skipper sailed her back and down near the first dory that had gone out. When this man had finished setting his trawl, the skipper luffed the vessel up close to his dory and picked him up and then the others in succession when they were ready to come aboard. The skipper then beat the vessel back, up to windward, near the windward buoy of the first trawl set, "jogging" her for perhaps two hours, and then sent the first man out to haul, getting his anchor and hauling to leeward. The skipper then sailed the vessel along to the second man's windward buoy, when he, too, would go out to haul, and so on, until all the crew had left and were out hauling their trawls. The skipper then went back, down to leeward of the first man, and when he had finished hauling, picked him up, and he would pitch his haddock out on deck. The others were taken care of in the same way in their turn. Most of these small "haddockers" out of Portland, made quick trips, often returning in twenty-four hours. Sometimes, however, in stormy or thick weather, they would be gone two or three days.

The vessels which went trawling for fresh haddock and cod, out of Boston and Gloucester, were larger. Most of them had been seining during the summer and were smart sailers and very able vessels. In the days of

SCHOONER "MYSTIC" DROPPING HER DORIES, UNDER SAIL,
ON GEORGE'S BANK, 1882

salt fishing (salt cod and mackerel), previous to 1870, there was no particular need for a vessel to be a fast sailer, for there was no quick change in the price of salt fish on the market. But when vessels went fresh fishing, the price of fish often changed quickly, either up or down, and it was necessary to have fast sailing vessels, to enable skippers to make a quick run to market with their trips of fresh fish. When the skippers and owners demanded faster sailing vessels, able to carry sail well in a blow, the designers and builders met this demand and built some of the finest, ablest, fastest vessels in the New England fishing fleet. Many fishing vessels built in the eighties and nineties, were famous sailers, and were known far and wide as the finest fishing vessels in the world. Those from Gloucester and Boston went off shore to George's Bank and to Western Bank, and often brought home large trips of fresh haddock and cod caught on trawls. This fishery was at its height from 1880 to 1890.

One of the finest vessels and smartest skippers in those days was the schooner *Mystic*, sailed by John McKinnon, who was "high-line" for the season of 1881-82, his vessel stocking $21,000.00, and his crew sharing $780.00 each. Another great fisherman was Charlie Martin, in the *Martha C.*, who landed one of the quickest and largest trips of that time, 93,000 pounds caught in only two days fishing on "George's," in February, 1882. Later on, such famous skippers as Tom McLaughlin, in the *Sarah H. Prior*; Maurice Whalen, in the *Harry L. Belden*; Johnnie O'Brien, in the *John H. McManus*; Linc Jewett, in the *Elsie M. Smith*; and Marty Welch, in the *Lucania* made many quick and large trips with fares of 100,000 pounds of fresh haddock and cod, caught in two or three days' fishing on "George's." They would be gone from home only three or four days and often made two trips a week. These men had very fine, able, fast-sailing vessels, among the best in the fleet of "haddockers" of that day, and they drove their vessels hard, through rough, stormy seas, in windy winter weather, often making port in a thick snowstorm, their vessels badly iced up from flying spray that froze where it struck, the running rigging frozen stiff, so that it was with great difficulty their crews were able to haul the sails down in time for skippers to shoot their vessels up alongside old T Wharf.

The haddock trawlers carried more ballast than the halibut trawlers, for they took only about ten tons of ice on their short trips, while the halibut vessels often took forty tons of ice on their longer trips to the Grand

Bank. The "haddockers" carried their ice and fish in the after-holds, for the fore-holds were their "bait-rooms," where the crews "baited up" their trawls in the winter time in very cold weather. Rough benches were arranged around the sides for the men to sit on while at work in the fore-hold, a lighted lantern fastened up on a tub in front of them. Of late years the crews use candles which are held in place by "stickin' tommies," when either "baiting up" or doing other work in the

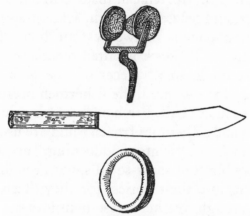

TRAWL-ROLLER, BAIT-SLIVERING KNIFE
AND WOOLEN HAND NIPPER

hold at night. Haddock trawls are "rigged up" much the same as cod trawls, but the hooks are smaller, and number five hundred to a "tub-o'-trawl," of three hundred fathoms. Each dory with two men sets from six to eight tubs.

The large vessels which go off shore to "George's," often carry twelve dories, fifteen feet in length. The haddock fishermen do not anchor on the Bank, as do the halibut and salt cod trawlers, but "set under sail," as did the Portland vessels, dropping their dories one after another as the vessel sails along with the wind abeam. When the trawls are all set, the skipper picks up the dories on the leeward end. They wait an hour or two, then begin hauling from the windward buoy, going to leeward. Often they "under-run" once or twice during the day, removing the fish and baiting up the bare hooks, then letting the trawl run out again in the same place. On the last haul in the afternoon, they take up their trawls and bring them aboard. When haddock are very plentiful, the trawls need to be set only a short time, and they often can make two sets a day, in fine weather, and secure many fish, sometimes forty to fifty thousand pounds in twenty-four hours fishing. The best bait for haddock is salted menhaden (porgy slyvers) cut up in small pieces of one inch square. When these can be secured, the fishermen prefer them to any other kind of bait. Fresh or frozen herring is the next choice, and sometimes frozen squid are used.

The men who go "winter haddocking," are exposed to the wintry blasts of snow-squalls, with rough, angry seas breaking into their dories, for they often fish in very windy, rough weather and sometimes a snowstorm shuts in quickly and they are lost. George's Bank is one of the roughest places on which to fish, off the New England coast, especially so during the winter months, for there is always a strong tide, and when it runs to windward, with a fresh breeze blowing, there is a very sharp chop, with wild, turbulant seas breaking continually. There are two reasons why the haddock fishermen haul their trawls from the windward to leeward. First, because it is very much easier work to haul the trawl into the dory when the ground-line is slack with her drifting off down to leeward, and second, because a haddock's mouth is very tender, and the hook tears out of its lips easily, when there is a heavy strain on the ground-line, as there would be if hauling to windward with the dory pounding into a head-beat sea, and many fish would be lost.

Most haddock fishermen work continuously while they are fishing on the Bank, either at baiting up, setting, or hauling their trawls. They have very little chance for sleep, often going without it from thirty-six to forty-eight hours at a time, improving the opportunity to catch a trip of fish quickly while it is good fishing weather. The skippers of these haddock trawlers were wonderful men, and it was just a little short of marvelous how they kept run of their vessels on George's Bank, while under sail all the time, night and day, in fair weather and foul, through gales and snowstorms, with the tide running strongly; yet they did it and always knew approximately where their vessels were. They could not get an observation of the sun with their sextants during thick weather, which would tell them the position of their vessels by latitude and longitude, so they kept run of them by dead reckoning. They made good use of their sounding leads often, for it told them many things. The lead was hollow on the bottom end; this was filled with hard soap or tallow and it would bring up particles of sand or gravel adhered to it.

An experienced fisherman can always tell, when sounding, when his lead has reached bottom, by "tunking" it up and down, just what kind of bottom he has, whether it be rocks, gravel, sand or mud. He knows by the feeling, as it is telegraphed up the line to his hand, just what he has found but this special sense is acquired only by years of experience as a fisherman. Each fishing skipper carries several charts of the New England and Nova Scotia coasts, including the several Banks, and these give him much information, for these charts are very accurate and are covered with figures showing the different depths of water in fathoms; with the shoal spots on the Bank and near the shore given in feet. So it is possible with the aid of the sounding lead and chart, and good judgment, to tell where a vessel was at all times and when ready to start for home, an experienced skipper knows what course to give the wheelsman to steer by and they invariably made the light or land-fall that they were running for, and port in safety.

When ready to leave the Bank and start for market, many of these skippers would set every inch of canvas the vessel had and drive her hard as long as she could stand to drag it, so that she would be the first of the fleet in, and get the best price for fish. For this reason many fast-sailing vessels, during the eighties, carried both their topmasts* winter fishing; so their skippers could set tops'ls, balloon-jib and stays'l on their way home. An inspiring, beautiful marine picture these handsome vessels made, running into Boston harbor with all sails set, in a fresh breeze, often making a good thirteen knots. Comparatively few were lost or even run ashore, while they were making port, although it was often "thick-o'-snow" or foggy weather, and Boston harbor is one of the most dangerous harbors to "run for," on our New England coast, as there are many outlying reefs, ledges and rocks at its entrance.

Great changes have taken place in this fishery during the past twenty years (1910-1930), both in the kind of vessels used and the new methods employed in catching trips of fish. With the advent of the gasoline marine engine, many sailing vessels had them installed,

---

*Later on many of these vessels had no topmasts when winter fishing and were called by the fishermen, "flat-roofers."

making them auxiliary powered craft. Then came the crude-oil-burning engine, of greater power, which was less expensive to operate, and a much better marine engine for fishing craft, either old or new. Most of the converted sailing vessels still catch their fish with trawl-line and hooks, but some of the larger ones have been converted into "draggers," using the "beam-trawl" to secure their fish. These older vessels have no topmasts and carry only enough sail to make them steady in a sea-way; they simply have a jib, jumbo, fores'l and a riding-sail set in place of the mains'l.

The fishing craft now being built each year (only a few vessels, to be sure, and most of them are steamers), are of an entirely different type from the smart sailing vessels of forty and fifty years ago, with their handsome, finely-modeled, graceful hulls, for they are being built rather full-bodied for seaworthiness and to carry a large load of fish. These auxiliary-powered vessels make quicker trips and their crews earn more money, for no time is lost during calm weather, as was the case with a vessel under sail alone, for these powered vessels go right along night and day, at a speed of ten to twelve knots an hour. The owners make more money now (1930) than formerly, for their vessels make quicker trips and bring in large fares of fresh fish, and the public is much better served with freshly caught fish of many varieties.

The once despised, lowly haddock has now come into its own, for thousands of people today prefer fresh haddock to fresh cod, and haddock often bring a higher price when sold by the fishermen at the Boston Fish-Pier. And it was only sixty years ago when the fishermen threw them away. Surely we mortals do change our ideas.

CHAPTER XII

THE FIRST FISHERMEN'S RACE, MAY 1, 1886

IN the early eighties, New England shipbuilders began to build fishing vessels from the lines of the blue-print designed on the drawing-board. This was a great change from building fishing vessels by the "rule-o'-thumb," from wood models, as had been done previous to that time. One of the most famous of all the New England designers of fishing vessels was "Captain of Arts" Thomas F. McManus, who sponsored the "first fishermen's race," sailed on May 1, 1886. He was at that time a young man of thirty, just coming into prominence as a designer of fishing vessels, and was full of enthusiasm for this race. It was through his untiring energy and hard work among prominent bankers, yachtsmen and fish merchants that the money ($1,500.00) was raised for the "first fishermen's race." Commodore Forbes was the first donor. He gave $100.00. He also promised to give a hundred dollar cup if the pilot's boat *Hesper* was allowed to race with the fishermen, with the understanding that if the *Hesper* won the race, she was to have the cup. If a fisherman won the race, she was to have both the cup and the money.

There was quite an argument among the fishermen as to whether they should allow the pilot boat *Hesper* to race against them. The matter was finally settled by Tom McManus who said to them: "You fellers are racing for money — not the cup." So it was finally agreed that they would allow the *Hesper* to race, and if she won, she should have the cup only, and the first fishing vessel to finish should have the $1500.00; but

158

if a fishing vessel won the race, she should have both the cup and the money.

There were several fishing vessels that entered in this race and also the pilot boat *Hesper*, making it a very interesting one. The fishing vessels and their skippers, as near as I can recall, were as follows:— Schooners: *Sarah H. Prior, John H. McManus, Gertie S. Windsor, Hattie I. Phillips, William Emerson, Belle J. Neal, Emily P. Wright* and *Edith Emery*. Skippers, Tom McLaughlin, Johnnie O'Brien, Maurice Powers, Ned Plunket, Bat Whalen, John Driscoll, John Carney and Pat Sullivan. The schooner *Augusta E. Herrick* (skipper Bill Herrick, of Swan's Island, Maine) was much larger than the others and a center-board vessel. She was not entered in the race but sailed over the course for the sport of sailing in a fishermen's race.

The course was a triangular one and the start was off Boston Light, to and around Davis Ledge buoy off Minot's Light, thence to and around Half Way Rock off the Marblehead shore, and back to Boston Light. The wind was southeast and very light at the start, so the first leg was a dead beat to windward; the second leg was a broad-reach with their sheets well off to port; and the third leg was a close-reach back to the finish line off Boston Light.

Before the race there was a great deal of talk and some argument among the fishermen as to whether the new fishing schooner *John H. McManus* was a faster vessel than the famous *Sarah H. Prior*, which was at that time the acknowledged "Queen of the Fleet," for the *Prior* was very fast close hauled by the wind, when it was blowing heavy and rough, and she could "trim them all" at this kind of sailing. She was not particularly fast in light winds close hauled, neither was she a fast running vessel with her sheets started. Both the fishing schooners *Sarah H. Prior*, and the *John H. McManus*, had been designed by a Boston man, Dennison J. Lawlor, who also had designed the handsome, fast pilot boat *Hesper*, which was sailed in this race by her proud owner and commander, Capt. George W. Lawlor.

Most of the fishing vessels were nearly of the same size, about ninety feet long, while the pilot schooner *Hesper* was larger, being one hundred feet or more. The *Augusta E. Herrick* was the largest of all, being one hundred and fourteen feet long. They all sailed vessel for vessel, for no time allowance is made in a fishermen's race.

There was a great deal of maneuvering before the start. The *Hesper* and the *McManus* were the first to cross the starting line, close together, near the windward stake-boat, with the *McManus* on the weather-quarter of the *Hesper*. The *Prior* was the next to cross, closely followed by the *Emery*, *Windsor* and *Phillips*. The *Hesper* held the starboard tack off shore, while the *Prior* and *Windsor* tacked to port shortly after crossing and stood inshore toward Nantasket beach. The *Prior* was under the lee of the *Windsor* for a time, but skipper Maurice could not hold her there and she soon pulled out ahead. The *Hesper* and *McManus* stood off shore for quite a long time on the starboard tack, the *Hesper* gaining slightly; finally she tacked to port and stood inshore, but the *McManus* held off shore for half an hour longer, then tacked and stood inshore on the port tack heading up for Minot's Light. At about this same time, the *Hesper*, which was inshore, tacked to starboard, heading out for Minot's. There was some interesting guessing at this stage of the race

SCHOONER "JOHN H. McMANUS," FIRST TO FINISH IN THE
FISHERMEN'S RACE, MAY 1, 1886

as to whether the *Hesper*, or the *McManus*, would be
ahead when they came together near Minot's. The
Hesper was too fast for the *McManus*, and crossed her
bow well to windward of her and turned the Davis
Ledge buoy some two miles in the lead.

The *McManus* was second around the buoy, followed by the *Neal*, *Prior*, fourth, *Windsor*, fifth, *Phillips*, sixth, the others trailing. The wind which had
been light, now breezed up and the *Hesper*, with her
sheets well off to port, did some fast sailing with the
wind over her quarter, her big balloon-jib drawing
well. The increased wind was just what the *Sarah H.
Prior* needed, and she soon passed the *Belle J. Neal*,
but could not sail as fast as the *John H. McManus*,
running off the wind, for the *Prior's* best sailing qualities were "by the wind." The *Augusta E. Herrick* also

did some fast sailing on this second leg, for she was a center-board vessel and was considered one of the fastest runners in the mackerel fleet in those days; but she was so far behind, having made a poor showing when "by the wind," with the others, that she could not overhaul the leaders.

The vessels rounded Half Way Rock as follows:— *Hesper*, first, *McManus*, second, *Prior*, third, and *Windsor*, fourth, and they finished with a light wind in this order. The pilot schooner *Hesper* was first, winning the race and the cup. The fishing schooner *John H. McManus* was second, she being the first fisherman to finish, and won the fifteen hundred dollars in prize money. She was two miles ahead of the *Sarah H. Prior*, which finished a few minutes before the *Gertie S. Windsor*. The *McManus* proved in this race, that she was much faster in light winds than the *Prior*; but Tom McLaughlin and his crew, as did many admirers of the *Sarah H. Prior*, claimed it would have been a different story had the race been sailed in heavy winds and rough seas. There is no doubt in my mind that the *Prior* was the ablest and fastest fishing schooner in the fleet at that time, when sailing in heavy winds and rough water.

"Captain of Arts," Thomas F. McManus, has now become famous as one of the great designers of fishing vessels, for he has had many famous sailers among the fishermen to his credit. He has designed more fishing vessels than others, having made a specialty of this class, while other designers have worked on both yachts and merchant vessels, as well as fishermen. While on board the U. S. S. *Bushnell*, viewing the "fishermen's races" held off Gloucester, between the *Bluenose* and the *Henry Ford*, in October, 1922, I enjoyed a long conversation with "Captain" McManus, and he told me that the *Henry Ford* was his four hundred and seventeenth creation. He has designed some others since then, so now he must have nearly five hundred sail to his credit. Tom McManus was a genius, and he had a great love for his work, as he greatly admired a beautiful vessel with graceful lines and a fine shear. He loved to see his vessels sail and it gave him a great deal of pleasure, especially when one of them made a fine showing and won a race.

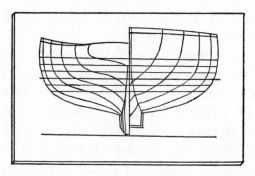

The Lines of a Fishing Schooner

CHAPTER XIII

THREE SKIPPERS WHO WERE
GREAT SAIL-CARRIERS

THERE have been many famous skippers of fishermen, who were great sail-carriers and I want to tell you about three of them who represent three different fishing ports and three different branches of the New England fisheries. First, there was Tom McLaughlin of Boston, who sailed the *Sarah H. Prior*, trawling for fresh haddock and cod on George's Bank; second, there was Tommy Bohlin of Gloucester, who sailed the *Nannie C. Bohlin*, trawling for fresh halibut on the Grand Banks; and third, there was Lincoln Jewett of Portland, who sailed the *Elsie M. Smith*, seining for mackerel.

When a boy, in the early eighties, while seining with father in the schooner *Astoria*, I often heard the crew tell about a wonderful vessel from Boston, by the name of *Sarah H. Prior*. They said, "She was the ablest vessel to carry sail in a blow, and the smartest sailer by the wind in a fresh breeze, out of Boston." Tom McLaughlin was the skipper of this able, fast-sailing vessel and he was not only a smart fisherman but a great sailing-master as well, and he dearly loved to sail this vessel, for she was his pride and joy. When he was trawling on "George's," and had caught a large trip of haddock, and was ready to start for market in Boston, often it would be blowing a heavy nor'wester ("a dead muzzler"), with a long, hard beat ahead of him; but he would set her "four-lowers" and drive her for all she was worth.

The *Prior* was a very able vessel and could carry

SCHOONER "SARAH H. PRIOR" BEATING HOME FROM
GEORGE'S IN A HEAVY NOR'WESTER

whole-sail as he beat her in to the "Cape," then across the "Bay," and on up into Boston harbor. He often beat this vessel into port during a heavy nor'wester, under "whole-sail," when other vessels had in "single-reefs," or some of them "hove-to" under their fores'ls. Sometimes when he arrived in Boston, the *Prior* was so badly iced up with frozen spray, from beating to wind'ard in a westerly gale, that it was quite impossible for his crew to get her sails down in time; so he would shoot her up under sail alongside old T Wharf. The crew would throw out her lines, make her fast, and let her sails shake the ice off in the wind and dry out, as they took out her trip of fish. Often, during cold winter days, I have seen vessels badly iced up, lying at the wharves in Boston, with their sails up, just as they were when they came into port, drying out in a fresh, off-shore wind.

Tom McLaughlin was proud of his vessel, for many times she would bring him into Boston ahead of the fleet and he was so enabled to get a good price for his fish. He was a good fisherman and made many large, quick trips, always up among the "high-liners," making a large stock, and his crew would share well for the season. He always had a fine crew of men, "the very best," as he could have his pick of the fishermen, for many men were anxious to "ship" with him, as they felt sure of making a good winter's work. These men were ready at anytime to swear by Tom Mc-Laughlin, for they thought him one of the smartest skippers in the fleet, and they also imbibed some of his spirit in his love for the *Prior*, and were always ready to bet their hard-earned money on her in a race.

One day in the fall of 1882, Tom McLaughlin was driving the *Prior* in from "George's," with a trip of fresh fish bound to market. As they neared Cape Cod they fell in with a large schooner yacht bound to Boston. It was blowing fresh from the west-sou'west, and the yacht was under single-reefs, but the *Prior*, as usual, had her four-lower sails set. Tom sailed his vessel up across the stern of the yacht, passing by her to windward, and when ahead of her, half a mile or so, he rolled his wheel up, swinging off, then jibing over, he sailed her along under the lee of the yacht, and when astern of her the second time, he tacked, then stood up across her wake and passed by her on her weather. When about a mile ahead of her, the second time, he turned to his crew and made this remark:

"I've heard a lot o' talk, 'bout that yacht being a great sailer! She's no sailer, for th' *Prior* can sail rings 'round 'er!"

They continued on to Boston and the *Prior* was tied

up alongside T Wharf, long before the yacht arrived in the harbor and anchored off the water front. The owner of the yacht came ashore soon after arrival and went up to his ship-broker's office on State Street and asked him this question:

"Do you remember that last spring you sold me a schooner yacht?"

"Yes, sir, I do, a fine vessel, too," replied the broker.

"I want you to sell her," said the owner.

"Why, Mr. Brown, what's the trouble?" asked the broker.

"Well, I don't want any yacht that a fisherman can beat as badly as we got beaten today, coming across from the 'Cape,'" replied Mr. Brown.

"What fisherman was that, Mr. Brown?" asked the broker.

"The *Sarah H. Prior*," he replied.

"Pshaw! Mr. Brown, you don't need to feel badly about that, for the *Sarah H. Prior* is called the ablest fisherman in a blow, and the fastest sailer by the wind, out of Boston," said the broker.

"I don't doubt it in the least, the way she sailed by us today. But I don't want a yacht that a fisherman can sail rings around; not for me! You sell her for what she'll bring!" said Mr. Brown to the ship-broker.

Tommy Bohlin was called by the fishermen: "The greatest sail-carrier and driver out o' Gloucester." I have heard several fishermen make this remark. Tommy Bohlin came to Gloucester when a young man and went trawling for fresh halibut on the Grand Banks. He was a smart young fisherman and was soon given command of a fishing vessel. He did well and in a few years the owners had a new vessel built for him, called the *Nannie C. Bohlin* and she proved to be a fine, able vessel and a fast sailer. Tommy sailed her for years, trawling for halibut, and made a fine record, bringing home many large trips; also, he made many quick trips, making money for the owners, himself and his crew. He not only made halibut trips to the "Flemish Cap" (Grand Bank), but he also went to Greenland, Iceland, and once he went over, off the coast of Norway, on a halibut trip. He was considered by the fishermen and owners of vessels, one of the smartest skippers out of Gloucester, for several years, in the fresh halibut fishery.

Tommy soon found out that the *Nannie C.* was a very able vessel to carry sail; also a fast sailer, both by the wind and running off. She was a fine sea-boat and handled well at all times. He tried her in many ways, driving her hard when it was blowing heavy and she would drag her whole-sail a long time, for she was a dependable vessel without any tricks about her. When they had caught a trip of fresh halibut with their trawls, on the Grand Bank, and were ready to start for home, Tommy would have the crew set whole-sail and then he would drive her hard the whole passage and make a quick run. Many a time when the *Nannie C.* arrived in Gloucester after a very stormy, rough passage in windy weather, both her topmasts would be missing, broken off from carrying sail so long.

At one time when they were bound home, Tommy made up his mind that he would drive her very hard on that trip, to see if he could make her quit, so he drove her harder than he had ever driven her before, but he could not make the *Nannie* quit. The day they arrived in Gloucester, Tommy went up to a barber shop to get a haircut and shave. There he met several skippers whom he knew and he soon began telling them about

SCHOONER "NANNIE C. BOHLIN" HOMEWARD BOUND
FROM THE GRAND BANKS

his trip home and about how hard he had driven the
Nannie that trip, to see if he could make her quit.

"But could I make her quit? No, sir! I couldn't do
it!" said Tommy, and to hear him tell his story, one
might think that he was driving spikes into a six-inch
plank with his clenched fist, for he said:

"I *drove* 'er, an' I *drove* 'er, an' I *drove* 'er! But
could I make 'er quit? No, sir! I couldn't make 'er do
it!" exclaimed Tommy most emphatically.

Sometimes when he was driving her hard on the passage home, some new member of his crew, not being
used to Tommy and his ways of driving the *Nannie C.*
so hard, might remonstrate with him and say:

"Don't you think she'd go erlong er little easier,
skipper, if we tucked er single-reef in 'er mains'l?"

"*What? Reef this vessel!*" exclaimed Tommy. "No
need to reef 'er, fer she's th' able *Nannie Bohlin*!"

Tommy Bohlin, although a great sail-carrier and a hard-driver of his vessel, was not a reckless man, for he watched the weather at all times and he always knew how much his vessel could stand before shortening sail. On one trip, when bound home, Tommy had been up all night watching his vessel, for it was blowing fresh. After breakfast he went below and "turned in" for a few hours sleep. Before leaving the deck he had said to the two men on watch:

"Keep er sharp lookout to wind'ard now, boys. If it should look like er squall, or if it breezes up any more, give me er call!"

"Aye, aye, sir!" replied the man at her wheel.

The two men on watch evidently were careless and did not heed their skipper's instructions, for he had been gone below only a short time when a heavy, white squall struck the vessel and knocked her down on her beam-ends, flat out on the water, and carried away her main mast. When she went over, it awoke Tommy, who sprang out of his bunk and rushed up on deck. The *Nannie* soon began to right herself and Tommy sang out lustily:

"Haul down th' jib an' jumbo. Take in th' fores'l. Lively, boys, lively! Now git th' sails off 'er 'fore they blow 'way."

There was urgent need for her crew to work quickly for the squall was a heavy one. The wind blew with terrific force, lashing the sea into a foam of feather white. In a few minutes the worst of the squall was over, but the wind still blew a gale, so the skipper told his crew to put two-reefs in the fores'l and set it; he then rolled her wheel down and hove her to. Skipper Tommy and his crew then set to work on the wreckage, trying to save the mains'l, the main-boom and main-gaff, clearing away the broken spar before it should punch a hole in the hull. While they were all busy at work on it, a large barque, bound from Turk's Island to Gloucester, with a load of salt, "hove-to" close by. Her Captain hailed Tommy, saying:

"Schooner ahoy! Do you want to be taken off, Captain, you and your crew?" Tommy looked up in surprise, for he didn't know that there was any vessel near them.

"Taken off? Why, no! We don't wanter be taken off! We're all right!" said Tommy.

The Captain then said to Tommy: "If you don't need any assistance, skipper, we'll be going along about our business!"

"All right, Captain! Much obliged; good luck to yer!" said Tommy.

The skipper of the *Nannie C.*, and his crew, saved the mains'l, the main-boom and the main-gaff, after a long, hard tussle and much dangerous work. They took in the reefed-fores'l, unbent it, took off the fore-boom and fore-gaff, rigged up the main-boom and main-gaff on the fore mast in place of the fores'l, bending on the mains'l, but first tucking a single-reef in the sail, because the fore mast was shorter than the main mast. With this sail set they started for Gloucester, the *Nannie C.* rigged as a sloop, instead of her usual schooner rig. She did well and made good time (blowing hard and rough though it was) as Tommy sailed her on through the winter gales and in a few days reached Gloucester. On the third day after they had arrived home, Tommy met the Captain of the barque on the street.

"Hello, Captain!" said Tommy. "When'd you git in?"

"Got in this morning!" replied the Captain.

"Ho! Where've you ben all this time?" asked Tommy and then before the Captain could make reply, Tommy said, "We got in three days ago!"

"Well!" replied the Captain, "We had a heavy gale for three days, so we hove-'er-to!"

"Hove-'er-to!" mused Tommy, "Is that what you call er heavy gale? Why, we was there at th' same time, an' we fixed up th' *Nannie* an' drove 'er erlong home, nice an' comfortable like, rigged up as er sloop."

Lincoln Jewett, when he was skipper of the famous fishing schooner, *Elsie M. Smith*, of Portland, Maine, in the eighties and nineties, was spoken of by the fishermen, as the greatest sail-carrier of all our "Down East" skippers. The fishing schooner *Elsie M. Smith* was one of the ablest vessels I ever saw under sail when the wind was blowing heavy, and she was a very fast sailer close hauled by the wind, in rough water. She was one of those rare vessels which would not roll out as some do, by the wind when it was blowing hard, for she seemed to settle down to her work, gradually heeling over until her lee-rail was down under water; there she would hold, walking right along about her business, going fast. When it was rough and she was in head-beat seas and hadn't time to climb over them all, she went right through them, minding it not at all, tossing the water from her deck, the able lady that she was. In conversation with skipper Al Miller, whose real name was Alvan Mallock, he told me this little incident about the *Elsie*:

"One day we was under single-reefs headin' to th' nor'thard on Cashe's Ledge. There was er smart breeze blowin' from th' east-no'theast an' it was rough; quite an old hubble o'er sea heavin' in from th' east'ard. We

Schooner "Elsie M. Smith" of Portland, Maine,
Close Hauled

sighted er speck o' sail 'way to th' sou'sou'theast, didn't think much 'bout it at th' first off, but pretty soon we saw it much plainer an' afore long we knowed it was er vessel comin' our way. I was skipper o' th' *Morning Star* then, an' we was goin' 'long fairly well, considerin' th' rough water an' heavy breeze blowin' at th' time. We had our purse-seine hauled out on deck an' our seine-boat was on er long painter out astern. We was bound to Portland fer er harbor, as th' fish (mackerel) was down to th' east'ard, off Monhegan, Seguin an' Cape Elizabeth. We didn't want to keep off an' run to Gloucester, which we could've done much easier, so I held 'er up by th' wind. In 'bout an hour's time, we saw that vessel was over-haulin' us, an' we begun to wonder what vessel it could be that was travelin' so fast. There was much guessin' an' speculatin' among our crew as to which vessel it was, some namin' one, an' others said 'twas 'nother. By an' by she was near 'nough so we could see she was under whole-sail; she even had both 'er gaff-tops'ls on 'er, so now excitement was intense erboard our vessel, wonderin' we all was who it could be. What kind o' er vessel was she that could carry whole-sail on er day like that? Fer we was under single-reefs! When she was 'bout half er mile from us on our starboard weather-quarter, I could see that it was th' *Elsie M. Smith*, an' I told th' boys what vessel it was.

"I was lookin' at 'er with my glass (binoculars), an' could see she had 'er seine-boat on deck; up to wind'ard it was, on 'er starboard side. I had met Linc Jewett, 'er skipper, an' knowed him quite well an' had o' course heard er lot o' talk 'bout him carryin' sail on th' *Elsie* an' how she was er very able vessel to lug 'er canvas in er blow, an' was er fast sailer by th' wind in rough water, but that was th' first time I had ever seen 'er under sail in er blow. I never would've believed that any fishin' vessel in th' fleet, could o' carried 'er whole-sail on er day like that, onless I had seen it with my own two eyes. Why, man alive! She went by us just as if we was anchored! I could hardly believe it was possible that there was er fisherman in th' whole fleet, what could sail as fast as that one was er doin' right then.

"'Did yer ever see enythin' like that afore in yer life, skipper?' said Joe to me, looking up to wind'ard after th' *Elsie*.

"'No, I never did, Joe,' I said.

"Then Joe started to go below, sayin' as he went down th' companion-way: 'It sure beats all my goin' to sea, skipper.'

"'It sure does, Joe,' says I," concluded skipper Al.

In 1887, when fishing with father in the *Lady Elgin*, mackerel were very scarce, during July, off the

Maine coast, so we went to Chaleur Bay looking for fish. We made the run in about four days, as we had a fine nor'wester which took us across the Bay of Fundy and ran us down the "Cape Shore." We stayed down there about ten days, having a good look around the "Bay" and over around the "Island," but found no signs of mackerel, so father decided shortly to start back home. When we reached the Straits of Canso, we found about forty sail of American mackerel seiners at anchor off Port Hawksbury. They, too, were on their way home, so we anchored that night, as it was stormy outside.

The next morning we all got under way and started for home. I noticed that the *Elsie M. Smith* was one of the vessels in the fleet as we beat across Chedabucto Bay. We went inside of St. Andrews Island, through "Little Gut of Canso," as father was well acquainted and a good pilot. Several other vessels also went inside, but the most of them went outside, especially the larger vessels which brought them to leeward. When we opened out by White Point, we found the wind was west-sou'west, right dead ahead, a very long, hard beat up the "Cape Shore," of two hundred and forty miles (if the wind still held from that quarter). The wind was light at first, but it soon began to freshen. It breezed up fast, and by ten o'clock it was blowing a good fresh breeze.

The *Elsie Smith* soon began to show her heels as the wind increased, which was just to her liking, and the way she "walked" up through the fleet that day was a caution. Skipper Linc was at her wheel, for we could see him there as she passed close by our stern once as we tacked off shore. She passed vessel after vessel and in two hours' time she was ahead, leading the whole fleet. The wind increased and by twelve o'clock it was blowing half a gale. Some of the skippers swung their vessels off and ran into different harbors along the coast for shelter. The most of us kept on, however, beating up the shore, off on the starboard tack, then up-shore on a longer port tack, "whanging" away all the afternoon. Our vessel, the *Lady Elgin*, was not a particularly fast sailer by the wind, but she was a good, able vessel and an average sailer, for there were as many vessels behind us, as there were ahead. We beat away all the afternoon and that night, at sunset, we just could see the *Elsie* from our masthead, for she was ten or twelve miles "away to windward" of the whole fleet.

What a vessel she was to sail, close hauled by the wind, when it was blowing fresh! And how proud her skipper must have been of her, as she sailed so well for him that day. She was, indeed, a wonderful vessel "by the wind." We beat away all that night, as the wind went down somewhat with the sun, but the next day, we had the wind off the land about nor'nor'west, a fresh breeze, and had a good reach up the Cape Shore. We were off Halifax the next night, and the following day we passed La Have, then Shelburne, and the third day we rounded the "Cape" and shaped our course for Monhegan. It was then August 13th, just three weeks since we had left home, and that evening about five o'clock, we sighted schools of mackerel as we crossed the "Seal Island Grounds."

We soon roused our purse-seine onto our seine-boat and went out and set our seine around a good school, pursed her up, dried her in and bailed out on deck, one hundred and fifty barrels of fine mackerel, that we dressed during the night.

The next morning early, the fish were up schooling

again, so we went out, set our seine and got one hundred barrels. That night, just before sunset, we got another fine school of one hundred and thirty barrels, which made us a full trip of three hundred and eighty barrels. We were up all the second night, dressing, and finished salting the following afternoon; then all "turned in," but the watch, and had a good sleep, and the next day started for home; the crew busy "heading up" and "stowing down" our barrels of fish in the vessel's hold. When we arrived home with this fine trip, the owner thought we had got our fish while in Chaleur Bay and was surprised when the skipper told him where.

This trip to the "Bay" goes to show how uncertain mackerel seining is, and also, how "lucky" the fishermen are sometimes; for we had started from the "Bay" bound home without any fish, but at last were made very happy by our "good luck" on getting this trip in the Bay of Fundy, while on our way home.

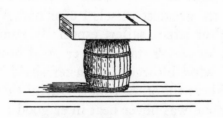

Mackerel Barrel and
Keeler

CHAPTER XIV

TWO FISHERMEN RACE TO MARKET

ONE of the secrets of the success of skipper Al Miller as a great sailing-master was his ability and excellent judgment in trimming the *sheets* of his vessel, so that her sails would draw well, thus enabling her to do her fastest sailing. I went cook with Al Miller, in the steamer *Lincoln*, for two seasons. One day when I was frying doughnuts he came into the fo'-cas'le and sat down on the locker near the range; a large pan partly full of freshly fried doughnuts stood nearby where I was at work. I told him to help himself. He reached over and took one and when he had eaten it he said: "These are pretty good doughnuts, cook, guess I'll have another!" When he had finished his second one, he was in a reminiscent mood and began telling stories. Here is one of them.

"Several years ago, back in th' year 1892, I had er new vessel built called th' *Edna Wallace Hopper*. She was one o' th' greatest vessels I ever had. Very easy to handle, an' er smart sailer, especially runnin' off th' wind with 'er *sheets* started in er good breeze, fer th' harder th' wind blowed, th' faster she'd sail, an' th' more she'd beat th' other feller. Durin' th' eight years I sailed 'er she was never beat in er good fresh breeze, but she wasn't fast in light airs.

"Now there was th' *Lucania*, an' th' *Oriole*, both of 'em very fast in light winds, more especially so, close hauled by th' wind, fer they would 'ghost erlong' in light airs, an' could beat th' *Hopper* er leetle mite then, but when there was plenty o' wind, she could trim anythin' in th' fleet in 'er day, with 'er *sheets* started er bit.

The winter she was eight years old, I took 'er to New-f'n'land after er trip o' frozen herrin'; we had er very severe cold spell that winter an' she got froze in th' ice an' I lost 'er. I felt very bad to lose 'er, fer she was er fine vessel, an' I had become 'tached to' er, same as er man will fer his good hoss, or his fine dog.

"Th' summer th' *Hopper* was new, one day we was down to th' sou'sou'theast o' No Man's Land, in company with Marty Welch who was in th' *Lucania*. We was th' only vessels there that day, an' we both sot 'bout th' same time, an' both o' us got good schools o' fish; couple o' hundred barrels in each school. Both o' us had ice, so we bailed 'em on deck, an' put 'em below, fer we intended to run 'em in fresh to Boston, instid o' dressin' 'em. Th' *Lucania* was er very fast sailer by th' wind in smooth water, an' moderate winds, fer she could trim most any vessel in th' fleet 'cept th' *Oriole*, an' Marty was rather proud of 'er.

"Now Marty had never ben in company with us afore, an' never had seen th' *Hopper* sail, so he didn't know nothin' 'bout what kind of er sailer th' *Hopper* was. I suppose he an' his crew thought they would have some fun at our expense an' could beat th' *Hopper* on th' run to Boston, fer when we was both ready to start fer market, Marty luffed th' *Lucania* up on our weather-quarter an' hailed us sayin': 'Hello Al!'

" 'Hello Marty!' says I.

"Then Marty says to me: 'Al, I'll race you to Boston, for fifty dollars!'

" 'All right, Marty, I'll take that bet. O' course you think th' *Lucania* can beat th' *Hopper*. Well, perhaps she can in er light wind, but if we have *wind 'nough*, we'll give yer er *good trimmin'*.'

" 'Ho! Ho! So you think th' *Hopper* can beat th'

Lucania! Well, try an' do it, Al!' shouted back Marty as he rolled 'er wheel up an' swung 'er off, bound to Boston.

"We swayed up our lower-sails, then set our balloon-jib, stays'l, an' both gaff-tops'ls an' started after him. There was er light wind that mornin' from th' sou'-west, but I thought likely it would breeze up in th' afternoon; you know it often does, cook, in th' summer time when th' winds is sou'west, an' I had this in mind when I bet with Marty. Well, it did breeze up that afternoon, cook, an' we had all th' wind we wanted, er regular old 'smoky sou'wester.'

"At th' start th' *Lucania* outsailed us er leetle mite with er light wind, as I had expected she would do, an' at th' end o' an hour's sailin', she was then perhaps, half er mile erhead o' us under our lee-bow. I think it was 'bout nine o'clock when we started, an' 'bout ten o'clock it begun to freshen er leetle an' it soon begun to breeze up fast an' by 'leven o'clock it was blowin' er good fresh breeze an' th' *Hopper* begun to travel faster, an' I could see that we was gainin' on th' *Lucania*. Th' wind increased an' th' *Hopper* was layin' over to 'er work in good shape, 'er lee-rail was under water, an' she was goin' erlong er good twelve knots, an' we was overhaulin' th' *Lucania* fast now, an' 'bout half past twelve at noontime, we passed 'er, close by on 'er weather. When passin' by 'er I saw out o' th' corner of my eye, one o' our crew down behind our lee-rail slyly reach over an' take th' end o' our main-sheet in his hand an' holdin' it up erbove th' rail he shook it at 'em, as much as to say, we'll give yer er line an' tow yer in."

We will let skipper Al have a breathing spell of a few minutes in telling his story while I tell you something about those two skippers. Both of them, Al Miller and Marty Welch, were great sailing-masters and

Schooners "Edna Wallace Hopper" and "Lucania"
Racing to Market

great sail-carriers. They knew how to sail their vessels well, to get the most speed out of them. Neither of them had the least idea of shortening sail on this run, for they were in a race to win, and they would blow their sails off their vessels before they would ever take them in.

There is a certain feeling among all fishermen, especially the skippers, that neither wants to be the first to shorten sail when racing, for if he should do so, he will never hear the last of it; the other fellow will be forever blowing about how he made so and so take in sail! "I made him douse his kites!" "I made him shorten sail!"

So these skippers would drag sail on their vessels and blow them away, before they would ever take them in. There is not much danger of capsizing an able, modern-built, New England fishing vessel, for the most of them are very deep, sharp and heavily ballasted with pig-iron, deep down in the bottom of their holds, floored over and stanchioned down securely under their deck-beams. It makes them very stiff and able and they will carry sail a long time, no matter how hard the wind blows, and if she should be flattened out, they know that she will come back again. Many of our modern fishing vessels have been knocked down, either by a severe squall or tripped by a heavy breaking sea, and they have come quickly back on their bottoms again.

"At four o'clock that afternoon," said skipper Al, "we was nearly up to Sankety Head, an' Marty in th' *Lucania* was fully eight miles astern of us, fer th' *Hopper* had ben doin' some fast sailin' an' we had gained on 'er stiddy since passin' 'er 'bout noon time. Th' wind was still blowin' strong, an' as we neared th' 'Cape,' th' wind come off th' land in heavy puffs an' when they struck th' *Hopper*, it made 'er buckle up in great shape an' 'er whole lee-side was under water, fer it was comin' in over 'er lee cat-head an' goin' out over 'er lee-quarter in er smother o' foam. After th' first puff was over, I said, 'This won't do, boys! We must do somethin' to hold our topmasts from goin' over 'er side.'

"I had ben watchin' 'em when th' first puff struck us an' they was bent over like whip-cords; it was then 'bout seven o'clock an' we was right off Chatham. I knowed we had er coil o' new riggin' down in our lazaret, so I took th' cover off an' told one o' th' boys to jump down an' pass me up th' end; then I sent er man aloft with it an' told him to make it fast to th' main-truck. I took th' wheel myself an' shot 'er up in th' wind, an' told 'em to sway it down good an' taut, an' make it fast to th' weather-bit-head. I had to swing th' *Hopper* off ag'in quick, fer we was close in under th'

beach an' would soon be ashore if I didn't. I had intended to have er man take t'other end o' th' new rope
up an' make it fast to th' fore-truck, but afore we could
do it, er heavier puff struck us an' I had to let 'er take
it, fer I dassent let 'er luff or we would be ashore. She
rolled down some, but I wasn't consarned erbout th'
vessel, but I was afeared that we would lose our fore-
topmast.

"All to once we heard er crash an' I knowed what
had happened; our fore-topmast was gone. It broke off
'bout ten feet up from th' cap on th' fore-masthead. I
told th' boys to clew up th' tops'l, an' haul down th'
balloon-jib; when this was done, we cleared erway th'
broken spar an' th' topmast-riggin', an' went erlong on
our way sorry to have lost th' use of our two sails. The
wind blowed hard that evenin', an' how th' *Hopper* did
go, cook! When them strong puffs struck 'er, she fairly
flew; fer if ever er vessel flew up by th' 'Cape,' we did
that evenin'. There was times when she made 'er *fourteen knots* an hour by th' log.

"What er vessel she was to sail in er breeze o' wind,
cook! What er pretty marine picture she must 'ave ben
fer them who could see 'er from th' shore as she tore
erlong, fer we was close in under th' land, er skimmin'
erlong th' beach!

"At sunset that evenin' we was up erbreast o' Nau-
set's Three Lights an' Marty in th' *Lucania* was out o'
sight fur astern. At ten o'clock that night we passed
Highland Light. Th' wind moderated some after dark,
but then we had er pretty good run ercross th' 'Bay,' an'
up th' harbor, an' luffed up erlongside old T Wharf
'bout four o'clock, just at daylight th' next mornin'.
We put out our lines an' made 'er fast, then furled up
our sails an' had breakfast.

"Just afore seven o'clock, I went up to th' Fish Exchange to be ready when th' Market opened to sell our fish. We was th' only mack'rel seiner in that mornin' an' th' fish buyers wanted our trip, so I let 'em bid 'til I got 'em up to ten cents, then I sold 'em our trip o' fish. We weighed out 60,000 pounds an' stocked $6,000.00 an' our crew shared $152.00 to er man.

"At seven fifteen o'clock, just as I come back from th' Fish Exchange down to th' wharf where our vessel lay, there was Marty in th' *Lucania* just luffin' up erlongside th' dock. Th' *Hopper* had beat th' *Lucania* three hours an' fifteen minutes on er hundred an' fifty mile run."

As an afterthought, with a twinkle in his eye, he said to me: "We led 'er more'n three hours! We beat 'er good, cook! But if we hadn't carried erway our foretopmast we'd er beat 'er worse'n that!"

PIGGIN. USED FOR BAILING

CHAPTER XV

THE KING OF THE MACKEREL FLEET

SKIPPER Solomon B. Jacobs of Gloucester, for many years was called by the fishermen, "The King of the Mackerel Fleet." He was born at Twillingate, Newfoundland, and when a young man, came to Gloucester, where he lived for more than fifty years, and there he died at the age of seventy-four. When he first came to Gloucester, he went fishing as one of the crew on a Georg'sman, hand-lining from deck. He was a smart fisherman and a bright capable young man, so was soon given command of the fishing schooner *Samuel R. Lane*. While skipper of the *Lane*, he was "high-line" of the "George's" fleet of hand-line fishermen, and made one of the greatest records ever attained in the cod fishery up to that time, 1875. Shortly after this he entered the mackerel, purse-seine fishery and soon was up among the "high-liners" in the mackerel fleet as well, and for many years was the most successful mackerel, purse-seine fisherman in the world.

In the year 1878, skipper Sol sailed in his new schooner, *Sarah M. Jacobs* and landed the second trip of mackerel in New York that spring. In the spring of 1879 he was the first to land a trip in New York in his new schooner, *Edward E. Webster*. In 1880, he was also the first to land a trip in New York in the same vessel.

Skipper Sol was a very smart, capable, energetic man, bound to be the first in all that he did. Here is an instance. In the early part of March, 1881, there were three of the seining fleet skippers, who were making plans to leave Gloucester in their vessels for the southern mackerel grounds very much earlier than usual. These three men were Solomon B. Jacobs, Eben T. Lewis and Frank Hall. Skipper Sol, in order to be the first, stole a march on the other two, which was characteristic of the man, for he sailed at four o'clock in the morning on Saturday, March 11, 1881. Nine days later, on March 20th, skipper Sol was in New York with a trip of mackerel; the *earliest* one on record. He was the first man to land mackerel for several years, and most of the time after 1881, he was "high-line," as well, for the season.

During those years from 1878 to 1881, when skipper Hans Joyce was "high-line" for the season, skipper Sol was a close second, for in 1881, the last year that skipper Joyce was "high" (and landed his record catch of 4,900 barrels), skipper Sol was close behind with 4,500 barrels; and the next year he was "high-line" for the season. From that time on during the next thirty-five years, he was "high-line" with the exception of a year or two in the middle eighties, when skipper Eben T. Lewis of Boothbay Harbor was "high."

Skipper Sol was a smart, progressive man and he soon made a lot of money, which enabled him to own his vessels, so that he did not have to sail a vessel from a fish firm, for he was his own master and owner and could sell his fish where he chose. He had many fine vessels in his day, and they were among the best in the fishing fleet, for he would not have anything but the very best, in either vessels or fishing gear. I recall several of his vessels, for I have seen the most of them many times. One of his first seiners was the *Sarah M. Jacobs.* Then he had the *Edward E. Webster, Molly Adams, Alice E. Jacobs, Ethel B. Jacobs* and the *Helen*

Miller Gould. The *Gould* was the first mackerel seiner to have a gasoline engine installed, making her an auxiliary-powered fishing schooner. This vessel caught on fire in Sydney Harbor, N. S., and was burned and lost.

Skipper Sol always had the latest and best in fishing gear, as well as the finest vessels. At one time he had a purse-seine made of Irish linen, a very long and deep seine that cost about $4,000.00. I have heard fishermen say that it was not a success and was used only a few times, when he gave it up and returned to the use of his ordinary cotton-twine seine. Sol was a great hustler and driver of his vessel, always hunting for mackerel and on the move somewhere. He very seldom stayed long in the fleet, but would go off by himself, and the next thing heard of him, would be that he was in Boston with a large trip.

If mackerel were scarce off the New England coast, in July or August, Sol would start for Chaleur Bay, and drive his vessel hard, night and day, as fast as she could sail (and most of his vessels were fast sailers). In three or four days he would be down to the "Bay." Sailing to the Magdalen Islands, then around Prince Edward Island, he sometimes would get a big trip and then make a quick run home. Other times he would not find any fish in the "Bay," so back he would come and as likely as not, catch a trip on "George's," or out around the South Channel somewhere.

Of the many fine vessels which he owned and sailed, the *Ethel B. Jacobs* was, in my opinion, the best one of them all. She was called by many of the fishermen, "The Queen of the Mackerel Fleet," and this was most appropriate as her skipper was called, "The King of the Mackerel Fleet." The *Ethel B.* was a large vessel for a fisherman, as she was 140 tons and could carry seven hundred barrels of mackerel. She was "hand-some, fast and able!" Yes, she was all three in one! For she was a very able vessel to carry sail in a hard blow; she was a very fast sailer, especially so with her sheets started while running off the wind when it was blowing fresh; and she was the most beautiful vessel in the seining fleet in her day.

Sol Jacobs was not only a smart fisherman, but a great sailing-master, and he dearly loved to sail and race the *Ethel B.* He drove her very hard once, making fifteen knots an hour for six consecutive hours; the only fishing vessel I ever knew that attained this speed for that length of time. It happened out south, one spring, when her skipper drove her to New York with a large trip of mackerel, in a heavy sou'wester, and beat the whole fleet into market.

As was his custom for several years, Jacobs, at the close of the mackerel season, went to Newfoundland after a trip of frozen herring. The winter the *Ethel B.* was a year old, Sol took her there on one of those trips. They had a very severe cold spell that winter, unusually so, even for that cold country. The *Ethel B.* got frozen in solid about the time she was loaded, and Sol had to stay there until the ice broke up late in March, so that it was about April 1st when they arrived in Gloucester. Most of the southern mackerel fleet had been gone for a week, and Sol was wild, for he was usually one of the first to sail south. Sol and his crew worked night and day unloading her cargo of frozen herring, and getting the *Ethel B.* ready for seining, and in a few days they were ready to sail. I have been shipmates with Joe Cash and he once told me the story of that trip, for he was one of the crew with skipper Sol that year.

"Just before we sailed that morning," said Joe, "I overheard a hanger-on say to another of his kind, in a cynical manner: 'I guess Sol won't be the first man into New York this spring with a trip of fish!' But that cheap guy didn't know Sol Jacobs very well, for skipper Sol was always doing the unexpected thing as you shall learn before I finish telling you my story about the quick trip we made out south that spring. When we had the *Ethel B.* all ready, a tow-boat come alongside, and away we went, hoisting our sails on the way out. When off Eastern Point, the tug blew her whistle, and we let go his line as the *Ethel* filled away, bound out south. We set every inch of her canvas and kept it on her night and day, for Sol drove her as fast as she could sail until we reached the southern fishing grounds and 'made the fleet.' They were 'on fish' and Sol acted like a wild man, for our seine-boat, as well as our seine, were on deck.

"You know, cook, it was the custom for large vessels when making a long passage, to carry their boats on deck for safety. So Sol began to yell for us to rouse the boat overboard, at the same time, he grabbed the wheel and hove the vessel to. 'Lively, boys! Lively, now! Hurry an' git th' boat-tackles hooked on,' he said, and every man was jumping to do his bidding as we quickly hoisted our boat out and dropped her overboard on the port side. 'Hurry, boys! Hurry an' git th' seine hauled onto th' boat!' yelled Sol as he turned the wheel over to the watch and started for the fore-masthead.

"Jack Campbell was our seine-heaver, a big, raw-boned, Cape Breton Scotchman, weighing two hundred and forty pounds, six feet and four inches in his sock feet, with a pair of hands on him the size of two good sized hams. The way Jack hauled our seine onto the boat that day was a caution. I never saw anything like it before in my life, for he hauled the seine on hand over hand, just as you would a cod-line, the roller on the rail singing a steady song and never stopping once, until the end of our seine went onto the seine-boat, for Jack Campbell hauled that seine onto our boat in eleven minutes, a *world's record*, so far as I know, for I never heard of any man doing it quicker.

"When the last bight went onto the boat, Sol shouted: 'Man th' boat!' He came down quickly and we went out and set around a good looking school of fish and got the mackerel, about three hundred barrels, or 90,000 pounds of fresh fish. The skipper luffed the *Ethel B.* alongside the boat and seine, and said: 'Hurry, boys! Hurry! Let's git these fish bailed out on deck!' Our crew worked like Trojans, every man pulling, hauling and hoisting for all he was worth; hats and coats were thrown aside that we might work the faster. When the fish had been bailed out on deck, the skipper said: 'Let's see how quick we can stow an' ice these fish! Lively now, lads, lively!'

"We passed them down in bushel-baskets, a steady stream going down both hatches at once, for we all worked fast, every man moving quickly and striving his best to do more work than the skipper, who was working like a beaver himself. When all our fish were below and iced in the pens, we hauled our seine on deck and hoisted the seine-boat in on the port side, so she would be up to wind'ard, for the wind was sou'west and we were bound to the nor'thard up the coast to a New York Market.

"The minute the seine-boat was in on deck and while some of the boys were lashing her to ring-bolts, the skipper rolled the wheel up and shouted: 'Haul in th' fore sheet, boys! H'ist th' jib, an' jumbo, lively now, lads,' and then afore she swung off, he sang out: 'Set th' stays'l, both tops'ls an' th' balloon-jib. Hurry, men! Hurry!' All hands jumped to their stations and quickly carried out his commands, and the *Ethel B.* was off with every inch of her canvas set, flying along fast after the mackerel fleet ahead.

"Do you know, cook, some of those vessels were out of sight ahead by the time we got started, for when we first reached the fleet, they were 'on fish'; some of them were 'bailing,' some of them were 'pursing' and others were 'setting'; so by the time we had got our fish and were ready to start, the most of them were gone.

"It was nearly noon when we first swung off and we had a fine scupper-breeze, and the *Ethel B.* was going along right smart, making her good twelve knots an hour. Pretty soon it began to breeze up and then the wind freshened still more and by one o'clock it was blowing a good stiff breeze, and our vessel was traveling a thirteen knot clip; we had put our patent-taff-rail-log out so we knew how fast she was going. Skipper Sol was watching her very sharp easing off a sheet here and having one hauled in there, when needed, to get every knot out of her that was possible. The wind was blowing half a gale and breezing on harder all the time. By two o'clock that afternoon, the sou'west gale was screeching right out loud, the *Ethel B.* was lying over on her side with her whole lee-rail under water. She was going like a house afire, with two men at the wheel to steer her, every inch of her canvas set and drawing like wild horses. How she did go, cook! She was making fifteen knots, and from *two* o'clock that afternoon until *eight* o'clock that evening, she made *fifteen knots an hour*, for six consecutive hours, or over seventeen land miles an hour. I have never seen any vessel sail so fast, before or since, in my life! Nor one driven so hard, as skipper Sol drove the *Ethel B. Jacobs* that afternoon. What a man he was to carry sail, cook! What a vessel she was to lug her canvas!

"I had been expecting something to give way all the afternoon, but everything held well, for she was only about a year old; all her running-rigging was new rope and she had preventer-back-stays; these kept her top-masts from going over her side. The wind moderated somewhat after sunset, but we still had a good breeze all night. During the night we passed vessel after vessel. Most of them had only their four-lower sails set; a few had single-reefs tucked in their mains'ls.

"At daylight the next morning we were off Sandy Hook, having passed the fleet during the night, and there was only one vessel ahead of us,—the *Grayling*, which was under her four-lower sails, and when Charlie Harty saw us overhauling him, he began to set his light sails, but we passed her off Red Hook and was the first vessel into Fulton Market. Our mackerel sold for a good price, making a large stock, and each man shared one hundred an eighty-two dollars for the trip.

"So Skipper Solomon B. Jacobs, in his schooner the *Ethel B. Jacobs*, was the first as usual to land a trip that spring although the last man away from home," said Joe Cash, as he concluded his story. Sol Jacobs loved to sail the *Ethel B.*, for he believed she was a very fast sailer and could trim any vessel in the fleet, in her day, and I think so myself; so when the fishermen's race was talked up among the fishermen, in the summer of 1892, Sol entered this vessel to sail in the race. I will tell about this race later on.

In 1901, mackerel were very scarce off the New

SCHOONER "ETHEL B. JACOBS" MAKING FIFTEEN KNOTS
AN HOUR, IN A SMOKY SOU'WESTER

England coast, so skipper Sol sailed his vessel across the Atlantic to try his luck fishing with the purse-seine on the European coast. He caught a few hundred barrels off the western coasts of Ireland and Scotland, and sent them home by steamer. The project was not much of a success, however, and in the end was very unfortunate for Sol, as he lost the *Ethel B.* one night, when she ran ashore on the rocks and was a total loss. He and his crew saved their lives, and later were sent home to Gloucester, by the American consul, on a passenger steamship. That winter he had another vessel built and continued purse-seining for many years, always known as "The King of the Mackerel Fleet" among the fishermen.

Chapter XVI

Some Smart Sailers

IT is very essential that a man should first of all be a fine wheelsman, in order to become a great sailing-master. Skipper Charles F. Harty had this quality. He also was called by the fishermen, "The greatest man to trim and sail a vessel out o' Gloucester." If ever a man loved to sail a fine vessel that man was Charlie Harty. He would rather sail one than eat his meals anytime. I have known him to sit on the wheel-box and steer his vessel for hours at a time, when racing with some other fast sailer in the seining fleet. Early in life he learned to be a fine wheelsman, and later on he became known as one of the greatest men in the fishing fleet to trim a vessel so she would do her best sailing. Often, when at the wheel, and his vessel was not sailing as fast as he thought she should, he would call the man on watch to take her wheel, and then go for'ard to look over her bow for a few minutes, and walk aft and look over her stern. If he thought she was a little too much by the head, he would have the crew roll a few barrels of mackerel aft, alongside the cabin-house; or, if he thought she was too much by the stern, he would have the crew cut a few barrels up for'ard, alongside the fore-rigging, on each side, to put her in the right trim; then he would take the wheel again to find out if she sailed any better.

I have laid great stress on the *right trim* of a vessel, for it is very essential that she should be in her *best trim* if she is to do her best sailing. Charlie Harty also was always trimming his vessel's sheets to make her sail faster, for he, like skipper Al Miller, thought this very essential, especially so when his vessel was "close hauled" by the wind, for he could make a vessel "eat right out to wind'ard," and lay a better course than the other vessel he was sailing with.

One summer afternoon, back in the eighties, he was sailing his new fishing schooner the *I. J. Merritt*, racing with Ben Spurling who was in the *Lizzie Maud*, also a new vessel at the time,—a fine little schooner built at East Boothbay, Maine. It was only a friendly "little brush" between two smart sailing fishermen, and both skippers were known as the very best of wheelsmen. As there were no mackerel schooling that day, the rest of the fleet tagged along behind, to see them sail it out. We were all away out in Massachusetts Bay, in the vicinity of Middle Bank, when we started. The wind was southwest, blowing a nice little breeze and the race was to windward. They beat away all the afternoon, and when they finished off the Gurnet's Lights, near Plymouth, Charlie Harty in the *Merritt* was ahead, and one mile to wind'ard; so he won the race.

Later on he had a vessel built called the *Grayling* and she soon proved to be an able vessel and a fast sailer. He won many races with this vessel and while sailing in her caught a lot of fish, for he was a smart mackerel purse-seine fisherman. When out on the fishing grounds he was always watching out to see what was going on in the mackerel fleet. If a vessel some distance away showed by her actions that she might be "on fish," skipper Harty would get his binoculars and after watching her for a minute or two, would call out to the watch on the fore-masthead: "What is that fellow doing down there to loo'ard?"

"I dunno, skipper, 'pears like he may be on fish!" the man on watch would reply.

"Is his boat out?"

"Can't tell whether it is or no, skipper, too fur away!" the man would answer.

The skipper with his binoculars slung over his shoulder, climbed aloft to the masthead and after looking intently at the distant vessel a few moments, called out to the man at the wheel: "Roll your wheel up, Ed!"

"Aye, aye, sir!" replied Ed.

Again came the command from the skipper on the masthead: "Set th' stays'l an' th' balloon-jib, boys! Steady your wheel, Ed!"

"Aye, aye, sir, steady!" replied Ed, and the *Grayling* was off on her run down toward the distant vessel. The skipper then came down on deck and in a little while the man on the masthead sang out loudly: "His boat's out, skipper, guess he's sot!"

By this time other vessels were on their way to the place where the distant seine-boat was out, and where her crew had set their seine around a school of mackerel. Skipper Harty, being the first man to take note of what the distant vessel was doing, was one of the first skippers to reach the place where the mackerel were schooling and got a fine school before the fleet got there and broke up the "bunch of fish."

Charlie Harty often got fish in this manner, for he was always on the alert, watching out, and his keen observation of what the other vessel was doing told him many things that often went unobserved by other skippers. He had charge of many fast-sailing vessels in his day, but one of the finest he ever had and, no doubt, the fastest in the mackerel fleet at that time, was the famous *Oriole*, for he called her the smartest sailer, in moderate weather, that ever sailed out o' Gloucester Harbor. He was very proud of this beautiful schooner and took great delight in racing her against other fast sailers, whenever the opportunity offered, and he would invariably win the contest, for a fast sailer, with Charlie Harty at her wheel, was a hard combination to beat.

There are several reasons why fishermen want fast-sailing vessels, when seining for mackerel. One is, that if you have a fast sailer, she will take you out on the fishing grounds ahead of the fleet; another, if mackerel are seen schooling, by some man on a vessel several miles away from where you are in the fleet, and the whole of them start in that direction, you, in your fast-sailing vessel, can get there first, make a set, and get your fish, before the bunch of mackerel are broken up by the fleet of vessels cutting through them. Again, when you have caught your trip and start for market with fresh fish, you can outsail the fleet, be the first in, and get the best price for your fish.

When Harty was out on the fishing grounds seining, and had been out there for several days, when the wind breezed up and the weather looked as if a storm was coming on, he was one of the first to swing his vessel off and run into some harbor for shelter. Not that he was afraid of the storm, but he didn't believe there was anything gained by a mackerel seiner staying out in a blow, "thrashing around," when the crew could be more comfortable, anchored in some good harbor. He was a great man to hunt for mackerel news and by going into port quite often, he found out many times where fish had last been seen schooling, and frequently got good trips by learning where the fish were to be found. I've known him several times to run into a harbor, when other skippers stayed outside, and the next morning when he was on his way out, he would find a school of fish and get a trip, while those who stayed out, wouldn't get any fish by so doing.

"Lucky Charlie Harty," the fishermen often called him.

One time when we were off to the sou'east of Monhegan several miles and it breezed up fresh from the sou'sou'west, Harty swung his vessel off and ran into Boothbay Harbor. The most of us stayed out that night, and the next morning when he came out, he got a large school of mackerel just outside of Bantum Ledge, near Damariscove Island.

Another smart sailer that he went seining in was the *Esperanto*. This vessel Marty Welch sailed to victory, when she won from the *Delawana*, off Halifax, in the International Fishermen's Race in October, 1920. Harty sailed in the *Esperanto* several years, seining for mackerel, and while in her he caught a lot of fish and made some money. He, it was, who found out that the *Esperanto* was a fine, fast-sailing vessel when she was in her right trim. She had a peculiar trim, much different from most vessels, for she trimmed about eight inches by the head when she was in her best sailing trim. Perhaps no one else but Charlie Harty would ever have found out her most peculiar trim, but he did, for he was always experimenting with a vessel's trim, until he found out where she would do her best sailing.

Skipper Al Miller sailed many of the fastest sailing fishing vessels, during the eighties and nineties, and he told me stories about some of them, when I was cook with him, seining in the steamer *Lincoln*, in 1926. One evening as we sat on the fore-hatch talking, I asked him this question: "Skipper, which was the best vessel 'by the wind,' that you ever sailed?"

"Th' *Carrie E. Phillips* was th' best an' smartest vessel, close hauled by th' wind, that I ever sailed, cook!" he replied without a moment's hesitation.

I waited a moment, hoping that my question would start a story, and it did.

"Th' second year I was in th' *Phillips*," he began, "we left Gloucester erbout th' 20th o' March bound south, seinin' fer mack'rel. We had er good run down, an' then cruised eround 'bout er week afore we found 'em schoolin' close inshore near Bodie Island. There was er light air o' wind from th' no'theast that mornin' when we went out an' sot eround er good lookin' school; we pursed 'er up, an' dried 'er in, an' got th' fish. Then we luffed th' vessel up erlongside th' seine-boat with th' fish in our seine, an' bailed 'em on deck, an' we had er hundred barrels o' fine mack'rel. We overhauled our seine aft in th' boat, an' hauled 'er out on deck, an' then I told th' boys to haul 'er back onto th' seine-boat so's to have 'er ready. I went aloft an' soon saw plenty o' mack'rel schoolin', an' erbout th' time th' boys had 'er on, I picked out er nice lookin' school an' we went out an' sot th' second time; that haul was er good one of three hundred barrels.

"By th' time we had th' second school o' fish erlongside our vessel in th' seine, it had breezed up fresh an' was pretty rough. Th' fleet had all left us an' worked to th' no'thard, fer they had sot only once. There we was, left all erlone, with th' no'theast wind er breezing on, er hundred barrels o' fish on deck, an' ernother three-hundred barrels o' fish in our seine erlongside th' vessel. It was er breezin' up an' gittin' rougher all th' time, so I said to th' boys: 'We must hustle them fish which are on deck down below an' git 'em iced, so's we can start bailin', fer it's gittin' rougher all th' time an' very liable to bu'st our seine an' we'll lose our fish!'

"Th' boys did hustle, an' we soon had 'em down below an' iced, an' then we started bailin'; an' we bailed,

an' bailed, an' bailed 'er deck full. She was full from
rail to rail, from 'er windlass to 'er wheel-box; three
hundred barrels o' fine fish on 'er deck. By that time
she had drifted close inshore an' th' wind was blowin'
fresh an' it was pretty choppy an' rough, so I said to th'
boys: 'We must scratch out o' 'ere, fer we're driftin' inter
shoal water! H'ist th' jib, an' jumbo an' haul in th' foresheet! All hands aft now, an' haul in th' mainsheet!'

"We trimmed 'er by th' wind an' I took th' wheel
myself, an' we beat that vessel off er lee-shore, it blowin' er gale o' wind, with 'er deck full o' mack'rel, an'
she never spilled five barrels off'n 'er deck, th' whole
time we was er beatin' 'er off shore that day. She stood
right up straight as er church-steeple th' whole time,
walkin' right erlong an' she er sailin' fast, an' not mind-
in' 'er heavy deck-load o' fish er 'tall. She handled like
er play-boat, fer when I rolled 'er wheel down to tack
'er, she would come erbout an' fill erway on tother tack
nice as you please. What er vessel she was, cook, 'by th'
wind!' I knowed what she could do, or else I'd never
o' stayed there that day to git that second school o' fish
when it was er breezin' up so fast from th' no'theast.
Fer th' spring afore, when beatin' up th' Jersey Beach
one day in er heavy nor'wester, I had found out that
she was er very able vessel to carry sail, an' er very fast
sailer by th' wind. I had put out my patent-taffrail-log
that time an' she made *thirteen knots*, as I drove 'er
hard under whole-sail in smooth water, with all th'
wind she could smother under, fer I wanted to find out
how fast she could sail, by th' wind.

"Now to git back to my story, cook! Th' boys was
er puttin' our fish below, as fast as they could, an' we
beat erway all that afternoon an' evenin' up th' coast,
fer we was bound to New York with our trip, an' we

SCHOONER "CARRIE E. PHILLIPS" BEATING OFF A
LEE SHORE WITH A DECK LOAD OF MACKEREL

was makin' short tacks off shore, an' longer ones up th'
coast. That night an' th' next day, we passed vessel
after vessel, as we worked our way up th' coast, an' th'
followin' mornin' at daylight we was right off Sandy
Hook, an' erhead o' th' fleet, fer I couldn't see any fishin'
vessels erhead o' us as I swung 'er off an' we eased
off our sheets to run up through th' 'Narrers.' When
we got up to th' city, we soon found out that we was th'
first vessel in, an' had th' market all to ourselves; so we
got er good price fer our fish, an' we made er large
stock. Our crew shared $202.00 to er man; th' best
trip that I ever made out south."

One summer when skipper Marty Welch was seining in the schooner *Lucania*, mackerel were very scarce
off the New England coast and some twenty-five seiners were lying idle at the wharves in Gloucester harbor.

Their skippers were up in the Master Mariner's Association's reading-room, talking the situation over about the scarcity of mackerel that season, and trying to decide whether to continue going seining any longer or changing over to go trawling for fresh haddock and cod. A trawler was fishing on Cashe's Ledge about that time, and the last day she fished there, her crew saw plenty of mackerel schooling. When she arrived in Gloucester, her crew soon spread the good news around: "Plenty o' fish schoolin' on Cashe's." As soon as the skippers heard this good news, they sent out word for their crews to come aboard to get their vessels ready to sail in the morning.

The next morning, early, the seiners began to sail out the harbor, and as they were luffed up around Eastern Point, their skippers found the wind was nearly dead ahead, for it was about east-no'theast. Marty, in the *Lucania*, soon began to work out through the fleet, passing vessel after vessel, and shortly he was out clear, well ahead of them, as she was very fast in light winds when beating to windward, for this was her best point of sailing. Marty was at her wheel himself and sailed her well, and by noontime she was three or four miles to windward and well ahead of the fleet. That evening about an hour before sunset, she was seven or eight miles out to windward,* on the western part of the Bank where the mackerel were schooling.

Marty picked out a good-looking school, and they went out and set and quickly "pursed 'er up." When they had "dried 'er in," they found they had a large school of fish in their seine. Marty and four of his crew then went aboard his vessel, in their dory, to bring her alongside the seine-boat, and shortly afterward the

* The *Lucania* at that time was about forty miles from Gloucester.

SCHOONER "LUCANIA" WORKING TO WINDWARD OF THE
FLEET, IN LIGHT WINDS

Lucania was luffed up alongside her seine. The crew
then threw out her lines, which were made fast to the
bow and stern of the seine-boat, and started bailing and
when all the fish were bailed on deck, they found they
had a fine school of two hundred barrels, — 60,000
pounds of fresh fish.

It was long after dark, perhaps nine o'clock, by the
time they had finished bailing, when some of the fleet
arrived, but too late to get any fish that day. They
knew, however, that Marty likely had got a good
school, for they had seen his vessel lighted up with
torches for sometime, and this told them (in the fishermen's language) that he must have made a good haul.

Marty was anxious to get started for market, as the
wind was moderate, so he called out to his crew: "H'ist
all th' head sails an' set th' stays'l, boys!" He then
walked aft and rolled the wheel hard up and the

Lucania swung off with a fair wind bound to Boston and market. The crew then set to work on her deck load o' fish and when they had them all stowed down below in her ice-pens, they washed down decks and went below, had a "mug up" and "turned in."

The next morning at sunrise, the *Lucania* was sailing up Boston harbor and before the bell rang at seven o'clock, Marty shot her up alongside T Wharf. He was up in the Fish Exchange when the market opened, and soon there was lively bidding for his fish among the wholesalers, as his was the only trip in that morning. The Boston Market was bare of mackerel as there hadn't been any fish in for more than a week. He let them bid until the commission men would go no higher and then sold his trip of 60,000 pounds for twenty cents a pound. His vessel stocked $12,000.00, and the crew shared $320.00 to each man.

This is a fine example of what it means to the fishermen to have a fast-sailing vessel that enables them to beat the fleet out to the fishing grounds, catch a good haul of mackerel, make a quick run to market, and get a good price for their fish.

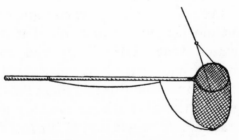

Mackerel Bailing Dip-Net

CHAPTER XVII

THE GREATEST FISHERMEN'S RACE EVER SAILED

THERE is an old saying "that a new broom sweeps clean." When skipper Maurice Whalen, in his famous fishing schooner, the *Harry L. Belden*, won the great fishermen's race in 1892, she made a clean sweep that day and beat some of the ablest and fastest sailing vessels in the fleet. Sol Jacobs was there with his *Ethel B.*, and Tommy Bohlin with his *Nannie C.* and so was Rube Cameron with the *Joseph Rowe*, and Charlie Harty with the *Grayling*; all of them large, able, fast-sailing vessels, and the little *Harry Belden* won the race, because she was able to carry sail in a hard blow, was a fast sailer "by the wind," and was well handled by her skipper, Maurice Whalen.

For several weeks previous to this fishermen's race, which was to be sailed on a Friday in August, the fishermen of Gloucester were talking about, and planning for, the event. When a fishermen's race is to be sailed off Gloucester, the city fathers make it a holiday for everybody and everyone is interested and making plans to see and enjoy it. On the day the race is to be sailed, thousands line the shores of Eastern Point, and hundreds of men and their wives, young men and maidens, go out on excursion steamers, fishing vessels, sailing yachts, motor-boats, government vessels and all kinds of craft to see the fishing vessels sail. On the day of this race, most of them were disappointed, and unable to see it at all, for the sun hid behind storm clouds and the wind blew a gale of sixty miles an hour. The sea was so rough that excursion steamers, and all other craft, would not go very far out beyond Eastern Point.

This weather, with a gale o' wind blowing, was just what the fishermen wanted for a race, as it would be a good test of who had the best vessel. The fishermen who went to the Grand Banks and drove their vessels on through the winter gales and snowstorms, were not afraid to race their schooners, in a little blow off Gloucester, in the summer time, so they went out just as if it had been a fine day.

For a week or more most of them had been in port getting ready for the race, over-hauling their running-rigging, reeving off new halyards and sheets, bending new sails, etc. Each skipper had his vessel hauled out on the Marine Railway and scrubbed and cleaned her bottom and then gave her a good coat of copper paint. Her top-sides were painted and also her rails, hatch-coamings, and houses on deck; in fact, they slicked her up, good and handsome, and put her in fine "ship-shape" and "Bristol-fashion." Skipper Tommy Bohlin in the *Nannie C.* had part of the ballast removed from his vessel, anticipating light winds on the day of the race, but he was very sorry that he had done so when he found a gale o' wind blowing on the morning of the race. He could not put any ballast back in his vessel on the morning of that day, for it was against the rules laid down by the committee, so he had to sail his vessel flying-light in a gale o' wind. She made a very poor showing, and he never got over trying to explain why she didn't sail better that day.

Skipper Maurice Whalen had entered his schooner, the *Harry L. Belden*, and was planning to be home in time to get ready for it. He was mackerel seining that summer, and previous to the race was out on a trip, away to the eastward, somewhere. The Sunday before the race was to be sailed on the following Friday, he said to his crew: "Boys, we'll have a look around today and start for home tomorrow!" The next morning it was calm weather and his vessel lay there becalmed all day and all that night. The next day was Tuesday and still it was calm weather, all that day and night. Early on Wednesday morning a light air o' wind sprang up from the no'theast and the skipper's "glass" was "high" and still "rising," indicating an easterly gale was on its way.

"We'll h'ist th' seine-boat in on deck," said skipper Maurice, to his crew, "for it's going to blow hard before very long, boys!"

They soon finished this work and he swung the *Belden* off for Gloucester, setting every inch of her canvas for he knew that he must drive her hard to reach home in time to sail her in the race. The wind breezed up fast and by noontime it was blowing half a gale, but still Maurice drove her hard, with every sail pulling well, and the *Belden* reeled off the miles at a twelve knot clip. The wind increased and that night at dark it was blowing heavy. She was then going very fast, and making thirteen knots an hour by her log, so Maurice very reluctantly gave the command: "Take in th' stays'l, an' haul th' jib-tops'l down! I hate to do it, boys, but I'm afraid we'll lose our topmasts, an' that won't do now, for we'll need 'em in th' race!"

Maurice drove her hard all night, with her four-lower sails and both her tops'ls set. All day Thursday he drove her, it blowing a gale of wind, and there were times when she made her *fourteen knots*. Thursday night at ten o'clock they tied her up alongside the wharf in Gloucester, too late to take out her trip of mackerel, too late to put her on the "Railway" to have her bottom cleaned and painted!

"We're goin' in th' race tomorrow, boys, just as she is, so come around early in th' mornin'!" said the skipper to his crew that night. The next morning they hoisted their seine-boat out and put it overboard, and tied it up in the head of the dock. Then they hoisted her sails, cast off her lines and away they went out to the starting-line, off Eastern Point.

The course was from a start off the whistling buoy near the "Point," to a buoy off Half Way Rock, leaving it to port; thence to and around Davis Ledge buoy off Minot's Light, leaving this buoy to port, also; thence back to the finish-line off Eastern Point; a distance of fifty miles. "What a day for a fisherman's race!" said many of the old salts about the water-front that morning. At the starting-line were several of Gloucester's fishing vessels, noted as fast sailers, each of their skippers feeling confident that his vessel was the fastest and would win the race. Some of them, however, never finished, for their vessels could not stand it in the gale that blew that day, for they lost their sails and were disabled.

The first leg was a broad-reach on the starboard tack, with the main-booms well off to port. Skipper Sol Jacobs in his handsome schooner, the *Ethel B. Jacobs*, got a fine start and was soon leading the fleet, for the *Ethel B.* was a very fast runner off the wind and when she reached the first buoy off Half Way Rock she was more than a mile ahead of the others. On a day like that, the safe and sane thing to do was to sail a short distance by the buoy, then roll your wheel down, haul aft your sheets, and "tack ship"; then swing your vessel off leaving the buoy on your port hand, for the next run to Minot's on a different course.

Jibing a vessel in a gale of wind, while running

under a whole mains'l with tops'l set (all other sails set also), is a rash and dangerous thing to do, for you are very likely to carry away something, break your main-boom, or your main-gaff, and perhaps part your main-sheet. Of course, some time is saved by jibing a vessel; also, some time is lost by hauling on the wind and tacking. In any ordinary breeze it is safe to jibe and the logical thing to do while passing a buoy when racing; but when it is blowing a gale, as it was that day, you are taking great chances by jibing. Sol chose to take a chance, however, so jibed his vessel, and when the mains'l swung over with a crash, the terrific strain broke the main-gaff. Instantly the mains'l split wide open from gaff to boom, tearing the sail from head to foot, and the crew had to haul it down and furl it up. Right then and there Sol Jacobs lost a fine chance to win the race, for his vessel was more than a mile ahead at the time, sailing very fast, and quite likely she would have gained still more on the next run to Minot's. She would have been so far ahead then that no other vessel could have overcome her great lead; and on the beat to windward, in all probability she would have won the race.

Skipper Sol kept on after the accident instead of quitting the race, and setting his riding-sail in place of his mains'l, he beat his vessel to windward, handicapped as she was by the loss of her large mains'l, and was the third to finish. Of course, there are no alibies or excuses offered and no allowance made to a vessel that has hard luck or meets with an accident during a fishermen's race. They take what comes and may the best vessel win. No doubt, every skipper racing that day was sorry for Sol's accident, for fishermen do not want to win a race at the expense of another's hard luck.

On the run to "Minot's," the *Belden* and *Rowe*, both had passed the *Ethel B.* and when they rounded Davis Ledge Buoy, these two vessels were side by side, for neither Maurice Whalen nor Rube Cameron would give way to the other, and both crowded through the narrow passage between the buoy and the ledge. Maurice had the weather berth, so when the *Belden* passed the buoy he luffed her up quickly, hauled her sheets in by the wind, and the "thrash to windward" was on. The beat to windward that day was one of the greatest battles ever sailed by New England fishing vessels, before or since that time, for the wind was heavy and the sea very rough. These vessels were driven hard under whole-sail and their skippers did not spare them, for they were out to win the race or blow their sails away in the attempt.

Skipper Maurice held the *Belden* on the port tack a long way off shore, and she lay over on her side with her shear-poles in the water, her whole lee-side buried under the rough seas. There were times when on the off shore tack, facing head-beat seas, that she buried her whole forward body under water, chock to her foremast. When she rose on the next sea she would throw the water clear aft along her deck so that the skipper at the wheel stood in water up to his waist and had a life-line tied around his body to keep him from being washed overboard. When near the finish line, an unusually heavy puff of wind struck the *Belden* and the crew watched their skipper to see if he would ease her up a little, but Maurice shook his head and rolled the wheel up, to swing her off a bit and let her take it with a full rap, and the *Harry L. Belden* shot across the finish line on her side, the winner of the greatest of all fishermen's races ever sailed. Some of the spectators

SCHOONER "HARRY L. BELDEN" RACING IN A GALE,
CROSSING THE FINISH LINE

on Eastern Point that day, jokingly told of seeing the
Belden's keel when she crossed the finish line.

When skipper Maurice and his crew tied the *Belden*
up alongside the wharf, that afternoon, the city went
wild with excitement; men, women and children
cheered them for winning the race, for the little *Harry
L. Belden* had sailed with no preparation, without even
having her bottom cleaned and painted. Soon one
of her crew was seen coming down the wharf with a
new broom in his hand. He went to her main rigging,
climbed aloft to her mast head, shinned up her top-
mast-shrouds, and lashed the broom to her main-truck,
thus proclaiming her "The Queen of the Fleet." For
several years afterward she carried a broom at her main-
truck, and often when sailing through the mackerel
fleet, some fisherman on another vessel would say to his
shipmates: "There she goes, the able *Harry Belden*!"

Chapter XVIII

The Swordfishermen of Gloucester

HARPOONS are used chiefly by the fishermen to secure swordfish for they very seldom take the baited hook. The harpoon-pole is usually about fourteen feet long and on the forward end is fitted an iron rod one-half inch in diameter, about two feet long and rather pointed on the end, so that it will fit into a socket on the side of the lily-iron, which is on the end of the rod. The lily-iron is usually made of brass or bronze composition, five to six inches long, and in shape, somewhat resembles an arrowhead. The edges are sharp on the forward end. It has a round hole through the center in which the running-line or warp is spliced.

The swordfish season is usually about four months long,—June, July, August and September. Most of the swordfishing fleet is composed of small vessels, from forty to sixty tons, which have been engaged during the winter months as "draggers"; also vessels which have been fishing during the months of April and May, out south, as mackerel gill-netters. About June 1st, these vessels change over and fit out for swordfishing during the summer. They have two very distinguishing features in their rig, namely: a fore-topmast on the fore-masthead rigged with "crows' nests," each seating a man as a lookout, part way from the masthead to the truck. They also have very long bowsprits, on the outer end of which is secured a stout plank; on this is the "pulpit," used by the "striker" to stand in and from which to throw his "harpoon-pole."

The gear carried by each vessel consists of several

THE CREW OF THE AUXILIARY SCHOONER "DORIS M. HAWES"
HOISTING IN SWORDFISH

harpoon-poles, two dozen or more lily-irons, a dozen quarter-barrels for buoys, and a dozen coils of fifteen thread rope for buoy-lines. The crew then put on board ice in large 300-pound cakes, which is stowed in her hold, to the amount of thirty to forty tons, in accordance with the size of the vessel. Swordfishermen use ice in large cakes, other fishermen use finely ground ice. Food enough to feed ten men for three weeks is then put on board and several casks of fresh water, or her tanks are filled up. Each vessel has a skipper, engineer, cook, and usually five to seven men in her crew. The "striker" is usually one of the crew. On some vessels the skipper is the "striker." Five to seven dories are carried according to the crew.

Swordfish frequent the mackerel grounds as these fish are their chief food. They secure them by rushing quickly into a school, and swinging their heads from side to side very rapidly, they kill several mackerel with their swords and then eat them at their pleasure. Swordfish have a habit of swimming near the surface of the sea, with the dorsal fin on their backs showing a few inches above the surface, and this is the only time that fishermen can harpoon and secure them. It takes a very practiced and keen-sighted man to see them at all, especially when the surface of the sea is troubled by the wind blowing and it has variable colors. When it is calm weather they are more easily seen by a man who knows what to look for. When out on the "grounds" most vessels have four or five men on the lookout, for five pairs of eyes can see more fish than one pair. In the early part of the season swordfish are found around Block Island, off No Man's Land, out by the South Shoal (Nantucket Lightship) and also along the South Channel and on George's Bank. Later on they are found on La Have Bank, Brown's Bank and over on the "Cape Shore," Nova Scotia.

When out on the "fishing grounds" and a swordfish is sighted, the skipper, who is usually one of those on the masthead, gives directions to the man at the wheel how to steer the vessel (which is under power with engine going) to bring her up near the fish, by saying: "Hard a starboard! Steady your wheel! Port your wheel! Steady now, as you go! Port, a little! Steady!"

The vessel must approach the swordfish from behind so that it cannot see her, otherwise it will quickly disappear. Often the fish turn quickly and see the vessel before she is near enough for the "striker" to use his harpoon. When the fish are swimming straight ahead, the vessel can approach from behind near enough for the "striker" to use his harpoon, which he skillfully drives down through its back, and the lily-iron turns flatwise on the under side of the fish and holds it fast. When the fish is struck it instantly darts forward at great speed, often going straight down to bottom, with the line spinning very swiftly out of the tub, in which it has been very carefully coiled so that it will run out clear without fouling, for if the line should foul, it will part and the fish will be lost.

When fishing on grounds where it is deep water, the line is always longer than the depth of water, so that the swordfish can reach bottom with plenty of line to spare without towing the buoy under. This is thrown overboard when the line is nearly out, the end having been made fast, previously, to the buoy. A dory is then hoisted out and one of the crew rows out following the buoy on the surface; this he takes into his dory. He then uses his judgment about playing the fish, until he is able to haul in on the line slowly and bring it up to the surface, alongside his dory, where he can use his lance, which is on a long pole, to kill it. Some swordfish are easily captured in a short time; others are crafty and hard to get up to the surface, so it takes a longer time to kill them, for some fish are very vicious and put up a hard fight, even attacking the dory.

I once knew of a case, out near Block Island, when a swordfish drove its sword right up through the bottom of the dory where the man was seated on the thwart. It came up between his knees. He grabbed the sword and held on until the fish was exhausted by its struggle and died; then the vessel picked him up safely and secured the fish.

When swordfish are very plentiful, the fishermen often strike and capture five, six or seven in succession, so that all their dories are out at one time. The skipper then directs the vessel, with the cook at the wheel, to near the first dory that went out, and most likely by that time the man has killed the fish with his lance. A strap is then put around its tail and hooked on the tackle when it is hoisted on deck. The rest of the dories are then picked up, proceeding in the same manner, and they then start to look for more fish while they are yet showing, for swordfish do not show every day. Sometimes when the fish show well, twelve to fifteen will be taken in one day. The next day may be stormy and so no fish can be seen or caught, or, perhaps the fish may not show at all, even though it is a fine day.

When no more fish are seen, the crew dress and put their catch below in the ice-pens, covering them completely with coarse chopped ice, with a large piece put inside each fish. When they begin dressing the fish, about the first thing they do is to saw off the sword which is from three to four feet long, and save it for some friend ashore who will be pleased to get such a curiosity. Then they cut off the head, fins and tail, open the belly, remove the entrails, wash the fish out clean, put a strap around the body where it will balance evenly and lower it into the vessel's hold.

Swordfish range in size from 80 to 100 pounds (for the babies), up to 600 pounds or more. Average size good market fish weigh 300 to 350 pounds each. Once in a while, a swordfish is captured that is very large, weighing from 650 to 700 pounds. The largest one I ever heard about weighed 712 pounds. Swordfishermen usually stay out on the "grounds" until they get a hundred or more for a trip, if it is possible, and are gone from home two or three weeks. When the fish are plentiful and they have "good luck," they sometimes bring in two hundred or more.

If they happen to strike a high market and get a

good price of twenty-five cents a pound, or more, for their fish, that will make a "good stock" and each man will share from $250.00 to $300.00 for the trip. The crews share and share alike. The skipper has a share and his percentage extra; the cook and engineer have their shares, with wages of $30.00 to $40.00 a month, as an extra.

Some seasons the swordfish are very plentiful and most of the fishermen do well and make good wages; but on other seasons the fish, for some unknown reason, are very scarce and, of course, the fishermen make very little money. Almost every fall a few vessels make a late trip to Brown's Bank, La Have Bank, or go over on the "Cape Shore" and get a fair trip, which is usually the last one for the season.

There are a great many more vessels engaged in this fishery today than there were fifty years ago; probably fifty sail from Gloucester alone, a few from Portland, and several from New Bedford and Edgartown. There are also several small sloops with power, and motorboats that sail from Block Island, Newport, and New London. These small craft carry only three to five men.

In the eighties, only a very few fishermen were engaged in this fishery, for there was very little call for swordfish. Many people thought they were not fit for food and consequently what few were sold, brought a very small price, often as low as three cents a pound. Today, most of the time swordfish retails at thirty-five to forty cents a pound. This goes to show how people will change their ideas about eating certain kinds of sea-food, for many today prefer swordfish-steak to any other of the several kinds of fresh fish on the market, and this change of mind on the part of the people, has also taken place in preferring fresh haddock to fresh cod, for the once lowly haddock is today consumed in larger quantities than cod, and also brings a higher price on the market.

Many trawling vessels that still retain their bowsprits, have a "pulpit" rigged on and carry swordfish gear and sometimes bring into market ten to fifteen swordfish which helps to bring their "stocks" several hundred dollars higher. There have been instances where halibut trawlers have caught swordfish on their trawls, but very seldom. There is a certain fascination for the fishermen and a "sport" that is found in no other of our ordinary New England fisheries, for the swordfish is a gamesome fish and often it will put up a great fight. There is also an element of danger, for fishermen have been injured in their dories while out capturing swordfish.

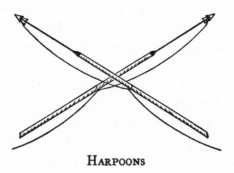

HARPOONS

CHAPTER XIX

THE FLOUNDER-DRAGGER AND BEAM-TRAWLER

FLOUNDERS are fine eating when cooked and and served as pan-fish. The delicious fillet of sole that is so much sought in the best hotels and restaurants, is taken from one of the flounder family. Flounder-dragging is a comparatively new industry in the New England fisheries, for only since the advent of the gasoline marine engine, installed in boats and small vessels about twenty-five or more years ago, somewhere about 1905, has this new flounder business been possible. Of course, some few flounders were caught by fishermen fifty or more years ago with a small "drag-net," which was set off the shore in some cove that had a beach of sand or mud bottom and hauled ashore by the fishermen who would secure a few barrels. These fish were iced and sent to market. The flounder fishery was in its infancy in those days for the general public had not then learned to eat them. When a small boy, I often caught many with a hook and line, and later on, when older, I caught them with a flounder-spear for lobster-bait. We ate them occasionally.

There are several kinds of flounders found along our New England coast, near the shore-line, often in very shallow water. They are found on either mud, sand or rocky bottom, of various sizes and colors, such as dark gray, light gray, brownish and some fish are nearly black on their backs; all are white bellied or nearly so. These fish live on the bottom where they find their food supply and nearly always swim close to the bottom. Flounders of a larger kind are found in deep water on the different Banks off our coast; also around Cape Cod, Nantucket Shoals and many places along the coast-line. These larger fish are mostly caught and brought to market by the modern, high-powered "flounder-draggers," and are known as: lemon-sole, black-backs, yellow-tails and dabs. This flounder-dragging industry has grown to be a very large business of late years, for these power-boats are found in nearly every sea-port from Portland, Maine, to New London, Conn. There must be from seventy-five to one hundred sailing out of Gloucester, one hundred or more from Boston (mostly Italian fishermen from these ports); and several from Plymouth and Provincetown and a large fleet from New Bedford, manned mostly by Portuguese.

The flounder drag-nets are of various sizes according to the size of the craft. The smaller nets are about fifty feet across the mouth of the net and one hundred feet in length, cone-shaped, with the rear end closed up to a point. The larger craft use larger and longer nets, from seventy-five to one hundred feet across and about one hundred and fifty feet long. Drag-nets are made of a special, heavy, soft-laid twine which is very strong, and they are knit with meshes close enough to hold any but the smallest fish. Each net has two heavy doors, ten feet high and six feet wide, one on each side of the mouth of the net, which, when set, draw at an angle of forty-five degrees. These doors have a tendency to keep the mouth of the net open wide when it is being towed over the bottom. They are made of heavy, three-inch oak planks with flat iron straps, which are bolted through with heavy bolts set up tight, making them very strong and enough iron is used in the construction to make the net sink readily to bottom.

When the flounder-dragger is out on the "fishing grounds," where the fishermen feel pretty sure that they have the right kind of bottom of either sand, gravel or mud, and likely to be comparatively free from large rocks or boulders (which would soon tear their drag-net to pieces), they get ready to make a set, carefully letting the net down over the side of their boat with the tow-line, which has been made fast to the bridle at the mouth. When it is on bottom, they start the boat slowly ahead, paying out on the tow-line until sufficient line is out, perhaps one hundred and fifty fathoms, or more, according to the depth of water. The drag-net which is then towing over the bottom, far out astern, will "draw right" and "fish well." The boat must not tow the net too fast, or it will lift it off the bottom and it will not fish well, but it must be dragged fast enough to prevent all the fish in the mouth of the net from swimming out clear and escaping. The right speed is from two and one-half to three miles an hour.

One can imagine that many fish which are near each side of the mouth may swim clear and not be caught, but they may be later on as the net is left out, towing, usually for an hour. It is hauled in with the aid of a drum on deck which gets its power from the engine below. The drum is worked by a lever and clutch, which revolves the drum and winds in the one-inch, galvanized, wire-laid rope (towing line), which is attached to the bridles at the mouth of the drag-net. After the net is up alongside the boat, straps are passed around it and tackles are hooked on and it is hoisted up to the masthead. When high enough to swing in over the rail, a man watches his chance, and pulls a trip-line and the fish fall out on deck. The net is then put out again and the boat continues dragging as before.

Several kinds of fish are caught by the flounder-draggers besides flounders, including cod, haddock, halibut, hake, cusk, pollock, butterfish, catfish, etc. While the net is out dragging, the crew dress, wash, sort and put the fish below in the hold and cover them with ice in the pens. Sometimes, when fish are plentiful, the drag-net is left out to fish for only half an hour or so, when a good catch of several hundred pounds will be caught in one haul. Other times, when fish are scarce, the net is left out longer, perhaps for an hour or an hour and a half, and when hauled in it may have only a few fish in it. The net sometimes drags afoul of rocks or boulders on the bottom and this brings the boat up short and causes much trouble before the crew can get it clear. Sometimes, the net gets caught on an old ship's anchor, which may weigh several hundred pounds and tears the net badly. Each boat has two drag-nets, one for each side, and when one is put out of commission, the other is brought into use and the crew must then put in long, tedious hours mending the torn net.

There is a good market today for flounders, nearly all the time, in New York City, New Bedford, Boston and Gloucester. On some days, thousands of pounds are landed at the Boston Fish Pier, that sell at prices of from two to ten and twelve cents a pound. Some days in January and February, when all kinds of fresh fish are scarce in the market, lemon-sole bring as high as fifteen cents a pound.

In the summer of 1926, when seining for mackerel in the steamer *Lincoln*, with Al Miller, we lay at a wharf in New Bedford for four days during a "fog mull." New Bedford sends out a large fleet of flounder-draggers, of all sizes, from small power-boats of 25 tons, with crews of four or five men, up to the larger

A FLOUNDER-DRAGGER FISHING OFF RACE POINT,
CAPE COD, IN 1928

power motor-boats of 150 tons, with crews of ten to twelve men. These larger boats have crude-oil-burning marine engines installed, of 200 to 250 h.p., and are powerful boats, well built and of a fine model, making a speed of 12 knots. They are good sea-boats, can stay out in all kinds of stormy weather, cruising about on George's Bank, riding out in safety the winter gales, and secure trips of fish which they take direct to New York City and sell at Fulton Market, often at good prices. Most of these fishermen are Portuguese. Some of these draggers catch very large amounts of fish during the year (for they fish the year around), and make "stocks" of $75,000.00 to $100,000.00 for the season, the crews sharing from $3,500.00 to $4,000.00 each.

One day with another man I sat on the cap-log of a wharf in New Bedford. We had been talking for some time, when a fine-looking, powerful boat, by the name of *Vagabond*, came in and tied up alongside the wharf. My new-found friend called attention to a smart, brisk-appearing young man, who had just stepped out of her pilot-house, saying: "That's the skipper of the *Vagabond*, one of our smartest fishermen."

"Tell me something about him," I said. He then told me this story about the young skipper.

"He's a college man, graduated from Yale a few years ago, the son of a wealthy, prominent lawyer of New York City. When the boy graduated, his father wanted him to come into his law office and start his life's work as a lawyer. The young man, however, had no taste for law and did not want to be confined in an office, and told his dad so.

"'Well, son, what do you want to do?' asked his father.

"'I want to go fishing, dad!' replied the son.

"The father thought the matter over a moment, then said: 'I'm disappointed, son, but go fishing if you want to.'

"The young man came down here and shipped in one of our boats as one of her crew, flounder-dragging. He was smart, quick to learn the business of fishing and in two years time he was given command of a small boat. He did well, caught a lot of fish, and soon was known as a smart skipper. One day his father came to New Bedford to see him; I suppose to find out how he was getting along. He found him skipper of a small power-boat, making a fine success as a fisherman, and after talking with him for awhile he said: 'Would you like to have a larger and better boat, son?'

"'Of course I would, father!' he replied, then added, 'I intend to, some day, when I get money enough saved up to have one built!'

" 'Well, go and have one built now, just the kind of a power-boat you want, I'll pay the bills,' said his father.

"So the son had a fine, handsome, large, high-powered steamer built which cost about $75,000.00, that boat lying there, called the *Vagabond*. He has done well; has caught a lot of fish and is making money fast. He made a great record the first year he had her, getting many fine trips and I understand he stocked $100,-000.00 and his crew each shared $4,000.00. They say that he found a 'spot' of lemon-sole on the sou'east part of George's Bank that first winter, where he caught big trips, taking them to Fulton Market where he got fifteen and sixteen cents a pound for them in February, when fish were scarce and high and he made a large 'stock' every trip. That was four years ago. He has been 'high-line' each year since, and I heard that he has paid his dad back what the boat cost, and that now he owns her himself, free and clear. What a shame it would have been for that lad to have spoiled his life by trying to be a lawyer (and no doubt a poor one too, for his heart was not in his work) when he wanted to go fishing and become skipper of a fine fishing steamer. Look at him, today! One of our smartest fishermen, a good useful citizen, and he has made a great success of his chosen work, doing the thing that he wanted to do most."

For many years the "beam-trawl" was used by the English, Scotch and Irish fishermen in the North Sea, before it was introduced into our New England fisheries. At first, many of our fishermen objected to its use here, for they contended that it would ruin our fishing grounds. They claimed that the beam-trawl, dragging over the bottom, would destroy the "feeding grounds" of the fish on the Banks and drive them away; but the use of it here has proved that to be untrue. The objectors also claimed so many fish would be caught, that the market would be flooded and fish would bring a very low price; fish, also, would become very scarce on the Banks, in a few years. Their predictions have not come true, however, and their theories have been exploded, for there are plenty of ground-fish of all kinds on the Banks and fishing grounds off our coast, today, where the beam-trawl has been used for several years past.

Boston, Mass., for many years, has been called the largest fresh fish port in the world, but Grimsby, England, surpasses Boston in the amount of fresh cod and haddock landed, so you can see that the fishermen must be catching more fish than ever in the North Sea, and that the use of the beam-trawl has not ruined or even diminished the fishing there.

The fresh fish industry of New England has grown to be an enormous business, due to refrigeration. Cold storage plants, refrigerator cars, artificial ice freezers and containers enable wholesale fish dealers, buyers and retailers to ship fresh fish in good condition to practically all parts of the United States. Another reason is our increased population of 120,000,000 people, many of whom are learning every day that they can buy good, fresh fish of several varieties and once tried, they call for more of these food products of the sea.

Of late years a large number of beam-trawlers have been built and are engaged in the ground-fish industry. They often bring in trips of fresh haddock and cod, of 100,000 pounds, and sometimes as much as 175,000 to 200,000 pounds, for they are steamers of 300 tons or more. Most of them burn coal and their engines are

A BOSTON BEAM-TRAWLER, ON GEORGE'S BANK,
BOUND TO MARKET

steam driven, as well as their deck machinery of winch-
es and drums for handling the heavy beam-trawls.
There are really three classes of vessels that use the
drag-net.

First, the small flounder-draggers, some of them
burning gasoline. The new power-boats burn crude oil
in their small marine engines. Secondly, the larger
power-boats and auxiliary-powered fishing vessels
which were formerly under sail alone. These schooners
have crude-oil-burning engines installed of 180 to 250
h.p. and both are called by the fishermen simply "draggers." The crews on these vessels use a drag-net larger
than the small flounder-draggers, which are from 75
to 100 feet across the mouth of the net.

Third, the fishermen on the steamers that use still
larger nets, called beam-trawls, which are from 100 to
120 feet across the mouth of the net with a length in
proportion. All these vessels use their drag-nets in the

same manner, as described. The large beam-trawlers often get large hauls of fish on George's Bank or out on the South Channel grounds. In the spring they sometimes go as far east as Western Bank. When fish are plentiful (mostly of cod) they often secure trips of 200,000 pounds and go into Portland when the Boston market is glutted. These steamers are equipped with wireless apparatus, carry an operator, and keep in touch with their owners, who may send information where other trawlers have found fish plentiful and also give them the prices of fish, etc. Nearly all fishing vessels today have a radio set on board and get the "fish news," twice daily, from station WHDH at West Gloucester.

The beam-trawler's crew go on a different "lay" from most fishermen, for they are on monthly wages of $65.00 to $70.00 per month. Most owners also give a bonus of five per cent on all over a certain amount of the "gross stock" for the trip. The crews on these steamers perhaps make more money at the end of a year than some other fishermen who go on shares, but they earn all they get. It is a hard life fishing on George's Bank during the winter, handling frozen lines and suffering from the cold during snowstorms and severe weather, contending with rough, angry seas, riding out the gales on the Bank. In fact, all fishermen who go fishing off the New England coast during the winter months, find it cold, disagreeable work; but these men are a sturdy lot who make the best of the situation at all times, for fish must be caught during cold weather as well as in the summer.

Chapter XX

Four Cup Winners: the *Esperanto* (1920),
Henry Ford (1923), *Progress* (1929),
and *Gertrude L. Thebaud* (1930)

MOST fishermen care very little about winning
a cup when they are sailing their vessels in a
fishermen's race, for most likely when the
cup is presented to them, the skipper will stow it away
in his locker and then forget all about it (as Marty
Welch did at Halifax in 1920) until it is called for by
the vessel's owner who wants to put it on display in
some show-window. What the fishermen enjoy most is
racing their vessels against other fast sailers, and winning the races, especially if there is plenty of wind.
They get a great deal of satisfaction and much pleasure
in handling their schooners merely for the sake of the
sport.

In the spring of 1920, a new fishing vessel named
the *Delawana* was launched in Lunenburg, Nova Scotia. She was soon known as a fast-sailing vessel and that
summer the "Halifax Herald" raised a purse of $4,-
000.00 and also offered the Dennison Cup for an International Fishermen's Race off Halifax in October,
1920. A sailing committee was appointed and they sent
a challenge to the Gloucester fishermen, for them to
send a fishing vessel to race against their fishing vessel,
the *Delawana*. The Gloucester fishermen accepted the
challenge and a sailing committee was chosen to select
a vessel.

Back in the eighties and nineties, the New England
fishing vessels were considered the fastest sailing fishermen in the world. Both Boston and Gloucester had

many fast sailers in their fishing fleets, but when this challenge was received from Halifax, there were very few all-sail fishing vessels in the Gloucester fleet for with the advent of the gasoline marine engine, most of them had had engines installed, their spars had been cut down and they carried only enough sail to make them steady in a sea-way, and all their new vessels, built between 1910 to 1920, had been designed for auxiliary powered fishermen.

The sail, fishing vessel conditions of Nova Scotia, in 1920, were entirely different from those at Gloucester, for their fishing vessels went salt cod fishing, while the vessels at Gloucester went fresh fishing. The all-sail fishing vessels of Nova Scotia, in 1915, were about the same in regard to model of hull for fast sailing vessels, as our New England all-sail fishing vessels were in 1875, forty years previous. For many years previous to 1870, most of the New England fishermen went salt cod fishing and there was no particular need of fast sailing vessels; but when they began to go fresh fishing, they had faster sailing vessels built. Between 1890 and 1915, many of our older fishing vessels were sold to Nova Scotia and Newfoundland and the vessel builders there had the opportunity to see their finely-modeled hulls. When the Nova Scotia fishermen began to go trawling on salt cod trips, using fresh bait for their trawls, they began to call for better sailing vessels, so the designers and builders in Nova Scotia built faster-sailing fishing vessels. By the year 1920 they had built several fine, fast vessels and their new schooner, the *Delawana*, was one of their fastest, so they sent a challenge for one of our vessels to come down and race her.

When the Gloucester sailing committee began to look around for a fast-sailing vessel, available for the race, they couldn't find one. They were nonplused. What should they do? While the committee were discussing the matter, very much perplexed, one of them (skipper Charlie Harty) saw a vessel that was just then entering Gloucester harbor. He soon made her out as the *Esperanto*, as he had been her skipper for several years, sailing her in the seining fleet for mackerel when she was new, eleven years before. As soon as he was sure that it was the *Esperanto*, he quickly turned to the others and said: "There's our vessel, gentlemen. It's the *Esperanto*; she's the best sailer in our fleet today."

The *Esperanto* was just returning from a salt trip of three months on Banquereau, where she had been handline dory cod fishing and was laden deep with a full fare. The sailing committee went directly to see her owners and asked for the *Esperanto* to compete with the *Delawana*. Gladly giving their consent they also said they would fix her up a bit for the races. When her fish had been taken out, she was scrubbed, washed and cleaned up, then hauled out on the marine railway, her bottom cleaned and painted, also her topsides, in and out. Her old sails were unbent and sent ashore to the sail-loft to be patched up, for there wasn't time enough to have new ones made. New running-rigging of halyards and sheets were rove off and she was soon made ready for the race. A gang of lumpers was put at work to ballast her, with skipper Charlie Harty in charge, for he alone knew how to trim her so that she would sail at her best.

Skipper Marty Welch was asked to sail her during the races and after much coaxing and some persuasion on the part of the committee, for Marty is a very modest man, he finally consented to take her and do the best he could, for Marty felt that he had a hard task ahead of him to win with the *Esperanto*, then eleven years old, in sailing against the new *Delawana*. When the *Esperanto* was ready to sail for Halifax, Charlie Harty took her out off Eastern Point and sailed her for an hour, trying her out to see how she handled and how well she would sail. Then being quite satisfied that she was in her *right trim*, he turned the wheel over to skipper Marty Welch, saying: "Take her, Marty, she's right! Go down to Halifax an' beat the *Delawana*."

Skipper Marty Welch with his fine crew of thirty men, part of whom were skippers themselves, made a quick run to Halifax, for the *Esperanto* was well handled and they had a good breeze.

In this first International Fishermen's Race, Nova Scotians were deeply interested and thousands of people witnessed the race as the start and finish line was at the mouth of Halifax harbor and the first few miles were sailed close to the land. At the start of the first race, the *Delawana* was the first to cross the line, closely followed by the *Esperanto*. Soon the pride of Gloucester began to overhaul the beauty from Lunenburg and the race was on. The good start that the Lunenburg skipper had secured did not worry Marty at all, for there were forty long miles to be sailed ere the race ended, and a few hundred yards' lead did not mean that his vessel would lose the race. Very quietly Marty smoked his cigar and watched every move, for the first few minutes of sailing would tell him something of his vessel's speed, compared with that of the new *Delawana*, at least on this point of sailing. He soon saw that the Lunenburg vessel was not outsailing the *Esperanto*, and in a few minutes she was up on even terms, and then, gradually passing the *Delawana*, took the lead. Twice that day the *Delawana* was leading, but the *Esperanto* beat her badly when "close hauled by the wind" and finally, after having sailed a fast race, Marty drove her across the finish-line, leading by three miles, some twenty minutes ahead, and won the first race.

Two days later, the second race was sailed and this race will go down in the history of fishermen's races as the greatest race ever sailed by skipper Marty Welch, for he showed the kind of stuff of which he was made and convinced the sporting world that a Gloucester fisherman could not be frightened into giving away his rights, when his vessel was nearly crowded ashore by the Lunenburg vessel. In these races, a Gloucester man sailed on the *Delawana*, and a Halifax man sailed on the *Esperanto*. They were placed there by the committee to see that there was fair play for both the contestants. When the *Delawana's* skipper crowded the *Esperanto* into shoal water, near Devil's Island, in this second race, Marty showed his iron nerve by not yielding and gave no outward sign that he was concerned about his vessel's safety. It was the Halifax man on the *Esperanto* who told the skipper of the *Delawana* that he must swing his vessel off (which he promptly did) and not drive the *Esperanto* ashore.

In justice to the skipper of the *Delawana* it must be said that most likely he did not intend to drive the *Esperanto* ashore, but thought he could frighten Marty into giving away his rights, and that the *Esperanto* might lose the race if Marty changed her course. The masthead-man called out that he could see bottom, in tones loud enough to be heard plainly by all those on the deck of the *Esperanto*; but Marty never let on that he heard what the man said and made him no reply. Marty held his course and won the race, the *Esperanto* crossing the finish-line nearly eight minutes ahead of the *Delawana*. He and his crew were given a great ovation by the thousands gathered to see the finish of this second and deciding race, which won the International Fishermen's Race for the Dennison Cup; also the first prize of $3,000.00.

THE FISHING SCHOONER "HENRY FORD"

THREE handsome New England fishing schooners sailed in the "Lipton Cup" race off Gloucester, August 31, 1923: the schooner *Henry Ford*, Clayt Morrissey, owner and sailing-master; the schooner *Elizabeth Howard*, Ben Pine, sailing-master; and the Boston-owned fishing schooner *Shamrock*, sailed in this race by skipper Marty Welch of *Esperanto* fame. The distance sailed was forty miles, over a triangular course off Gloucester. The starting-line was off Eastern Point, about a mile south, with the whistling-buoy at one end and the judges boat at the other. The first leg was east by north, a distance of five miles to the first buoy off Milk Island; then south by east, ten miles to the second buoy; then west by north, ten miles to the third buoy; thence northeast, ten miles back to the first buoy (a triangle of thirty miles); then west by south, five miles back to the finish-line. This course gave the people along the East Gloucester shore a fine view of the vessels for the first five miles. The thirty miles sailed over the triangle off shore, gave the vessels a beat to windward of ten miles, a close reach of ten miles, and ten miles dead before the wind. The last five miles sailed back along the East Gloucester shore, gave the people a good chance to see the finish.

The wind was southwest and the start was a pretty

one, the *Ford* leading slightly, with the *Howard* close behind, and the *Shamrock* last across the line. It was a very close and pretty race for the first five miles, with the *Ford* still leading, and as she luffed up around the first buoy, the *Howard* was so close that her bowsprit was almost over the *Ford's* stern, with the *Shamrock* close behind the *Howard*. A beautiful sight they made as these three handsome vessels rounded the mark so closely bunched; the *Ford's* fine lines and handsome black sides glistening in the sunlight, with the white hull of the *Howard* in strong contrast, for she, also, had fine lines and was called the "White Ghost" by the fishermen. The *Shamrock* was a new and handsome vessel sailing in her first race.

After rounding the first buoy they hauled up sharp, close by the wind, with their sheets flattened, and all three stood off shore on the starboard tack with both the *Ford* and the *Howard* outsailing the *Shamrock*. The *Ford* was the first to tack to port heading inshore, but Pine in the *Howard* held her on a long starboard tack well off shore, for the *Howard* did her best sailing on that tack, as she had been ashore once and her starboard side been damaged, so she would not sail so fast on the port tack. When these two met near the outer buoy, the *Ford* was still slightly ahead and crossed the *Howard's* bow with only a few yards to spare, for the *Howard* had gained slightly on the beat to windward.

The run to the next buoy was a close reach. The wind had increased and they tore along at a good twelve knots, passing the *Shamrock* which was still on her way up to the outer buoy. On this leg both the *Ford* and *Howard* sailed very fast on about even terms, skipper Clayt jibing his vessel smartly around the third buoy, closely followed by Ben Pine. Then both vessels running off before the wind, the *Howard* dropped astern a little, for the *Ford* was very fast, with her sheets well off, down the wind. When the *Ford* rounded the leeward buoy, off Milk Island, and Clayt hauled her up by the wind, on the last five miles, he had a good lead on the *Howard* and gained still more, for as Pine rounded the buoy and hauled the *Howard* up by the wind, her fore-gaff-tops'l-sheet parted (having been chafed badly across the spring-stay while on the run down the wind) and she lost a few seconds time while the masthead-man was reeving off a new sheet.

On the last five miles the wind increased again and both vessels did some smart sailing, with their lee-scuppers down awash and with a big white bone in their teeth, they tore along at thirteen knots as only large, heavy, fishing vessels can sail, with every inch of canvas set and drawing well. Pine, in the *Howard*, made a grand try to win the race on this last five miles, and was gaining on the *Ford*, for the *Howard* was sailing faster in the increasing breeze.

A grand marine picture these two handsome vessels made that beautiful afternoon, with the ocean a dark blue, reflected from the sky overhead, the sunlight sparkling on the wave crests and long silvery white trails of foam from the vessels' wakes as they sailed along the East Gloucester shore like great sea-birds. Thousands lined the shore to witness the finish as the *Howard* rapidly lessened the few hundred yards that separated her from the handsome black racer, the *Ford*, which, however, crossed the finish-line, and won the race with only two minutes to spare. A gun boomed, whistles blew, and many horns proclaimed a noisy serenade for skipper Clayt and his crew, for winning one of the closest fishermen's races ever sailed.

The *Shamrock* was more than a mile and a half behind. Marty Welch had sailed her well and had done the best he could with her, but she proved to be only an ordinary sailer.

The Fishing Schooner "Progress"

FOUR of Gloucester's fine-sailing fishing vessels entered the race sailed on Labor Day, in 1929: the *Arthur D. Story*, Ben Pine, skipper; the *Elsie*, sailed by Captain Norman Ross; the *Progress*, sailed by Domingoes, her skipper; and the *Thomas S. Gorton*, sailed by skipper Wallace Parsons. At nine o'clock that morning there was a very light air from the sou'sou'-west, so the sailing committee postponed the race half an hour, making the starting time ten-thirty instead of ten o'clock. The start was a beautiful one as all four skippers sent their vessels over the starting-line closely bunched, with Ben Pine leading in the *Story*. Close behind was the *Elsie*; then followed the *Progress* and the *Gorton*.

This race was sailed over a triangular course of six miles to a leg, twice around, then one and five-eighths of a mile from a buoy off Eastern Point to the finish-line inside the breakwater in Gloucester harbor, making a distance of thirty-seven and five-eighths miles. The first leg was a close reach to the southeast buoy. The wind had freshened and the *Story* sailing fast, made twelve knots (the best sailing of the day), and gained slightly on both the *Elsie* and the *Progress*. After rounding the southeast buoy, it was a "broad reach" to the buoy off Thatcher's Island. On this run it was very even sailing by the first three vessels; for the *Gorton* was then trailing behind. The *Story* rounded first; then Pine hauled her up sharp by the wind, standing inshore on the port tack. Then came the *Elsie*, closely followed by the *Progress* and both of them, also, stood inshore on the port tack and did not come about until close in, their skippers thinking to find more wind and also expecting to get a slant of wind off the land.

When they had hauled on the wind, after passing the buoy, and were on the port tack heading inshore, I could see that the *Progress* was pointing higher than either the *Story* or the *Elsie*, in fact she was half a point nearer the wind than the *Story* and one point nearer than the *Elsie*. Now this is what makes a smart sailer by the wind for a vessel that will point high and foot equally as fast will surely beat the other vessels and win the race, if there is any windward work over the course sailed.

On the second tack, beating up the shore, the *Progress* went out to windward of the *Elsie* and had her beaten right there. The *Progress* went after the *Story* and nearly caught up with her at the windward buoy, gaining more than two minutes on this beat of six miles up the East Gloucester shore. She held her position on the next reach and run and when the *Story* rounded the buoy off Thatcher's, and Pine hauled her up by the wind, for the second beat up the shore, the *Progress* was close behind her. The *Story* held her port tack for about half a mile inshore, then came about and headed off shore on the starboard tack. The *Progress* held her port tack inshore for about a mile, then tacked and stood off shore. The *Story* then tacked again, heading inshore on the port tack.

All was excitement then for when they came together, that would tell the tale of which was ahead. If the *Story* could cross the bow of the *Progress* she would

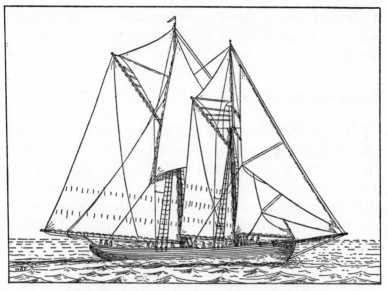

The Schooner "Progress" Winning the Fishermen's
Race, in 1929, by Fine Windward Work

be ahead, for the *Progress* was on the starboard tack
and had the right of way. But Ben Pine could not make
the *Story* do it and he had to roll his wheel down and
tack her, under the lee-bow of the *Progress* which then
lay to the windward blanketing the *Story* and soon passing her. The race was decided right then and there.
The *Progress* was doing fine sailing, pointing high, and
footing fast, going right out to windward in good
shape, and continued to gain on the *Story* until the finish of the race.

The *Progress* won the race because she was a smart
sailer "by the wind." She was the smallest vessel of the
four, but had no time allowance, for fishermen sail vessel against vessel regardless of size. She was only 96
tons, while the others were all of about 140 tons each.
When fishing, she went to the Grand Banks fresh halibut trawling, both winter and summer. The following

winter she caught fire and was burnt off Cape Cod; a
sad ending for a smart little vessel. All hands were
saved.

THE FISHING SCHOONER "GERTRUDE L. THEBAUD"

TO Ben Pine should be given the credit for keeping
alive the sporting spirit of racing fishing vessels.
He has done more than any other man during the past
ten years, to promote fishermen's races. The tendency
of the times has been to build auxiliary-powered vessels, rather than the all-sail fishing vessel. Consequently, the fast-sailing fishing schooners are rapidly disap-
pearing and would soon be only a memory to those of
us who remember them in their former glory, but for
the good work done by Ben Pine to keep the spirit alive.
Ten or more years ago, Pine chartered the beautiful
knockabout schooner *Elizabeth Howard*, built by Irving Adams & Son, at East Boothbay, Maine, and
brought her to Gloucester. He sailed her in the elimi-
nation trials held off Gloucester, in 1922, against the
fishing schooners *Henry Ford*, the *Yankee*, and the
L. A. Dunton. In the first race, the *Howard* met with
an accident, losing her main-topmast when the trestle-
trees gave way, and Pine withdrew from the race. In
the second race she came in second, the *Ford* winning
both of the trial races. The next year, 1923, was
Gloucester's Three Hundredth Anniversary, and Pine
was the leading spirit in arranging for a Fishermen's
Race for the "Lipton Cup." The *Henry Ford* won that
race by only two minutes, for Ben Pine sailed the *Elizabeth Howard* well and gave Clayt Morrissey a hard
and very close race. The following year, 1924, Pine
was the leading spirit in raising money among the

merchants of Gloucester, to build the beautiful, fast-sailing *Columbia*, which he took down to Halifax that fall and sailed against the *Bluenose*. In the fall of 1926, a fishermen's race was sailed off Gloucester between the *Henry Ford* and the *Columbia*, which was sailed by Pine who won that race, evening up the score with Clayt Morrissey who had won from him in the race of 1923, when the *Ford* beat the *Howard*. During the summer of 1929, Pine had the old schooner *Mary* rebuilt, and renamed her the *Arthur D. Story*. He was also the leading spirit in starting the arrangements that led up to the race held on Labor Day, 1929, won by the *Progress*.

There is a pretty story about the fishing schooner *Gertrude L. Thebaud*, and how she happened to be built. Previous to the Labor Day Race in 1929, during the summer, a wealthy New Jersey man, Louis G. Thebaud (who owns a beautiful summer home at Eastern Point) was in the habit of cruising about the fish wharves at Gloucester and one day he met Ben Pine. They saw each other several times later and finally became well acquainted. During one of their talks, Pine invited Mr. Thebaud to sail with him on the *Story* and see the vessels race on Labor Day and he gladly accepted the invitation. On the morning of the race, Mr. Thebaud was on hand, bright and early, and had a fine time that day, enjoying himself immensely, talking with the skipper and his crew, who told him "fish stories"; and he even had a "mug up" with the cook in the fo'cas'le. After the race, Pine was rather downcast about losing the race.

"Don't feel so badly about it, Ben," said Mr. Thebaud, "we'll have a new vessel built this winter that you can sail to win the race next fall," and right then and there, he wrote his check for a large amount and gave it to Ben Pine. When the papers were drawn up and signed, Frank C. Paine, who designed the sloop yacht *Yankee*, was chosen to design the new fishing schooner *Gertrude L. Thebaud*.

Her builder was Arthur D. Story of Essex, and the *Thebaud* was launched in the spring of 1930. The launching was a notable affair with a large party from Gloucester, who saw Mrs. Thebaud christen the beautiful new vessel named for her. Both the designer and builder should feel proud of their new creation for she is certainly a beauty, one of the handsomest vessels that ever came into Gloucester harbor. She has a very long overhang, both forward and aft; a graceful bow, which is very sharp at her waterline; and she slips through the water very easily. She has a beautiful stern, slender and very fine, and the lines of her run under her counter are as clean as a hound's tooth. With a very handsome shear she is as graceful as a swan.

The *Thebaud* went fishing during the spring and summer of 1930, for a fishing vessel must be a bona fide fisherman to be eligible for entry in any fishermen's race, especially so in an International Race. During the summer a challenge had been sent to the owners in Nova Scotia, for the *Bluenose*, to come to Gloucester and race the *Gertrude L. Thebaud*. This was accepted and a few days before the race was scheduled to start, her skipper, Angus L. Walters, brought the *Bluenose* to Gloucester.

The race between the *Bluenose* and *Thebaud*, sailed in October, 1930, was not an International Fishermen's Race for the Dennison Cup, but just a local affair. The start was a fine one, both vessels going over the line together. The first leg was a beat of six miles to

SCHOONER "GERTRUDE L. THEBAUD" WINNER OVER THE
SCHOONER "BLUENOSE" IN THE FISHERMEN'S RACE OF 1930

windward, on which the *Thebaud* outsailed the *Bluenose* four minutes, but on the run of six miles to the southeast buoy, the *Bluenose* gained two and a half minutes. After rounding the outer mark, both skippers hauled their vessels up by the wind on the third leg, when the *Thebaud* quickly increased her lead and when the race was called off, for lack of wind to finish inside the time limit, she was more than five minutes ahead of the *Bluenose*.

After several postponements (due to lack of wind), the unfinished race was sailed on Thursday, October 16th, and the *Gertrude L. Thebaud* won this first finished race handily by fifteen minutes. The second and final race was sailed on Saturday, October 18th. At the start the *Bluenose* had the best position, for she was to windward of the *Thebaud* and soon passed her, sailing fast for the first six miles, and was leading the *Thebaud* when she jibed around the first buoy off Milk Island. On the "broad reach" to the second buoy off to the southeast, the *Thebaud* gained slightly, but the *Bluenose* was still leading, and she rounded the mark one minute and four seconds ahead of the *Thebaud*. But right there skipper Angus made his big mistake and lost what chance he had to win the race; for instead of keeping his vessel to windward of the *Thebaud*, between her and the next windward mark, he chose to "split tacks" and stood inshore on the port tack a long way to the nor'west, and lost out by so doing.

When a man has rounded a buoy in a race ahead of another, he should never split tacks when working to windward, but should keep his vessel to windward of the other one, always, tacking whenever she tacks, thus keeping his vessel between her and the windward mark, so that the other vessel cannot get any favorable slant of wind over his vessel. It is all right for a man who is behind and to leeward to split tacks, for he has nothing to gain in following the vessel that is ahead and to windward of him, and quite often he may gain by splitting tacks and get a favorable slant of wind that will enable his vessel to overcome her handicap and beat the other vessel, as was the case in this race.

When the *Thebaud* rounded the southeast buoy, the crew quickly hauled in her sheets, as the skipper luffed her up sharply, close hauled by the wind, and still on the starboard tack. He then made a long hitch to the west-sou'west, and when the wind headed her off, tacked her to port, for the wind had backed out more to the westward, which gave them a good slant and she was able to fetch the windward mark, more than two miles to windward of the *Bluenose*, and the *Thebaud* passed the buoy leading her by fifteen minutes. The *Thebaud* beat the *Bluenose* almost seventeen minutes on the "thrash to windward" of six miles. On the second time around the triangle of eighteen miles, the *Bluenose* gained almost six minutes on the reach and run, and held her own fairly well on the second beat to windward, but the *Thebaud* won this race by more than eight minutes. Had skipper Angus Walters kept his vessel on the starboard tack to windward of the *Thebaud*, it would most likely have been a very close and exciting finish.

The skipper of the *Thebaud* that day, was Charlie Johnson, as Ben Pine was on the sick list, and he sailed her in an able manner, showing excellent judgment and good seamanship. She had a fine-setting suit of sails, with a very large mains'l which held her up well when she was by the wind. It had a very long main-gaff that peaked up high, and was a handsome sail. In fact, all her sails set finely and drew well, which was a very important thing in her equipment, for they brought out her fine sailing qualities and drove her at her best speed. Poorly fitted sails are a great handicap to any vessel. The *Bluenose* is much the larger vessel of the two, yet the *Thebaud* draws more water, for she has a very deep body with sharp easy bilges, designed for windward sailing.

HALIBUT-GAFF, BAIT CHOPPER, AND
GOB STICK

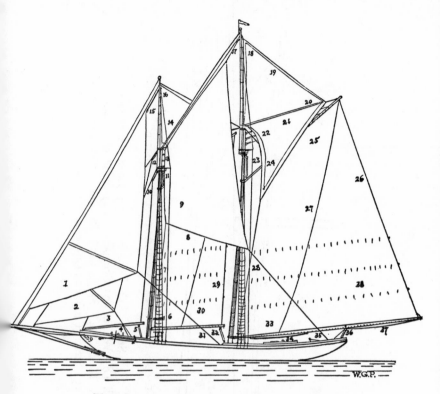

The Sails and Running Rigging of the Schooner "Gertrude L. Thebaud"

(1) Jib-topsail. (2) Jib. (3) Fore staysail* (or jumbo). (4) Jib-sheet. (5) Fore staysail-sheet. (6) Throat. (7) Luff. (8) Foresail. (9) Fishermen's staysail. (10) Fore staysail halyards. (11) Fore throat-halyards. (12) Jib halyards. (13) Fore peak-halyards. (14) Fore gaff-topsail. (15) Jib-topsail halyards. (16) Fore gaff-topsail halyards. (17) Staysail halyards. (18) Main gaff-topsail halyards. (19) Gaff-topsail clew-line. (20) Gaff-topsail sheet. (21) Main gaff-topsail. (22) Main peak-halyards. (23) Main throat-halyards. (24) Topsail tack. (25) Head of mainsail. (26) Leech of mainsail. (27) Mainsail down-haul. (28) Luff. (29) Leech of foresail. (30) Fore-sail down-haul. (31) Jib-topsail sheet. (32) Foresheet. (33) Foot of mainsail. (34) Main-boom tackle. (35) Staysail-sheet. (36) Main-sheet. (37) Foot-rope. (38) Reef-points.

* In the '80s when fishing schooners carried a flying-jib-boom the three head sails were called the (1) Balloon jib. (2) Flying-jib. (3) Jib.

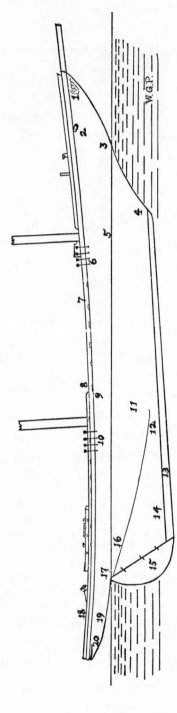

PROFILE PLAN OF THE FISHING SCHOONER "GERTRUDE L. THEBAUD"

(1) Bow. (2) Hawse-hole. (3) Stem. (4) Fore-foot. (5) Load water-line.
(6) Fore chainplates. (7) Rail. (8) Waist. (9) Scuppers. (10) Main chainplates.
(11) Bilge. (12) Floor. (13) Keel. (14) Skeg. (15) Rudder. (16) Counter.
(17) Quarter. (18) Taffrail. (19) Stern. (20) Fashion-piece.

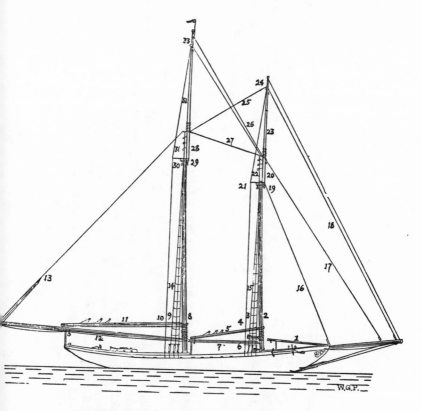

THE SPARS AND STANDING RIGGING OF THE SCHOONER "GERTRUDE L. THEBAUD"

(1) Fore staysail-boom. (2) Foremast. (3) Fore shrouds. (4) Fore topmast back-stay. (5) Fore-gaff. (6) Shear-pole. (7) Fore-boom. (8) Mainmast. (9) Main shrouds. (10) Main topmast back-stay. (11) Main-gaff. (12) Main-boom. (13) Topping-lift. (14, 15) Ratlines. (16) Fore stay. (17) Jib stay. (18) Jib-topsail stay. (19) Fore cross-trees. (20) Fore trestle-trees. (21) Fore topmast-spreader. (22) Fore masthead. (23) Fore topmast. (24) Fore truck. (25) Fresh-water stay. (26) Main-topmast stays. (27) Spring-stay. (28) Main trestle-trees. (29) Main cross-trees. (30) Main topmast-spreader. (31) Main masthead. (32) Main topmast. (33) Main truck.

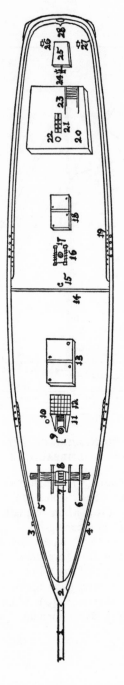

DECK PLAN OF THE FISHING SCHOONER "GERTRUDE L. THEBAUD"

(1) Bowsprit. (2) Knight-heads. (3, 4) Starboard and port cat-heads. (5, 6) Starboard and port windlass bits. (7) Pawl-bit. (8) Windlass. (9) Foremast. (10) Stovepipe funnel. (11) Forecastle companion way. (12) Fore hatch showing grating. (13) Main hatch. (14) "Break" of quarter deck. (15) Foresheet traveler. (16) Fiferail. (17) Mainmast. (18) After hatch. (19) Pinrail. (20) Trunk or cabin house. (21) Skylight. (22) Stove funnel. (23) Companion slide. (24) Steering wheel. (25) Wheel box. (26, 27) Starboard and port bit heads. (28) Mainsheet traveler.

CHAPTER XXI

THE FRESH MACKEREL SEINER OF TODAY

ALL the mackerel purse-seine fishermen today have a gasoline-purser installed in their seine-boats, for by its use the seine is pursed easily and quickly, saving much hard labor formerly done by hand. In the early mackerel purse-seine fishery, the fishermen went in a sailing vessel, depending on the wind to take them out on the fishing grounds. When they were "on fish" they rowed out in their seine-boat, and during calm weather, sometimes had to row both the seine-boat and dory a long distance from the vessel to reach a school of fish where they could set. After rowing around the school, setting their seine by hand, the crew had to purse it up by hand-power, a hard and laborious job. When they caught a school of mackerel, they had to bail them out on deck, hoisting them in by hand-power, using the fore and main-stays'l halyards as tackles. In those days, most of the fishermen dressed and salted all their fish, and when they had caught a large school, it was a long, tedious job of 24, 36 or 48 hours before they had them under salt. Then they had to "pack, head up, and stow down" the barrels of mackerel in the vessel's hold. When they had a full trip of 300 to 500 barrels, they sailed into port and landed them by hoisting the barrels out on the wharf with the fore and main-topping-lifts; later, some of them used a horse to hoist out their fish. That method of catching mackerel meant a great deal of hard labor for the fishermen.

The mackerel purse-seine fishermen of today go fishing in either auxiliary powered vessels or in steam-

251

ers, having crude-oil-burning engines installed, of from 120 to 260 h.p., according to the size of the craft. They are rigged with only enough sails to keep them steady in a sea-way, when hove-to on the fishing grounds. All of them have a four h.p. gasoline engine on deck to hoist fish, and another in the seine-boat, called the purser, to purse the seine. Very few mackerel are dressed and salted on board a seiner today, for the fish are mostly brought directly to market, fresh, iced in pens in the hold, saving time and also much manual labor. There are several reasons why mackerel are brought in fresh.

First: there is not much call on the part of the public today for salt mackerel, such as was the case in former days. Second: people have been educated by judicious advertising on the part of the wholesale and retail fish dealers, to call for and eat more fresh mackerel. Third: modern refrigeration has enabled the wholesaler and shippers to send fresh mackerel to inland points in good condition for the use of the consumer. Fourth: fishermen can earn more money and make quicker trips, saving both time and labor.

During the World War our government had 25 submarine chasers built of wood at various shipyards for service in the navy. They were known as 110 footers, were of a fine model, long, sharp and narrow, about 14 feet wide, with a shallow draft of seven feet. After the War they were dismantled and the boats sold, mostly bought at Gloucester by the fishermen, who used them for mackerel seiners, netters and draggers. The fishermen had them rebuilt inside with fo'cas'le and cook's pantry in the forward end, the hold for pens and fish in the center, with large crude-oil-burning, high powered engines of 180 to 240 h.p. installed in the after-hold giving them a speed of 10 to 12 knots an hour. Most of them had two short masts with mains'l, fores'l and jib, used mainly to keep them steady in a sea-way. They cost the fishermen, when ready for sea, from eighteen thousand to twenty thousand dollars, saving about ten thousand dollars over the cost of a new boat.

I went cook with skipper Al Miller, mackerel purse-seine fishing in the steamer *Lincoln*, one of those sub-marine chasers that had been converted into a seiner. I sailed with him for two seasons, 1926 and 1928. On our first trip, after putting my clothes-bag and bedding aboard in my berth, I looked around the store-room and lockers to see what she had on board for stores, and then went up on the wharf, found the skipper and asked him how long I should "fit out" for. He replied: "Fit out for three weeks, cook!"

"Aye, aye, sir!" I said, and then not knowing just how well he wanted his crew to live, I said to him, "Skipper, I should like to order some fruit for the trip, a few bananas, oranges and grapefruit, if you are will-ing."

He turned to me and said: "Cook, get anything you want!"

"Thank you, skipper," I said. "I'll order a bunch of bananas, a crate of oranges and a crate of grapefruit."

"That's right, cook. I want the 'boys' to have plenty to eat!"

Some of my readers may be under the impression that fishermen live chiefly upon fish. Of course, we eat them occasionally, as people do on shore; but when we do have them they are very fresh. I have often cooked fish that haven't been out of the water an hour before I had them on the range cooking. The fishermen of today have plenty of good things to eat and live well, for we have fresh meat of several kinds and plenty of ice to keep it fresh. We have fresh fruits and vegetables in their season, canned goods of good quality and of several kinds; a barrel of sugar, a case of fresh eggs, a case of milk, several pounds of good tea and coffee, and many kinds of small stores. A cook who understands his business and knows how to cook well, can set a fine table. The fishermen expect it and if you are unable to give it to them, the "Old Man" (skipper) will "turn you ashore" and "ship a new cook."

The cook on a fishing vessel is a very busy man in any branch of the fishery. When seining in the summer, mackerel often come up schooling at sunrise, so the cook "turns out" at three o'clock, has breakfast at four, dinner at ten and supper at three in the afternoon. The crew are allowed to go to the "shack cupboard" and "mug up" several times a day, besides their three hearty meals, and with a crew of fifteen men on a seiner, some one is at the cupboard nearly all the time, and the cook has to hustle to keep enough food cooked ahead for them to eat.

The "shack cupboard" is not to be confused with the cook's own cupboard where he keeps his food supply for the table. He makes his own bread, baking eight loaves each day, makes pies by the dozen, fries doughnuts, half a bushel at a time, makes puddings of various kinds, bakes cake of several kinds and often frosts them. We live high, work hard and sleep well.

In the old days of sailing vessels, the "bunt" was in the center of the purse-seine, half way around from each end, one of which was the dory's end; the other, the boat's end; also called "wings." When we had been out and set the seine around a school of mackerel and had "pursed it up," we then began to "dry in" on the corks and twine, with the crew along the length of the boat, from bow to stern. When it was nearly dried in, if we had the fish, they would be in a small bag down under the boat. We then took the corks onto the boat, brought the vessel alongside and bailed the mackerel out of the seine on deck. If we did not get the fish at that set, we hauled all the seine into the boat, then hauled what twine and corks were in the bow of the boat, aft, and when the vessel picked up the seine-boat, we made her fast to the boat-boom on the port side and hauled the entire seine out on deck. The seine-heaver, cork-thrower and bight-passer, standing in the seine-boat, then hauled the seine onto the boat over a roller on the vessel's rail, making it on in bights. It usually took about an hour to haul the seine aft in the boat, haul it out on deck, and then haul it back onto the boat, making it ready to set.

About ten years ago the Italian fishermen of Gloucester, began to use a new method, by having the "bunt" in the dory's end, or wing of the seine, at the third ring, fifteen fathoms from the end. All the mackerel purse-seine fishermen today, have adopted this new method and have their seines "hung" with the "bunt" in the "dory's wing" and when the crew start to haul in the corks and twine, after the seine has been set around a school and pursed up, instead of drying the seine into the boat, her entire length, the crew make the seine onto the boat out of the water, in the after end, ready to set again. Three men haul in and flake the twine across the boat and the cork-thrower makes on his corks at the same time the foot-rope and purse-line is also made on across the boat just in front, forward of the bulk of the twine, near the center of the boat. As the seine is made on, the seine-boat swings slowly around the seine towards the dory's end, and if we have the mackerel in the seine, we haul in about ten fathoms of it into the forward end of the boat, then take the corks onto the boat, and when the steamer comes alongside, we bail the fish out on deck. After the fish are all bailed out of the seine, the crew throw out the part which is in the forward end, then we make it onto the boat in the after end, out of the water, and in a few minutes are all ready to set again.

This new method saves about an hour's time, which is very important if mackerel are schooling and we want to make another set right away. Sometimes when we have made a set in the evening and perhaps missed the first school (or got only a few fish which we have bailed on deck), by the new method, we are ready in a few minutes to make the second set, before the fish sink or before darkness comes on.

When under power on the fishing grounds, and a school of mackerel is sighted, we hoist out the dory, the two men in her towing astern of the seine-boat, which has been hauled up on the starboard side of the steamer and made fast to the towing-boom. Most of the crew get into the seine-boat. The skipper is on the fore-masthead and the cook goes to the wheel in the pilot-house, to steer the steamer under directions from the skipper who calls out loudly from time to time: "Starboard your wheel! Port your wheel! Steady, now," as the case may be, until the steamer is up near the school, which is off on the starboard side.

"Give him a bell!" says the skipper to the cook, meaning the engineer, and the steamer slows down, as it is very essential that the skipper should know in which direction the fish are going; just how they are moving, whether fast or slow, before he starts to set the

The Steamer "Lincoln" Encircling a School of
Mackerel, the Skipper on the Foremast Head

seine, for the steamer should be going in the same direction as the fish, so they will go into the seine. It
takes a very practiced eye and keen sight to tell just
how the fish are moving. If they are going fast, it is
important to be some distance ahead of the school before setting the seine, so as to make a complete circle
around the school. If we start to set when the fish are
going in the opposite direction, they will go out of the
seine and we will be unable to completely encircle
them, for the length of the seine limits the size of the
circle, and the two ends must meet to allow of pursing
the seine. Sometimes the school turns with the boat, as
fast as she turns, and will swim out by the dory's end of
the seine before we can encircle them, and once in a
great while, a school will "cart-wheel" (go around in
a small circle). When they play in this manner, it
makes no great difference where we start to set, so long
as we are near enough to make a complete circle.

When the skipper has made up his mind to set, he
calls for a bell to start the steamer and when she is in

the right place, he calls out loudly: "Let go th' end o' th' seine! Give 'em twine!" The seine-heaver then throws out the end and a few bights of twine and when this settles in the water, it drags the rest of the seine out over the side and stern of the seine-boat as she moves ahead towing from the boat-boom on the starboard side of the steamer, both of which make a great circle

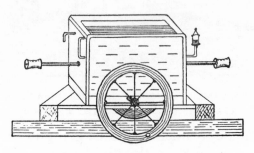

GASOLINE MOTOR FOR PURSING THE SEINE

around the school, back to the dory and the end of the seine. The boat's painter is then cast off at the right time by the man in the bow of the seine-boat, the steamer going along, and the seine-boat is held at the end of the seine. The crew then reeve off the purse-line through the purse-blocks on the purse-davit, start the purser, catch a turn with the line, and purse the seine with the aid of the gasoline four h.p. purser, which saves time and much hard work. If the tide is running, making the seine purse high, the purse-weight is put on the purse-line and run to the bottom of the seine to the bridles, where, by its weight of eighty pounds, it helps to make it purse deeper under the school of fish.

Mackerel are wild and hard to catch, on some days, for they will dive and go out under the seine before it is possible to purse it and entrap the school. On other days they are easy to catch, and will school on the surface in the seine until it is pursed up. Sometimes when it is rough the seine is burst open or ripped down, even when it is up alongside the steamer, and the fish are lost. Fishermen are never sure of their mackerel until they are bailed out on deck.

Once off Seguin, in the *Lincoln*, we set around a large school, pursed our seine and caught the fish, dried in the corks and twine, and then brought the steamer alongside the seine-boat and started bailing. It was rough, with an old sea heaving in from the south'ard, and the steamer was rolling badly. Before we had a thousand pounds of fish bailed out on deck, our seine started to rip off and tore along the cork-line on the rail, so that we lost a large school of fish, estimated at 100,000 pounds or something over 300 barrels. Our seine was an old one and very tender, not strong enough to stand the great strain of that large school when it was rough.

Often when setting around a school, the fish will settle away and that will be the last ever seen of them. Sometimes, when half way around the school, they will disappear, but we keep on and make the set, and by the time the seine is partly pursed up, they will come up again, schooling in the seine, and so we get the fish. Often when pursing, we are able to see the school in the seine until it is nearly pursed up, when the fish will suddenly dive and go out under the seine-boat. Once when setting off Cape Cod, the fish settled away as we started to purse, and we did not see any until we had the seine pursed up and half dried in. All at once, without any warning, we were startled by a sudden rushing sound, and saw the whole school fling themselves several feet up into the air and fall back into the sea, right in the center of our seine. They had been badly frightened by a mackerel-shark, in our seine, underneath the school. We killed the shark and saved the school of 24,000 pounds.

When the crew had pursed the seine and dried it into the boat until it was nearly all in, except the part in the water enclosing the fish, we then took the corks onto the boat and the fish were held in a bag down under the seine-boat. The engineer and cook, who were left on the steamer while the crew were out in the seine-boat, kept close by, and when the skipper was ready, he, with four men, got into the dory and rowed aboard the steamer which the skipper soon put up alongside the boat, with the fish in the seine between the boat and steamer. We then took the corks up on the rail, made fast with the rail-board and rope-stops, and put a canvas tarpaulin over the rail to prevent the large dip-net from tearing the seine while hoisting out the fish. The dip-net holds about three hundred pounds, and is hoisted in over the rail by a tackle and the hoisting engine on deck. The skipper holds the long-handled dip-net, which he fills by pushing it down in the seine under the swimming fish and when ready, he sings out: "H'ist away!" The man running the hoister on deck, catches a turn and when the net is high enough, and as it swings in over the rail (the skipper guiding it), he lets go a trip-line which opens the bottom of the dip-net and the fish drop out on deck.

The old style dip-net had no trip-line, and was turned bottom-up by two men as it came in over the rail, dumping the mackerel out on deck. Years ago when seining in sail vessels, we bailed on deck and then passed them below in bushel-baskets where the fish were dumped into ice-pens in the vessel's hold. Today, most mackerel seiners have several deck-plates set in their decks, about fifteen inches in diameter. These plates are removed during bailing and the fish allowed to fall through the deck-plate holes into the ice-pens below, where two men ice them. This saves much time and labor and the mackerel are iced in better condition for they are fresh, right out of the water.

When all the fish have been bailed out of the seine, the crew drop the boat astern, haul the seine aft in the boat and then haul her up on the port side and make her fast to the boat-boom. The seine is then hauled out on deck, salting it at the same time to kill the gurry and slime on the twine. This is always done after getting a school, for if not done, the seine will heat and rot the twine, making it very tender, and in a short time it will become unfit to use. There are, of course, exceptions to this rule, for when we get small hauls and expect to set the seine again soon, it is made onto the boat without salting.

After a good school has been caught and the seine is salted on deck we put the long painter on the seine-boat and drop her astern, and start for market. If possible, the skipper makes his plans to be in port at the Fish Pier, before the market opens at seven o'clock in the morning. Most of the fishermen enter the harbor during the night, which is easily done in clear weather, as the channel is well marked with lighted buoys and most skippers are good pilots, and have no trouble in finding their way in, even in foggy weather. When the market at the Fish Exchange is opened, all the skippers in port are on hand to sell their trips of fish. If it happens to be a morning when there are only a few seiners in, with small trips, mackerel will sell for eight or ten cents a pound, and make a large stock, the crew sharing a hundred dollars or more. A large trip of 60,000 pounds with fish at twelve cents will make a gross stock of $7,200.00 and after expenses are deducted, the crew will share around $220.00 for the trip.

One of the largest stocks in the mackerel fishery, of recent years, was made by skipper Wm. Corkum in the seiner *Lois H. Corkum*, when she brought in 60,000 pounds and sold for twenty cents. As fish were very scarce and the market bare, she got a high price for her trip, as she was the only vessel in that morning, and made a gross stock of $12,000.00, her crew sharing about $380.00 to a man.

Sometimes when in with a large trip, there would be a fleet of forty sail in, also with large trips, and down would go the price to two or three cents, making only fifteen or twenty dollars a share for the trip. At three different times in 1926, we came in with good-sized trips and finding the market glutted with a million pounds of fresh mackerel, sold to the cold storage plant for a very small price, and shared only about twenty-five dollars apiece for the trip. That is the way it goes with the fishermen who are either "lucky" or "unlucky" about striking a market, for sometimes a small trip will bring more money than a large one.

Once in a while we are unfortunate and not in the right place where mackerel are schooling and so miss the "spurt," and are gone from home three weeks without getting a trip. For when our crude oil is nearly gone and "grub" is getting low, we have to return home with a "broken trip," and in debt. But this doesn't happen often. We usually get some fish, enough to pay expenses, at least, on a hard trip. On one trip in the *Lincoln*, we had "hard luck," not finding any fish for nearly three weeks. We had cruised all around Boston Bay, out around Cape Cod, then went over "The

Shoals" out through Vineyard Sound, then out around Nantucket Lightship, back around Block Island, and into New Bedford, where we stayed for four days during a "fog mull." When it finally cleared off, the skipper decided to leave at midnight, and we went down across Buzzards Bay, out through by Cuttyhunk Island, then up Vineyard Sound and down over "The Shoals." The next morning, when we passed out through Pollock-Rip-Slue, we could see some vessels away off shore to the eastward, and when we got nearer we saw they were working on fish. Before long we sighted a school, made a set and got 26,000 pounds and that night went to Boston and the next morning sold our fish for a good price, each man sharing $48.00, a lucky ending for what we thought was going to be a very disappointing "hard luck trip."

Another time we went to the eastward and the next day it breezed up from the no'theast, so the skipper headed her up for Portland, intending to make the harbor; but the wind increased and the sea got rough, so he changed his mind and swung her off and ran into Portsmouth instead. We stayed there for two nights and a day during the storm, then when it cleared off, we came out and near Boone Island sighted a school of fish, made a set and got 19,000 pounds. That night at nine o'clock (after dark) we got another school of 9,000 pounds, which made us up a small trip of 28,000 pounds so we started for Boston and sold our fish for a good price and shared $56.00.

We did well, night fishing, during the fall of 1926, sharing about $400.00 from September 15th to November 17th. One day about four o'clock, while I was washing the supper dishes, we left Gloucester and ran off east-no'theast from Thatcher's Island, about 25 miles, and that night, after dark (about nine o'clock) sighted a good school, made a set around them and got a good haul, bailing out about 40,000 pounds. We were back in Gloucester at four o'clock having been gone from port only twelve hours. When the market opened our fish sold for ten cents a pound, stocking $4,000.00, and each man shared $134.00 for his night's work. The same week we got another good trip, one night off Cape Cod, of 38,000 pounds and shared $84.00, but the following week was stormy, foggy weather, and we didn't get a fish.

John Seavey was a "high-line" mackerel fisherman for several years. He started in fishing early in life, at Boothbay Harbor, Maine, and went skipper for many years. He was very successful, especially so during the last of his life. When most men retire he kept on going, had a long, useful life, and followed seining until his death in 1925. Unlike most skippers he didn't go winter fishing for he made a specialty of mackerel seining as his life's work and he made the longest record (45 years) as skipper, of any man in the fishery. During that long period he landed an immense amount of mackerel. In early life he went skipper in vessels from Boothbay Harbor and Portland, and later on he went to Gloucester and sailed out of that port for many years, in several different vessels, and was skipper of the schooner *Mary F. Curtis*, in the spring of 1925. That fall he died, active to the last, at seventy-five years of age.

John Seavey made his greatest record in the schooner *Arthur James* of Gloucester, during the four years, 1916-1920. He was "high-line" of the mackerel fleet, making a record stock each year: in 1916, $42,000.00; in 1917, $36,000.00; in 1918, about $40,000.00; and in 1919, it was $24,000.00. The last year was for only part of the season as the fishermen's strike was on during that summer. The *Arthur James* was a very "lucky vessel" (so the fishermen say), for she made a great record during her thirty years in the mackerel fishery, earning a lot of money for her owners, skippers and crews. Several years ago, at the very close of the mackerel season, she brought in three good trips, one each morning, for three successive days, and was then struck by a steamer in Boston Harbor during a thick fog and sunk while bound in on her fourth trip, but soon raised and repaired.

In June, 1926, we lay alongside a wharf in New Bedford, for nearly a week, during a long fog spell. One day while the "first gang" were eating their dinner, I went up on deck to get a breath of fresh air and soon fell into conversation with a young lad, about fifteen, the brother of the skipper of the seiner *Bethulia*, which lay on the outside of our steamer, the *Lincoln*.

"I understand the *Bethulia* did well out south this spring," I said to him. "Did her crew share $1,400.00 during April and May?"

"Yes, sir, they did," he replied.

"What do you get, half a share?" I said.

"Yes, sir, I get half a share!" he replied.

"You must have earned $700.00 out south this spring."

"Yes, sir, I did!"

"You did well, my lad," I remarked, "but I am a little curious about what you did with your money."

"I gave it to my mother and she put in it the bank for me!" he said.

"Good for you, my boy, that was the right thing to do with it," I said to him as I went below.

By the time that Italian lad is twenty-one years old, very likely he will have several thousand dollars saved up in the bank, so that he will be able to buy an interest in a seiner and most likely go skipper of her himself. The Italian fishermen of Gloucester are industrious, save their money, and own their own fishing steamers, which are among the best in the mackerel fleet. They are great workers and most of them are good seine-menders, capable of taking care of their own purse-seines; and they are smart fishermen for some of their skippers have been "high-liners" of the fleet for several years past. In 1923-25, the mackerel seiner *Annie and Mary*, with an Italian skipper and crew, was "high-line" for those years, making a very large stock each year and her crew shared $3,300.00, $2,800.00, and $2,400.00, the largest amount being the most money ever made by any crew on a mackerel purse-seine fishing vessel in any one season.

Most Maine fishing vessels, especially those from the small ports, were not sent winter fishing. Many went hand-line, dory cod fishing, sailing about the first week in April for the Western Bank on the spring trip and usually arriving home in June. They were then fitted out for the mackerel purse-seine fishery. A few vessels went back on the "second trip" for cod on Banquereau, fishing for the most part on the "Rocky Bottom" in August, arriving home about September, and then going seining during the fall months.

Some few vessels went "south" in the spring, following the mackerel purse-seine fishing throughout the whole season of eight months. About the last of October most vessels were "hauled up" for the winter. Owners believed they saved money by so doing, for the vessel's sails would last longer (three years) and a saving was also made on the wear and tear of the vessel and her rigging by not sending her winter fishing.

Southport, Maine, had a fleet of eleven vessels left in 1889, and they went hand-line, dory cod fishing to the Western Bank each spring, usually for one trip, and then went seining for mackerel (salt fishing) during the rest of the season. William T. Maddocks had a fish firm on the west side at Ebenecook harbor, and owned six vessels; and Freeman Orne & Sons had five, on the east side at Townsend Gut. These two firms continued in business until about 1893, and then sold their vessels and closed their doors for good, chiefly because of the scarcity of both cod and mackerel.

In 1860, Southport had a fleet of forty sail of fishing vessels and did a thriving business for many years, but for the past forty years her chief industry has been the "summer boarder."

The fish firm of S. Nickerson & Sons at Boothbay Harbor, did a large business for twenty-six years, and then sold out in 1903. They had a fleet of twenty vessels, bankers and seiners, and some of their vessels were large and brought in big trips of salted cod, one of them, the *Bertha D. Nickerson*, carrying 3,000 quintals. The firm carried on quite a business in salt, of various kinds, for salting fish, furnishing the nearby vessels with this commodity for their fishing trips. They also had a large general store filled with food supplies for their vessels, and also sold goods to the families of the men who sailed in their vessels. Their business for many years totaled $250,000.00 annually. Their fleet of vessels, with seine-boats, dories, and fishing gear, cost about $200,000.00, and their plant consisting of general store, several large fish-houses, sail-loft, etc.; cost at least $150,000.00. Today, the entire fishing business of Boothbay Harbor, and Southport, Maine, is gone, a thing of the past.

Bucksport, Castine, and Lamoine, sent several vessels hand-line, dory cod fishing for many years, but did not fish in the mackerel purse-seine fishery, confining themselves wholly to the salt cod fishing. Most of these vessels were "laid up" during the winter. Today, they are all gone, only a memory.

The vessels sailing from Swan's Island, Deer Isle, Vinal Haven, and North Haven, were, for the most part, engaged in the mackerel fishery. In the early days these vessels (mostly pinkys) were sent to the North Bay and Magdalen Islands, "jiggin' mack'rel." Later on, during the seventies, eighties, and nineties, new and larger vessels were built for the purse-seine fishery, and this fleet of about fifty sail did well and landed a very large amount of salt mackerel annually.

It was the custom for skippers to land their trips in Portland, where the mackerel were packed and sold. They bought their empty barrels and salt there, and also most of their food supplies and fishing gear. The fishermen from these islands manned not only their own fleet, but many of the men went seining in Portland vessels. The men who lived on the islands in Penobscot Bay depended almost wholly on the mackerel fishery for their living during the days of sail. For the past thirty years many of the younger men have found employment on yachts, some of them as sailing masters, captains, officers and crews, and some are famous up and down the Atlantic coast, as "yacht seamen."

Portland was the largest fishing port in Maine, and for many years had a fleet of about seventy-five sail of Bankers, seiners, and trawlers. Many of her fleet "laid up" for the winter months, especially the older vessels, but some went "haddocking." Several went to Grand Manan after herring, and during the early winter, a few went to Prince Edward Island for a load of potatoes.

Portland, during the days of the sailing fishing vessel, was the headquarters for about all the vessels owned along the coast of Maine, in her numerous harbors and among the many islands from Kittery to Eastport. It was there the vessels went to "fit out" during the spring, summer, and fall, for they could buy salt, bait (salted clams), ice, barrels, food supplies and all kinds of fishing gear, and the merchants did a fine business, selling goods to these outside vessels, as well as supplying their own fleet.

At Boston, and Gloucester, it was quite a different matter as regards winter fishing, as most of their vessels went to sea the year around. Some of the seiners changed over at the close of the mackerel season and went winter "haddocking." Many of the large seiners went to Newfoundland after frozen herring, bringing their trips home to either Gloucester, or Boston, where they were sold mostly for bait, but some of the herring were sold for food. Others went trawling for fresh halibut in the Grand Bank fishery. A large fleet went in the George's Bank (hand-line from deck) fishing after both cod and halibut, bringing their trips in as fresh fish. Some went trawling for cod on salt trips to the Western Bank, and also to Banquereau. Only a very few of the older vessels in the seining fleet were "hauled up" for the winter season at Gloucester.

The large Provincetown fleet of hand-line dory cod fishermen, for the most part went to the Grand Banks. Many of them were large vessels, and often were gone from home three or four months on a salt trip. When they returned in the fall with a large fare, they were laden deep with 2,500 to 3,500 quintals of salt fish. After unloading and "washing out," men spread them on the "fish flakes" to dry. Some vessels took on board the dry fish and sailed for the West Indies during the early winter and returned with cargoes of fruit, molasses, or sugar. Very few vessels from Provincetown went seining. Several years ago the large fleet of handliners were sold, one by one, until all were gone. Of late years a small fleet of fine fast-sailing vessels are engaged in the trawl-line fishing out of Provincetown. They are owned and manned by Portuguese fishermen who sell their trips of fresh cod and haddock at the Fish Pier in Boston.

Nearly all the Cape Cod fleet of fifty sail of seiners, from Wellfleet, Harwich, South Chatham, Dennis, and Dennisport, were "laid up" for the winter, during the years from 1870 to 1890, when they prospered during the summer season in the mackerel purse-seine fishery.

A few vessels sailed from Plymouth, Scituate and Cohasset in the eighties, mostly Bank fishing.

Marblehead, in the old days, sent out a large fleet of fishermen in the hand-line from deck fishery, and during the years between 1860 and 1890, she sent a large fleet hand-line dory fishing to the Grand Banks, and these vessels were among the first to go "dory fishing." The Marblehead hand-line dory vessels followed a method of their own in dressing fish on the Bank, for they had a "dressing gang aboard" who worked on the fish all day, while the rest of the crew were out in their dories. I have seen some Marblehead fishermen out in their dories as late as six o'clock in the evening, when we, on our vessel, were dressing fish, for our crew had all come aboard at three o'clock to get supper, after which all hands worked on the fish caught that day.

There have been greater changes in the models of fishing vessels out of Boston, and in the methods of catching fish, than from any other New England fishing port.

In 1870 there was quite a fleet of "Irish smoke boats"; plumb-stem sloops, painted black, wide and very deep-bodied, but short in length which made them rather chunky. They were able sea-boats and some of them went trawling, but many comprised the herring fleet. They were of a type peculiar to Boston harbor. In 1880, a son of Boston, Thomas H. McManus, began designing fishing vessels and in a few years his vessels began to attract attention, for they were of a handsome, fine model and very able, fast sailers. He did more to develop the New England fishing vessel than any other man in Boston.

About 1905, the gasoline marine engine was installed in a few fishing vessels; and later came the crude-oil marine engine. This was the beginning of the end of the all-sail fishing vessels of Boston, and elsewhere in New England. Then came the draggers, and beam-trawlers. Boston now has the largest fleet of beam-trawlers (steamers) in the New England fisheries, and all are engaged in the ground-fish industry and bring to the Boston Fish Pier large trips of fresh cod, haddock, halibut, pollock, cusk, hake, scrod, whale-cod and flounders (lemon-sole, gray-sole, black backs, yellow tails and dabs). The fishing industry of New England has changed from salt fish to fresh fish, almost wholly, for very few vessels engage in the salt fishery today.

Appendix I

Nautical Terms Used on Fishing Vessels

ABEAM. The wind is abeam when it is blowing directly on the windward side of a vessel.

ABLE. A skipper who has skill in seamanship and is a capable, high-line fisherman. An able vessel is one that can carry whole-sail in heavy winds and rough seas.

ABOARD. To go aboard a vessel. To row alongside in a dory.

ABOUT. To change the vessel's course from one tack on the wind to another. "Ready-about": an order given by the skipper when he is ready to tack his vessel.

ALOFT. On the masthead, the lookout watching for a "school." "Lay aloft and furl the gaff-topsail."

ANCHOR. A fisherman's anchor is designed to hold on well; more so by its shape than by its weight, for it has a longer shank and stock than other kinds. Fishing vessels carry three sizes, — *sheet anchor*, *best bower*, and a *spare anchor*. "Anchor's aweigh," when it is clear of the bottom as the cable is hove in while getting the vessel underway. The "anchor comes home" when it is dragged from its bed on the bottom, during a heavy gale, and the vessel breaks adrift. An "anchor watch" is kept when a vessel is riding at anchor on the fishing Banks.

ASTERN. The vessel in the rear; behind another. When the seine-boat or dories are made fast to the stern.

BAILING. A fishing vessel hove to, her crew bailing mackerel out of the seine on deck, with the large bailing dip-net.

BAIT. The bait used on fishing vessels consists of salted clams, menhaden (porgy-slyvers), fresh mackerel, herring, squid, capelin, lant and Bank clams. "Baiting up"— the crew cutting bait and baiting their trawls.

BEAT. "Beating to windward"—the vessel going against the wind by alternate tacks.

BECKET-ROPE. A half-inch rope, two fathoms long, seized in the middle to a staple in the vessel's deck directly under her wheel, the two ends used to make the wheel fast.

BELAY. To make a rope fast to a cleat, belaying-pin, or the bit-head.

BELOW. To go down below into the cabin or forecastle. "Below decks"—the vessel's hold. To pitch fish (dressed cod) "below" in the hold. "Stand from under below"—when lowering a barrel into the vessel's hold while men are at work under the hatch-way.

BENDING-SAILS. The crew lacing the head of the sail to the gaff and the foot to the boom; seizing the luff to mast-hoops as the sail is hoisted up.

BERTH. The berths in cabin and forecastle where men sleep. Berth—three feet at the rail where men stand to fish with hand-lines. "Berth on the fishing-bank"—vessel lying at anchor. "Making a berth"—changing position of the vessel to new fishing grounds. "A good berth" (trawling)—two miles to nearest vessel. When hand-line dory fishing one mile to the nearest vessel.

BLANKETING. When a vessel passes close by another on her weather, her sails "blanket" the one under her lee.

BOAT'S-OUT. When the masthead lookout reports seeing a seine-boat out, whose crew have made a set around a school of mackerel.

BOUND. A vessel on the fishing Bank with her colors at the main-truck, indicating that she is "Bound home." "Bound to the west'ard"—a Grand Banker bound home. "Bound to market"—a trawler with a full trip. "Outward bound"—a vessel sailing for fishing grounds.

BREAK. Where the quarter deck ends near amidships and steps down to the main-deck. A vessel breaks adrift, when *foul anchor comes home*. "To break out" barrels stowed in the vessel's hold. "Break out the anchor"—when heaving in on the cable. "Break 'er down"—the crew heaving hard on windlass brakes. "Break out the sails"—"break out the flag."

BREAK-DOWN-THE-DORIES. When hoisting them in on deck a man passes out the anchor, bait-bucket, and water-jug, then knocks down the thwart and kid-boards into the bottom of the dory, so that the next one can be "nested" (set inside).

BROACH. When a vessel swings to windward of her compass course in heavy weather while running free.

CALL-THE-WATCH. When it is time to call the men below to come on deck.

CARRY-AWAY. The loss of topmasts and light sails by heavy winds.

CAST-OFF. To unfasten a rope; "cast off the line"; "slack up the line."

CAT-THE-ANCHOR. To reeve the cat-stopper through the ring and haul it from the hawse-pipe up to the cathead.

CATCH-A-TURN. To hold a turn under a cleat while the crew are swaying hard on a rope.

CLEW. "Clew up the gaff-topsail"—to haul down on the clew-line which draws the sail in close to the masthead.

CLEW-LINE. A small rope which runs (through blocks) around the outside edge of the gaff-topsail.

COIL. All new rope comes in a coil. To coil a rope, is to lay it around from left to right (with the sun) in a small circle, one layer upon another, so that it will run out clear when used.

COME-UP-BEHIND. To slack up quickly when hauling on a rope, so that the man can catch a turn and make it fast.

COURSE. The direction a vessel is sailing by point of compass.

CULLING-FISH. Sorting out the different sizes and grades.

CUT-AWAY. To roll a barrel of fish away nearly upright on its edge. To "cut the cable" when a vessel is drifting down afoul of yours during a heavy gale.

DEAD-RECKONING. Is to keep run of a vessel (by the use of the chart, mariner's compass, patent-log and the sounding-lead while sailing on a course) without taking an observation of the sun with the sextant to find out her exact position by latitude and longitude.

DORY-POD. A very small school of mackerel caught with the purse-seine.

DRAGGING. A vessel adrift with her anchor out on bottom. To catch fish with a drag-net or beam-trawl.

DRAUGHT. The depth (in feet) of a vessel from her load-water-line to the bottom of her keel. A school of fish caught with the drag-net or the purse-seine.

DRAW. Most fishing vessels "draw" from twelve to fifteen feet of water. A fine setting suit of sails "draw well." "Draw-away"—to let go the tail rope on the jib-sheet after tacking a vessel. Draw-bucket—a wooden water-pail fitted with a bucket-rope for drawing water over side.

DRESSING-DOWN. The crew at work dressing a "deck of fish."

DRIVER. A skipper who drives (sails) his vessel hard when making a passage in heavy winds.

DROP-THE-DORY-OVERBOARD. To hoist out and lower away the dory with the fore and main topping-lifts, when a school of mackerel is seen by the skipper on a seiner.

DROP-THE-BOAT-ASTERN. To unfasten the (towing boom) painter and make fast the long painter, then push the seine-boat astern of the vessel.

DRY-IN-THE-TWINE. To haul the twine into the boat, out of the water, after making a set of the purse-seine.

DRY-'ER-UP. To haul up hard on the twine while bailing mackerel out of the seine when alongside the vessel.

EASE-HER-UP-A-LITTLE. To luff a vessel or boat up slightly when a sudden puff of wind strikes her.

EASE-OFF-THE-SHEETS. To slack off the sheets when a vessel swings off.

EVEN-KEEL. When the vessel is setting even at water-line, with no list to starboard or port.

FALL-OFF-HER-COURSE. A vessel making leeway when by the wind.

FATHOM. A fathom is six feet long. All ropes and lines are measured in fathoms, by seamen who take the rope in their hands, extending them in a horizontal position sidewise.

FETCH-BY. A vessel sailing off a leeshore and weathering a point or headland without tacking.

FILL-AWAY. When a vessel falls off and the sails fill with wind while getting underway or after tacking.

FITTING-OUT. The skipper and crew at work getting the vessel ready for a fishing trip by stowing on board gear, grub, bait, ice or salt, coal, wood, etc.

FLAKING-THE-TWINE. When the crew are hauling the seine off, or on the boat, they flake the twine back and forth so that it will not pile up too high.

FLATTEN-THE-SHEETS. All sheets are trimmed down flat when a vessel is close-hauled.

FLOW-THE-HEAD-SHEETS. To slack up the leeward sheets on a vessel when she is tacking.

FOOT-AHEAD. Some vessels "foot-ahead" faster than others when by the wind.

FOUL-ANCHOR. If the cable has a half turn over the stock when a vessel is riding at anchor, she will drag and go adrift.

FRESH-FISHING. To bring in fish fresh, iced in pens in the vessel's hold.

FURL. To furl and roll a sail up on the boom and fasten it with stops.

GANG. While hand-line, dory-fishing on the Bank, the crew are equally divided into "two gangs," the "starboard-gang," and the "port-gang." The skipper always eats with the first-gang. His seat is on the starboard-locker at the foot of the table near the gangway.

GANGWAY. The entrance to the forecastle and the cabin.

GEAR. A general term for all running-rigging and "fishing-gear." Trawl-men go out in their dories to haul their "gear." When in port they over-haul their "gear" to repair it.

GEORGE'SMAN. A vessel whose crew fish with hand-lines for cod and halibut, from deck, on George's Bank.

GOOD-HOLDING-GROUND. A bottom of hard mud is the best.

GROUND. To run a vessel aground; to strike bottom.

GROUND-BAIT. Mackerel toll-bait, menhaden (porgy slyvers) ground up in the bait-mill, to bring fish alongside.

GROUND-SWELL. An underrunning sea (sometimes heavy) heaving in usually from the south or southeast, indicating that there has been a heavy gale in that direction.

GROUND-TACKLE. The anchors and cable on a vessel.

GUNWALE. The top planking around a dory's side.

GUST. A sudden squall, of short duration.

HADDOCKER. A vessel trawling in the fresh haddock fishery.

HALIBUTER. A vessel trawling in the fresh halibut fishery.

HAND. A fisherman, one of the crew, an old hand. To "give a hand" and furl the sail. A "new hand"—a man recently shipped on a vessel. A "green hand"—a man on his first trip; a "peddler." "All hands on deck," to take in sail.

HANDLINER. A "cod fisherman," whose crew fish from dories with the hand-line on a salt trip.

HARD-UP. To roll the wheel "hard-up" and swing the vessel off.

HARD-A-LEE. When the skipper is ready to "tack ship," he calls out: "Hard-a-lee!" and then rolls the wheel hard down.

HAUL. When the wind "Hauls 'round" with the sun. To close up on the wind. To catch a large "haul" of mackerel with the purse-seine. A large trip. "Haul aft the mainsheet!"—the crew haul the sheet in. "Haul in alongside the wharf!"—to warp her in. "Haul in your lines, Boys!"—says the skipper. "Haul up the boat!"—to haul the boat up alongside when school of mackerel is seen. "Haul the seine out on deck!"—to haul it out of the seine-boat. To "haul out"—to put the vessel on the railway to clean and paint her underbody. To "haul up"—to make a vessel fast alongside the wharf and remove gear, sails and stores.

HEAD. All sails on a vessel have a head, foot, leech and luff. Head sails, those forward of the foremast. The figurehead on a vessel, under her bowsprit. A head wind is one blowing directly from the point of destination.

HEADING. The point on the compass card at "lubbers mark"; the course the vessel is sailing. "How is she heading?" asks the skipper of the man at her wheel: "East-south-east, Sir!" he replies.

HEAD-OFF. When the wind hauls ahead, it "heads off" the vessel so that she will not lay her course.

HEEL. To lean to leeward side when the wind is blowing.

HIGH-LINE. The vessel that makes the largest stock during the season. The skipper who lands the most fish during the season. The man who catches the most fish during a trip.

HITCH. A short tack on the wind.

HEAVE-AHEAD. To heave in the cable and weigh the anchor.

HEAVE-THE-DORIES-OUT. To hoist out and drop them overboard.

HEAVE-THE-LEAD. To heave it well forward alongside the vessel.

HEAVE-IN-THE-STRAD. To man the windlass and heave in the cable far enough to remove the *strad* (chafing gear) when it has been badly chafed across the bobstay during rough weather.

HOIST-AWAY. To haul down on the halyards and hoist the sails. "Hoist-away!" says the skipper, when bailing mackerel out of the purse-seine on deck.

HOLDING-ON. A vessel that rides out the gale when others drag their anchors and go adrift.

HOOKING. A crew catching mackerel with the jig and hand-line; the mackerel fishery of former days.

HOVE-DOWN. A vessel "hove down" on her beam ends by a violent squall, or tripped by a heavy breaking sea.

HOVE-SHORT. When the slack of the cable is hove in taut.

HOW-DOES-SHE-RIDE? Asks the skipper. "Ride, why she shames the gulls, Sir!" the man replies.

HUNG-UP. When the purse-seine has been set and is afoul of the bottom, so that it is impossible to purse it. When a vessel proves to be a fast sailer and handles well, she is said to be "hung up" just right. When a purse-seine is assembled (when new) the twine is "hung up" to the cork-rope; also the bottom part is "hung to the foot-rope." When a purse-seine is "hung full' in the bunt and fishes well, it is said to be "hung up right."

IN-IRONS. When a vessel loses headway and misstays while tacking.

JIBE. To turn a vessel with wind astern, so that the sails swing over to the opposite side.

JIGGING. To catch mackerel with the jig and hand-line.

JOGGING. A vessel heading nearly up into the wind with her jib-sheet made fast to windward and her wheel rolled hard down.

KNOT. A nautical mile of 6,082 feet. The statute mile is 5,280.

LAY. On some vessels the crew, "share and share alike." On others, the crew fish on the "square halves."

LAY-TO. The same as hove to: the vessel lying nearly side to the wind.

LEE. A vessel at anchor under the lee. The side opposite to the wind.

LEE-HELM. A vessel inclined to fall off to leeward of her course,—a bad fault.

LEEWAY. A vessel makes leeway, when "by the wind." When a vessel is hove to jogging.

LEEWARD. Pertaining to the part towards which the wind blows.

LEE-SHORE. The shore under the lee of the vessel. Beating off a lee-shore in a gale of wind.

LET-GO-THE-ANCHOR. The command given by a skipper when ready to anchor his vessel.

LOCKER. Lockers extend around the sides of both the cabin and forecastle on which the fishermen can sit. Inside the cabin-lockers are stored small gear, lines, blocks, spun yarn and marlin; in the forecastle lockers the cook stows vegetables and canned goods.

LOWER-AWAY. To cast off the halyards and lower the sail. To lower barrels into a vessel's hold.

LUBBER'S-MARK. A black vertical line or mark in the compass-bowl in the direction of the vessel's head by which the angle between the magnetic meridian and the vessel's line of course is shown.

LUFF. To roll the wheel down and swing the vessel up by the wind.

LUFFING. To head the vessel up into the wind.

LUMPERS. Men who work around the wharf getting a vessel ready for her trip to sea.

MAINSAIL-HAUL. A vessel lying to under her mainsail, while her crew are at work dressing a large haul of mackerel out at sea.

MAKE-FAST. To fasten a rope to a cleat, belaying-pin, or to the bit-head.

MAKE-THE-LIGHT. When a vessel is approaching the land during the night.

MAKE-SAIL. To hoist the sails and fill away.

MAKE-ON-THE-SEINE. To haul the purse-seine into the seine-boat from the deck of the vessel.

MAN-THE-BOAT. An order given by the skipper for his crew to get into the seine-boat when a "school" is seen.

MAN-THE-WINDLASS. An order given by the skipper for his crew to heave in the cable and get the anchor.

NEST-THE-DORIES. To hoist them in and stow them inside of each other, on top of the cabin-house, out of the way when hand-line dory fishing. When trawling—to stow them on the main deck.

NETTER. A vessel fitted with gill-nets which the crew set on the surface of the sea to catch mackerel and herring. The gill-netter who fishes for cod in Ipswich Bay, sets his gill-nets near the bottom.

ON-FISH. When a vessel, or a fleet of vessels, are cruising where mackerel are schooling at sea.

ON-SOUNDINGS. When a vessel reaches the fishing Banks outward bound; also when returning, as she nears the land along the coast-line.

OUTSAIL. To sail faster than; to leave behind in sailing.

OUTSIDE. When a vessel is outside the harbor; out at sea.

OUT-OF-TRIM. When a vessel is not in her best trim for sailing; ballast or cargo too far forward or aft.

OVERHANG. That part of a vessel's hull which extends out over the water from her water-line at both the bow and stern.

OVERHAUL. To overtake and pass another vessel. To overhaul and mend the purse-seine. To overhaul the running-gear on a vessel. To overhaul and repair all fishing gear.

OVERSPARRED. The masts too long and sails too high, for the size of the vessel.

OWLING. A crew fishing on a mackerel seiner during the night.

PACK. To pack in more fish before heading up a barrel.

PACKING. Culling, salting and packing a trip of mackerel.

PAINTER. A four-inch manilla rope used to tow the seineboat. A dory has a painter three fathoms long.

PART. Parting (pulling apart) the cable while a vessel is riding out a heavy gale on the fishing Banks.

PAY-OFF. When a vessel's sails fill with wind after tacking. When a vessel's wheel is rolled up, she "pays off."

PAYING-OUT. To pay out more cable when the wind increases. To pay out more slack on a running-line.

PITCHING. The rising and falling of the bow and stern of a vessel as she sails over the waves.

POINT-HIGH. When a vessel is held close up into the wind. Some vessels will point higher than others.

POLLOCKER. A small vessel whose crew fish with the hand-line from deck during the fall months.

PORT. The left side of a vessel looking forward. The port light is red. "Port the helm." The Port (harbor) of Boston.

PURSE-UP-THE-SEINE. To haul in on the purse-line which closes the bottom of the seine.

QUARTER. A quartering wind is a breeze over the vessel's weather-quarter. A vessel's quarter is aft near the stern on each side.

QUICK-IN-STAYS. A vessel which comes about quickly when tacking.

QUINTAL. A quintal is 112 pounds of dry salt fish, sometimes written and pronounced kentle.

RAFT. A very large school of mackerel.

RAISE-THE-FISH. Throwing toll-bait to bring mackerel up alongside when jigging or hooking.

RANGE-AHEAD. A vessel luffing up with good headway.

RANGE-LIGHTS. To keep the vessel in the channel while entering a harbor.

REACH. "Close reach"—when the vessel is sailing with the the wind abeam, blowing directly on the windward side. "Broad-reach," when the vessel is sailing with the wind abaft the beam, or over her weather-quarter.

REEF. To tie the reef-points on a sail and reduce its size.

REEFING-DOWN. To reef a vessel's sails in windy weather.

REEVE. To pass the end of a rope through a block, thimble, ring-bolt, cringle, purse-rings, etc. To reeve off new halyards, or sheets, for the sails. To climb aloft and reeve off the pennant halyards.

RIDE. When heaving in on the cable it will often "ride" on the windlass and has to be slacked up a bit. "Riding out a gale"—a vessel at anchor on the Bank.

ROUNDING-TO. A vessel luffing up alongside her seine-boat. A vessel luffing up to "speak" another at anchor.

RUN. "A good run," is a fair wind for the course sailed. The after part of a vessel's hull down under her quarter on both sides.

RUNNING-FREE. A vessel sailing with her sheets well off.

SAIL. A spread of canvas set to the wind, drives a vessel on her course. To sail—to set sail and put to sea. "Sail 'O!" When the lookout sights a sail out at sea.

SAIL-CARRIER. A skipper who knows what his vessel will

do and has the courage to carry whole-sail in increasing heavy winds when she is laboring hard in rough seas before he will reef her down. "A good sail carrier" is an able vessel to carry sail.

SAILER. A vessel that sails well: a fast sailing vessel.

SAILOR. An able seaman (A.B.). A sailor before the mast.

SALT-FISHING. To bring in fish that were dressed and salted in the vessel's hold while out on the fishing grounds.

SCHOONER. A New England fishing schooner has two masts, booms and gaffs, rigged with fore and aft sails. A coasting schooner has from two to seven masts.

SCOPE. The length of the cable out, when a vessel is riding at anchor; she may have out a "short scope," or a "long scope."

SCROD. Small fish such as haddock, cod, hake, or pollock, brought in by the ground-fishermen (trawlers and draggers).

SCUD. To swing a vessel off and "scud under bare poles" before the wind during a very heavy gale. Loose fog clouds driven swiftly by the wind.

SEA-BOAT. A good sea-boat, is any kind of craft that behaves well in rough seas during a gale of wind.

SEA-LEGS. A fisherman has "good sea-legs" when he is able to walk on a vessel's deck while she is pitching and rolling during rough weather.

SEA-PORT. A harbor near the sea (where there are buildings and wharves) from which vessels sail.

SEA-ROOM. Ample room at sea, far enough from land for a vessel to heave to without drifting ashore on rocks, shoals or bars.

SEA-WAY. A vessel with sail enough set to keep her steady, when cruising slowly ahead.

SEINER. A sailing schooner previous to 1920; at present an auxiliary vessel or steamer engaged in the fresh mackerel purse-seine fishery.

SEIZE. To fasten the masthoops to a sail. To seize on the jib-hanks. To put a seizing on the lanyards.

SET. To "make a set," is to set the trawls from dories.

SETTING. To row the seine-boat around a "school" and to heave out the purse-seine, enclosing the fish. To encircle a "school" with the steamer towing the seine-boat, the seine going out over the stern.

SETTLE-UP. The crew go to the office of the firm and the owners of the vessel pay off the crew at the end of each trip.

SHACK. Strips cut from cod, haddock, hake, or cusk, and used to "bait up" the hooks on a halibut-trawl.

SHAPE-A-COURSE. The course to be sailed is taken from the chart with a parallel rule.

SHAKE-OUT-THE-REEF. To untie the reef points and set the full sail.

SHIP. "To ship"—a verbal agreement with the skipper to go on a fishing-trip as one of his crew. "Sign on"—to "sign the articles" (ship's papers) as one of the crew for the trip. To "ship a hand," the skipper "ships" the man as one of his crew. To "ship" the windlass brakes and "heave ahead." To "ship" the pump brakes and "pump ship." To "ship" a heavy sea on a vessel during a gale.

SKIPPER. The master of a fishing vessel, sometimes referred to as "The Old Man."

SLANT-OF-WIND. A wind that changes favorably so that a vessel can "head up" better when beating to windward.

SMACK. A small vessel rigged as a sloop, formerly used on the Maine coast as a lobster-smack, with a "well" in her hold, which had auger holes in the bottom to let in salt water, to keep the lobsters alive.

SOUNDING. Heaving the lead to get the depth of water.

SPLICING. To join the two ends of a cable, rope, or line by tucking the unlaid ends under the strands three times. There are three kinds of splices, the long-splice, the short-splice, and the eye-splice.

SPLIT-TACK. A vessel that is sailed on the opposite tack while beating to windward "splits tacks" with the other vessel.

SPURT-OF-FISH. When schools of mackerel are caught

by the fleet at about the same time, the fishermen speak of it as "a good spurt."

STAND. To "stand a watch" on "ship-board"—to go on duty. To "stand off shore"—a vessel "by the wind" on the "off shore tack," heading out to sea. To "stand by," a vessel in distress and render aid.

STARBOARD. The right side of a vessel looking forward. A vessel close-hauled on the starboard tack has the right of way. "Starboard your wheel," is to swing the vessel to port.

STAYS. In stays—the point between one point and another, when a vessel is headed up into the wind while tacking. The head-stays. The topmast backstays.

STRIKER. The man who stands in the "pulpit," on the end of the bowsprit, and throws the harpoon at a swordfish, is called "the striker."

STOW-DOWN. To lower away and "stow barrels" in a vessel's hold. To "stow fish" in her ice-pens, or salt pens. To "stow the seine"—to haul it into the seine-boat from off the vessel's deck.

SWAY. To sway up a sail, the crew sway their bodies backward, pulling down hard on the halyards. When the vessel is rolling (at anchor), the dories sway to and fro while the crew are hoisting them in, or while lowering them out.

TACK. To turn the vessel against the wind so that the breeze will be on the opposite side. The gaff-topsail "tack" (a small rope) is used to haul the foot of the sail down taut.

TAKE. "Take in the staysail"—to lower the sail down on deck.

TAUT. To haul and stretch a rope tight.

THRASH-TO-WINDWARD. Beating a fishing vessel to windward in rough seas and heavy winds.

THROW. To "throw toll-bait," when jigging mackerel. To "throw a line," to the seine-boat when the vessel is luffing up alongside. "Throw down your fish," when the "salter" wants more fish.

THWART. The seat for the rowers to sit on; placed athwart the dory or seine-boat.

TRAWLER. A sailing schooner, formerly; at present, an auxiliary vessel whose crew set trawls from their dories to catch cod, haddock and halibut when either fresh or salt fishing; incidentally, all salt-water fish are fresh when first caught.

TRICK. "Your trick at the wheel"—when it is "your watch."

TRIM. To "trim the sheets," is to haul them in so that the sails will draw better when a vessel is close-hauled. To put ballast in a vessel and bring her down to her load-water-line. To move part of the ballast forward or aft, for better trim.

TRIP. A "full trip"—a vessel loaded with a full fare of fish. A "round trip"—from time of leaving port until return. A "broken trip"—when a vessel returns with only a few fish. To trip (spill) mackerel out of the purse-seine into the "pocket," by hauling up on the twine in the seine-boat.

TROUGH-OF-THE-SEA. The space between two high waves.

TUCK. To tuck the ends of the strands of a rope when splicing. To "tuck a reef" in the sail.

TURN. To hold a turn when swaying on a rope. "Turn in"—to lie down and sleep in a berth. "Turn out"—to get up out of a berth. "Turn to"—an order given by the skipper for the crew to go to work.

UNBEND. To unbend the sails, is to unlace them from the gaffs, booms, and stays, roll and tie them up, then put them ashore on the wharf and send them to the sail-loft.

UNDERWAY. A vessel with sails set. To "get underway"—to hoist sails, and heave in the anchor.

WAKE. The wake of a vessel—the track it leaves in the water, caused by the hull passing through it.

WALL-KNOT. A wall-knot is made by untwisting the end of a rope, and making a bight with the first strand; then passing the second over the end of the first, and the third over the end of the second, and through the bight of the first.

WATER-LINE. A horizontal line drawn around a vessel's hull at the water's edge when she is in her ballast trim.

WAY. Headway—when a vessel is luffing up into the wind. A vessel gathers headway as the sails fill, after tacking. "Way enough!" says the skipper as the seine-boat approaches the dory's end, after setting the seine.

WASH-DOWN-DECKS. To scrub and clean the deck and rails after "dressing down" a "deck of fish."

WATER-HAUL. To fail to catch the school with the purse-seine.

WEATHER. The windward side of a vessel. "Weather berth"—a vessel sailing to windward of another. "Weathering the Cape"—a vessel beating to windward with difficulty, during a gale without "tacking ship." Weather helm—a vessel is said to carry a weather helm when she is inclined to come up too near the wind; a good fault.

WEAR or WEIR. To swing the vessel off before the wind and jibe over.

WHALE-COD. Very large, old fish which are thin and flabby.

WHIP. A small rope with a long tackle and two, two-fold blocks, one block made fast on the opposite end of both the throat and peak halyards, and used to sway the sails up taut.

WINDWARD. Direction from which the wind blows. "Working to windward"—beating a vessel up against a head wind by tacking. A vessel doing good "windward work" often wins the race.

YAW. To steer wild and fall off the course while running free in heavy winds and rough seas.

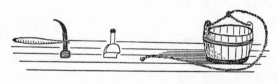

COOPER'S ADZE, DRIVER, AND DRAW-BUCKET

Appendix II

Fishermen's Lore and Superstitions

The Barometer

Long foretold, long last; short notice, soon past.
First rise after very low, foretells stronger blow.
When the glass falls low, prepare for a blow;
When it rises high, let all your kites fly.

At sea with low and falling glass,
Soundly sleeps a careless ass.
Only when it's high and rising,
Truly rests a careful wise one.

Wind and Weather

A red sky in the morning, fishermen take warning;
A red sky at night is a fisherman's delight.

The evening red and morning gray are sure signs of a
fine day;
The evening gray and morning red makes the
fisherman shake his head.

On the Atlantic Seaboard

Fair weather winds, are "off shore" winds, blowing from the southwest, west and northwest, while most of our stormy winds, are "on shore" winds, blowing from the northeast, east and southeast; there are exceptions to this rule, for sometimes we have a "clear easterly."

Fishermen speak of the wind as "hauling out," when it changes from the northeast to the south and "hauling in" when it changes from the south to the northwest (going around with the sun).

Reverse this and they speak of the wind as "backing out" when it changes from the northwest to the south, and "back-

288

ing in" when it changes from the south to the northeast (going around against the sun).

An "ash breeze" is when it is calm weather and a man is rowing a dory with a pair of ash oars.

A "fog breeze" is when the wind is blowing about 20 miles an hour in foggy weather.

A "smoky sou'wester" is a wind of 35 to 40 miles an hour.

VELOCITY OF WIND PER HOUR

1 mile, hardly perceptible.
5 miles, light air of wind.
10 miles, light wind.
15 miles, brisk breeze.
30 miles, fresh breeze.
50 miles, high wind.
60 miles, gale force.
80 miles, hurricane.
100 miles, destructive hurricane.
120 miles, typhoon (Indian Ocean).

SQUALLS

When rain comes before wind, halyards, sheets and down-hauls mind.

When wind comes before rain, soon you may make sail again.

LIGHTS

When a vessel is underway, green light on starboard fore-rigging, red light on port, both side-lights fifteen feet above deck. Auxiliary fishing vessels and steamers also show a white light at masthead. When a vessel is at anchor, the side-lights are taken down and a riding-light (white) is shown on the starboard forward shrouds fifteen feet above deck.

RIGHT OF WAY OF SAILING VESSELS

When both side lights you see ahead,
Port your helm and show your red;
Green to Green, or Red to Red,
Perfect safety, go ahead.

If on the port tack you steer,
It is your duty to keep clear
Of every close-hauled ship ahead,
No matter whether Green or Red;

But when upon your port is seen,
A stranger's starboard light of Green,
There's not so much for you to do,
For Green to Port keeps clear of you.

Both in safety and in doubt,
Always keep a good lookout.

When on the starboard tack close-hauled, your vessel has the right of way, but when on the port tack you must keep clear of the other one. When your vessel is running free (off the wind) you must keep clear of all vessels close-hauled. In foggy weather when by the wind with starboard tack aboard, blow one blast of your horn, when on the port tack blow two blasts, and when running off before the wind, blow three blasts. When your vessel is at anchor, blow one long blast frequently or ring the bell often.

THE SOUNDING-LEAD AND LINE

At   2 fathoms, leather with two ends.
     3 fathoms, leather with three ends.
     5 fathoms, white cloth.
     7 fathoms, red bunting.
     10 fathoms, leather with a hole in it.
     13 fathoms, blue serge.

15 fathoms, white cloth.

17 fathoms, red bunting.

20 fathoms, strand with two knots in it.

The above numbers are called "marks"—"By the mark seven."

The intervening eleven numbers as follows: 1, 4, 6, 8, 9, 11, 12, 14, 16, 18 and 19 fathoms are called the "deeps"—"By the deep six."

Starboard and Port Watches on Sailing Ships

Eight P.M. to midnight — first watch.

Midnight to four A.M. — mid watch.

Four A.M. to eight A.M. — morning watch.

Eight A.M. to noontime — forenoon watch.

Noontime to four P.M. — afternoon watch.

Four P.M. to six P.M. — first dog watch.

Six P.M. to eight P.M. — second dog watch.

Watches on Fishing Vessels

Two men are in a watch of two hours, one at the wheel for one hour, the other man on the lookout forward for one hour, then they exchange. The anchor watch is of one hour, one man in the watch.

The Mariner's Compass

Every boy should learn to "Box the compass," that is, he should be able to name every point on the compass card; starting with North, then North one-quarter East, North one-half East, North three-quarters East, North by East, completing the circle of 360 degrees. The compass has eight cardinal points, eight intercardinal points, sixteen whole points, thirty-two half points, and sixty-four quarter points, making one hundred and twenty-eight in all.

SPEAKING A VESSEL ON THE "BANK"

One vessel under way, the other at anchor.

"Schooner ahoy! Hello, skipper George!"

"Hello, skipper Mark!" George replies.

"How'd you find th' fish here, George?" asks skipper Mark.

"Plenty o' fish here; we got 42 tubs yesterday," replies George.

"How much water you got here, George?" asks Mark.

"Twenty-eight fathoms under the vessel; give us a short 'berth' to the east'ard and anchor, plenty o' large fish on a Bank-clam spot two cable lengths north of us," replies skipper George.

A "BREEZE"

The average fisherman seldom dignifies the most furious gale by any other name than a "breeze." "Were you out in the last breeze?" he may ask his friend when he meets him on the street, referring to the last unusually heavy gale, when several men were lost. He speaks of a "smart staysail breeze" when a vessel has all she can carry a staysail with, close-hauled. A "whole-sail breeze" is one in which the four lower sails can be carried and no more.

A "double-reef breeze" signifies that a vessel can carry only double-reef sails.

RIDING OUT A GALE AT ANCHOR ON THE "BANK"

"I tell you what 'tis, this is a tough one," said Joe as he came below after his watch on deck. "If this haint a regular old-fashioned screamer I never saw one," he added.

"How does she ride?" asked the skipper.

"Ride? Why, she shames the gulls, skipper!" Joe replied. Later on when the gale had moderated somewhat, as the man on watch came below, the skipper awoke and asked Bill why he had not called him. Bill replied, "Well, skip, I didn't know but it'd blow agin; it looks nuff like it."

The skipper said to Bill, "Go for'ard an' rouse 'em out, Bill, we'll heave in part of our cable afore it drags afoul o' some sharp rock an' parts."

Fishermen's Superstitions

To start a trip on Friday is unlucky.

It is unlucky to launch a vessel on Friday.

A vessel that sticks on the ways while being launched will be unlucky. The fishing schooner *Ambrose H. Knight*, stuck on the ways twice and was a very unlucky vessel all her short life and was finally lost with all her crew.

It is considered very unlucky to turn a hatch-cover bottom up, or drop it into the vessel's hold.

It is bad luck to take an umbrella aboard a fishing vessel. It is bad luck to turn a dory with the left hand, swinging her around against the sun; if you expect to get any fish that day, turn her with the right hand around with the sun.

A fisherman will not drive a nail on Sunday for that will invite bad luck.

Fresh Fish

A little advice to the ladies about buying fresh fish for dinner. When making a purchase of fresh fish, see if the gills are a bright red color, rather than one that has pale and faded gills. Select a fish that has bright clear eyes, not one that has dull sunken ones. Be sure that the fish is good and firm of flesh, not flabby and soft. Then you can serve a fine, sweet-tasting fish on your table. So long! — W. G. P.

Appendix III

New England Fishing Vessels

THE first boats used by the settlers in fishing were wooden canoes, made by the Indians. In Maine these canoes were usually made of the bark of birch trees, sewed on ribs of ash wood, and made so light that an Indian would carry on his head for several miles one which would hold eight or ten persons, while in Massachusetts they were usually made from the trunk of a large tree. Wood (1634) says:

Their Cannows be made either of Pine trees, which, before they were acquainted with English tooles, they burned hollow, scraping them smooth with clam shels and Oyster shels, cutting their outsides with stone hatchets: These boats be not above a foot and a halfe or two feete wide, and twenty foote long. Their other Cannows be made of thinne Birch rines, close ribbed on the inside with broad thinne hoopes, like the hoopes of a tub; these are made very light, a man may carry one of them a mile, being made purposely to carry from River to River and bay to bay to shorten land passages. In these cockling fly-boates, wherein an English man can scarce sit without a fearfull tottering, they will venture to sea, where our English Shallope dare not beare a knot of sayle; scudding over the overgrowne waves as fast as a wind-driven ship, being driven by their paddles; being much like battledoores; if a crosse wave (as is seldome) turne her keele upside downe, they by swimming free her, and scramble into her againe.

The majority of canoes would carry only four or five men; the larger ones, twenty, thirty, and even forty men; and they were round-bottomed and very crank. The bodies of the log canoes were straight, the ends sharp, and the fore foot and heel cut away as in a modern whale-boat. Their narrowness gave them great speed, and three men, with paddles, could drive them faster than a shallop could be propelled with eight

NOTE:—Appendix III is reprinted, in part, from Henry Hall's "Report on the Ship-building Industry of the United States"—10th Census of the U. S., Washington, 1884.

oars. An Indian, by going into the woods and giving his time to it, would make a canoe in ten or twelve days.

When the English settled at Plymouth, Salem, Ipswich, Portsmouth, and other places on the New England coast they bought these strong and handy boats in large numbers, both for fishing in smooth waters and for crossing streams and visiting their neighbors, and nearly every family in towns like Salem owned its canoe, as every farmer today does his horse. Canoes were the universal oyster boats for the first fifty years on the whole American coast, and were so well adapted to that use that they are still employed by American oystermen in many localities.

It is not probable that log canoes ventured more than two or three miles from shore, and then only in calm weather, as they could not be launched through the surf nor taken into very rough water. A larger class of boats was required for taking cod and for other work in the open sea. The first ones were ships' boats left behind by the vessels which visited the coast; but in 1624 boat-building began regularly at Plymouth, some ship-carpenters having been sent over for the purpose. Two chaloupes, or shallops, were built, one of them afterward making a voyage as far eastward as the Kennebec. They were open boats, like others of their class, having, however, a little deck amidships, to keep the crew dry. In 1625 one of these boats was sawed in two and lengthened 5 or 6 feet by putting in more frames amidships. A deck was laid the whole length of the boat, and she did the colonists good service for at least seven years afterward. A great many shallops were built in subsequent years, as there was need for them at Salem, Ipswich, Gloucester, Medford, Portsmouth, and the other settlements all along the coast. Some were used for trading purposes, but the majority were fishing boats. They usually carried one mast, with one sail hoisted from the deck; but in the larger ones, instead of fitting the shallop with a tall mast and a large sail, the owners usually followed the safer and more convenient plan of adding another mast with its own sail. Two small sails were more easily handled than one large one, and in a fresh wind the after sail could be lowered and the boat allowed to scud under the foresail alone. The ancient shallop probably carried lug sails.

A great many shallops were built in the winter time by the fishermen and their sons, who thus employed their idle season with useful work. The lumber for the boat was gathered little by little, a good deal being cut in the common woods and some picked up on the beach, so that it cost them next to nothing, and the boat, when built, was found to have cost them little more than the outlay required for nails, paint, iron fittings, blocks, cordage, and canvas. These boats were constructed in door yards, often in barns, and sometimes in the woods two or three miles from the water, whither they were dragged on sledges of timber. The home company sent over a number of shipwrights among their early dispatches of emigrants; many others came voluntarily among the crews landed from the large fishing vessels from England; and boat-building became an established industry in nearly every village in twenty years after the landing at Plymouth.

The first vessels sent from New England to the banks to fish set sail in 1645, and comprised "a ship and other vessels," their rig not known; but a style of smack which became popular as soon as something larger than the shallop was required was the "catch," or "ketch." The Dutch called them the "pinkie," a name borrowed from the Mediterranean and meaning a hull round at both ends, the outside planking ending on the stem and on the stern-post, in distinction from ships having a broad or "square" stern above the water, which were planked straight across. The "pinkie" hull was popular with the Dutch, and there is reason to believe that the hulls of the vessels in the northern fisheries of Europe were of that class. The first catches carried one mast amidships, with a large square sail. Afterward a small mizzen was added away aft, the mainmast being planted in that case one-ninth or one-tenth of the vessel's length forward of amidships. The mizzen-mast carried a lateen or a lug sail, which is a lateen with one-half of the forward part cut off. The mainmast bore two square sails, perhaps three. The popularity of the ketch was due to its simplicity of construction, as no ingenuity was required in framing either the bow or the stern and the planking was easily put on. It was a good sea boat, pretty fast and safe on account of its breadth of beam, easily handled, and, when required for the coasting trade, was useful for its great capacity, the bottom being broad and round. The probate records

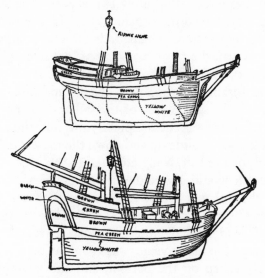

HEEL-TAPPER FISHING SCHOONER OF 1770
Drawing by C. G. Davis

of Suffolk county, Massachusetts, indicate that ketches and shallops constituted the whole fleet of the fishing merchants up to about 1700. The ketches were 9 or 10 feet deep in the hold, drew 7 or 8 feet water, were decked throughout, had cabins aft, and were built of white oak, except the deck and cabin, which were of white pine, and the masts, which were usually of spruce. The broadest part of the hull was two-fifths of the vessel's length from the bow.

Salem was the principal center for the building of ketches, and it is said that the people of that town clung to the model and rig longer than any other community on the coast, using ketches both in fishing and in general trade. The average size was about 30 tons register, but a few were as large as 80 tons; the majority were below 30 tons, and cost about £3 5s. per ton to build. Before the independence of the colonies the ketch had ceased to exist, and had become, through slight modifications of hull and rig, the brigantine of today—a class of vessel used only in trade.

Out of the old shallop grew two classes of small vessels which have remained in permanent use. In one of them the two small masts were retained, but were planted a step farther forward, the foremast being set not over 4 feet from the bow, and, in 30-foot boats, the mainmast 10 or 11 feet aft of the foremast, bringing it about amidships. A change took place in the sail. A part of the sail and of the yard forward of the mast was cut completely off, and the end of the yard was shaped to slide up and down the mast, the fore edge of the sail, or the luff, being attached to the mast by wooden hoops, which would also slide up and down with ease. The head of the sail was narrowed, and the foot was spread by means of a "sheet," attached to it at the lower after corner, carried aft and hauled taut. The boat remained open and without deck for many years, was round at both ends, being moderately sharp on the bottom, and the prow was often pointed. These changes in the fishing shallop culminated at Essex, Massachusetts, formerly called Chebacco, the story being that the first Chebacco boat, probably not much larger than the yawl of a modern schooner, was built in a garret, and was taken out of the house through a window and dragged to the water's edge by cattle. The shrewdness of the inventors of this new and handy rig brought a great deal of business to Chebacco, and the Chebacco boats, as they were called (or pinks, from the shape of the hull), became famous along the whole of the New England coast. First used in fishing at Sandy Bay, these boats soon came into general use, the majority of them being built in the village in which they originated. They ranged from 3 to 5 tons burden at first, and their owners put out in them to the ledges and shoal grounds for

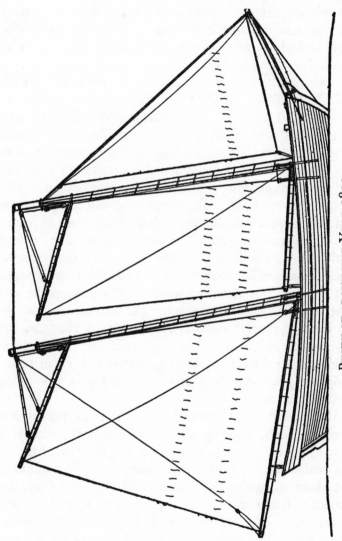

PINKY OF ABOUT THE YEAR 1800
Drawing by C. G. Davis

cod, hake, and pollock early in the day, always to return at night; but in later years, especially after the independence of the colonies, they were built larger and decked, and were fitted with a cabin, sometimes being of 30 tons register. When they reached a large size the foot of each sail was fitted with a boom. The Chebacco boats were always framed and planked with white oak, cut from the abundant forests of that timber which grew all around the town, and nothing except heart of oak was used, all of the sapwood of every tree being sawed or hewed off and thrown away. Thus the boats were built of wood which would scarcely perish. The deck beams were usually of oak, but the deck plank and cabin were of white pine, and the masts of white pine or spruce. These boats were often built in the woods, or, at any rate, a long way from the water, and as late as the Revolutionary War fishing boats of from 10 to 20 tons were thus built and were dragged to the river by cattle. Though built in Chebacco (or Essex), the boats were chiefly owned in Gloucester, and by 1792 this latter town had 133 boats of this class, registering 1,549 tons, in the shore fisheries; but by 1804 the number had increased to 200, with the tonnage nearly doubled. From 1800 to 1840 the boats were built for $18 a ton, a good price for the times, but much smaller than the builders got afterward. From 1861 to 1865 the price was about $65 a ton, but it is now (1880) about $40 a ton.

About 1820 the fishermen began to put bowsprits into the Chebacco boats, shearing off the pointed prow, and calling them "jiggers." The planking of the low bulwark of the boat was carried out beyond the sharp stern 3 or 4 feet and nailed to a short triangular stern-board, like that of a dory. This projection had a seat for the use of the crew, and the boom of the mainsail rested on it while the boat rode at anchor. Fishermen built "jiggers" of 40 tons register for mackerel catching, on account of the abundance of that fish at the time, the first great year being 1825, when one jigger, with 8 men, caught 1,300 barrels of fish; but when the mackerel began to disappear, which was about 1845, the large jiggers disappeared with them. Chebacco boats of moderate size remained in use for many years, but are now obsolete in New England. A few pinks, with bowsprits, were still to be seen occasionally at Gloucester as late as 1880, and especially in the waters around Eastport, Maine, and they were also to be seen, usually without decks and always without projecting prow, but in other respects like the Chebacco boats of the earlier times, at Block Island, where they were almost the only style of boat employed. Full in the forward body, a trifle leaner aft, sailing with a drag of from 2 to 4 feet, broad of beam, and carrying a great deal of stone ballast, they were a cheap and excellent fishing boat, safe, comfortable, and almost non-capsizable. At Block Island, lying 20 miles out to sea from Newport, Rhode Island, the little community of resident fishermen had 100 fishing boats and 200 men employed as early as 1800, as appears from a petition sent by them to Congress in that year, all under 5 tons each. It is probable that the islanders originally built their own boats from the timber which anciently covered their lands in a dense growth, but of late years they have been obliged to send to the mainland to buy, as the island has become entirely denuded of trees of all kinds. The cod banks being within two leagues of the shore, the men go out to them early in the day, returning at dusk, and, drawing up their boats on the beach, fasten them to poles planted in the sand, to protect them from the fury of the waves. The secluded life of the islanders prevented the newer fashioned boats from creeping in among them for any purpose (as in the case of most of the fishing islands on the northern coast) until about 1860, when people from the mainland began to spend their summers there to enjoy the cool air and the surf bathing.

The other style of vessel which grew out of the old "chaloupe," or shallop, was the modern sloop whose name is a contraction of that of the foregoing. The sloop is a vessel with one mast, spreading a large fore-and-aft sail, the foot of the sail attached to a boom and the head to a gaff, and with a bowsprit spreading a large jib. This class of vessel appears to have

been used in America originally for trading purposes; there
was certainly a large fleet of them owned in the towns adja-
cent to Massachusetts Bay, employed in freighting fire-wood,
hay, and goods along that part of the coast. The hulls were
built with broad decks, square sterns, and pretty full models.
After the sloop came into existence it was extensively employed in the fisheries, and is now popular among yachtsmen,
the rig being generally regarded as the handsomest in existence for pleasure boats. When properly designed, the sails
present the appearance of a large and showy triangle of canvas, reviving in outline and effect the old lateen sail. The
sloop was in vogue at an early day in England, and may have
come to America from that source. Square topsails were fitted to the larger sloops in England, and a picture of an English war fleet is extant in which there is a sloop with two square
upper sails. In 1714 the *Hazard*, a sloop, was sent expressly
from England to America to carry the news of the accession
of George I to the throne and orders for the colonial government. This vessel, after crossing the Atlantic in safety, was
wrecked on Cohasset rocks on the 12th of November and
dashed to pieces. No papers of any consequence were saved,
and of all her company only one man came to land alive. The
rig of the sloop was a handy one for boats between 10 or 12
tons register and 30 or 40 tons burden, and came into favor
rapidly after 1700, both for large fishing vessels on the New
England coast and for trading purposes everywhere in America. Many of the "bankers," and all of the early mackerel
boats, were sloops, and the first vessels with which whales
were chased out to the Gulf Stream, and thence to distant
latitudes, were of this class, the larger ones probably being
fitted with a square topsail, to catch the air in light weather.
The majority of sloops were not over 10 or 15 tons register,
but some were as large as 30 tons. In the little fleet of 10
vessels hurriedly fitted out in Massachusetts, manned by fishermen, the smartest and ablest of sailors then, as now, and
sent in 1745 to capture the great fort at Louisburg with its
200 cannon, 3 were Yankee sloops, and of the 34 vessels

burned by the British in 1778 at New Bedford at the time of the capture of that town 10 were sloops. Many of the fishing sloops were very fast vessels, and they and their crews were accordingly much in demand during the Revolutionary War for privateering, their exploits forming a romantic chapter in the naval history of the United States. The principal places at which sloops were built were Boston, Scituate, Salem, Charlestown, Gloucester, and Newbury, but the boat-yards all along the whole coast began about 1700 to devote considerable attention to this class of vessels, which, as before stated, were employed partly in fishing and partly in trading, entirely superseding in both employments the ancient "catch."

In after years the square topsail was given up and a gaff topsail was bent in its place, being a large triangle of canvas hoisted along the mast above the mainsail, and the jib was divided into two smaller head sails. A great number of sloops were built before the Revolutionary War for the open sea fisheries, chiefly at Boston, Charlestown, Scituate, Essex, Salem, Beverly, Marblehead, Gloucester, Ipswich, New Bedford, Portsmouth, and the fishing towns along the coast of Maine. In the cod-fishery Massachusetts alone had 4,000 men and 28,000 tons of shipping before the Revolutionary War, the fleet being largely composed of sloops. The great advantages of the sloop were its safety, and particularly its cheapness, arising from the small size of the vessel and from the abundance of native oak and pine near the fishing towns. The fishing vessels built in New England before the Revolutionary War cost only one-half what the fir-built vessels of the Baltic did, and the result was that American fishing vessels continually increased in the cod and whale fisheries of the Atlantic, while European vessels continually decreased. Jefferson reported in 1791 that no other nation except the Americans could make a profit in the Newfoundland fisheries without national aid, and the governmental machinery was invoked to secure the widest possible market for American-caught fish.

In 1745 Andrew Robinson, of Gloucester, built a vessel

with square stern, which was fitted with two masts, bearing a sloop sail on each and a bowsprit with jib. She was sharp on the bottom and fast, and, on being launched, sped over the water so fast from the impetus gained by descending from the ways as to elicit from a bystander the remark, "See how she scoons." "Scoon" was a word used by plain people to express the skipping of a flat stone over the surface of the water when skillfully thrown, and the builder of the vessel, having been somewhat at a loss for a name for the new rig, seized upon the trifling incident referred to and replied, "A scooner let her be," and two-masted vessels, with jibs and fore-and-aft sails, have since been called by that name. The advantage possessed by the "schooner" (as the name is now spelled) is that the canvas of the vessel is divided into a large number of sails, which are more easily handled than the large sails of a sloop could be, each containing the same amount of cloth. The schooner quickly superseded the sloop in the banks fisheries and in all others requiring voyages of any duration. Carrying twice as many men as a sloop, and making quick trips, a schooner could catch as many fish as two vessels of the other style, and were large enough to carry their own fish to foreign markets. Since the Revolutionary War they have been the only vessels employed by Americans in the banks fisheries.

The American fisheries were annihilated during the Revolutionary War, and the vessels were captured, the utensils and apparatus destroyed, the ship-yards closed, and both fishermen and carpenters were driven into other employments. The business revived promptly after the peace of 1783 both on shore and out to sea. By 1788 the New Englanders had an aggregate of 540 vessels, registering 19,200 tons, and 3,290 men in the deep-sea fisheries, and for more than half a century, interrupted only now and then by war or by small profits, the business went on increasing steadily. These statistics are from Jefferson's report to Congress in 1791.

The largest schooners were those sent to the Grand Banks, and for many years after 1800 about 70 sail of vessels were annually sent thither, chiefly from Cape Ann. The original "banker" was strongly and substantially built of oak. Her decks and cabins were of pine; her spars of either pine or spruce; her rigging and cables entirely of hemp. The ship-yard was usually located at the water's edge (although a vessel of 100 tons has been built one or two miles from the water and dragged on sledges over the snow in winter by 200 cattle to a spot suitable for launching), and the ways were planted so that the hull of the new vessel should just escape the water at high tide. The keel was laid of oak or other hard wood. Beginning at the fullest part of the vessel, the frames of the forward body were put in, going forward, and the stem, with its apron, knight-heads, and hawse timbers bolted together, was then raised to its place. The frames of the after body were then raised, and the stern-post, with the frame which belongs to that part of the vessel bolted to it, was fitted to its place. The keelsons were put in, the vessel was ceiled, planked, and decked, and in due time was launched, often with her principal spars in place. The only tools used in the ship-yard were those wielded by hand—saws, axes, hammers, augers, squares, chisels, and calking irons—the largest being the great saw, for cutting timbers lengthwise, worked by two men, one at each end, the timber being placed across two wooden horses, and one man standing on the top of the log, the other in a pit below the surface of the ground. All the beams, planks, keelsons, etc., were carried into the vessel on the shoulders of the men, but the masts were raised and set by means of an extemporized derrick. In model the vessels would be thought uncouth at this day. The bows were nearly as full as half an apple, the bottom as round as the side of a barrel. They sat low in the water, and there were no bulwarks amidships other than the covering plank, with a chock, which rose in all about 15 inches above the surface of the deck. Aft there was a quarter-deck extending nearly half the length of the vessel and rising 4 feet above the main deck, reached by a flight of steps. The cabin was large, and, as this was before stoves were invented, was furnished with a large fireplace and chimney, the smoke sometimes going out by way of the chimney and sometimes through the open door of the apartment. The masts were rather short, and there was no topmast, except on the mainmast. The bowsprit was set high, sometimes at an angle of about 30°. The cutwater was a large and strong knee, securely bolted to the stem, and served as a means of securing the bowsprit in place, that spar being lashed to the knee with hemp or iron. There was not much beauty to the old-time "bankers," but they were staunch and durable vessels. Built for strength, well calked, and immediately repaired when showing a leak or weakness anywhere, they often lasted for forty or fifty years. The last of them owned at Gloucester was the *Manchester*, which, after long service on the banks, was sold to go into the coasting trade, and was a successful vessel in that business for more than twenty years. The bankers used to make about three trips a year, beginning in March and ending in November, and then either went into trade or were laid up for the winter.

The clipper schooner succeeded the banker. A few good years, in which fish were plenty and prices profitable, and the anxiety to make rapid trips and as many as possible in one year, led to great improvements in form. The body of the vessel was made leaner and sharper under the water, the bow longer and finer, the run cleaner, and the angle of entrance forward was sharpened from 85° to 45°. The spars were lengthened, and the schooner put under a heavier press of canvas. The clipper fashion is said to have been set at Essex, and the models of the carpenters of that town were so much admired as to bring a great deal of business to their yards. The Essex men have always shown originality in the shapes of their vessels, and have always led every other town upon the New England coast in the production of tonnage for the fisheries. Of the 475 schooners, sloops, and boats owned at Gloucester in the year 1880, 218 had been built at Essex, 133 only having been built by the Gloucester men themselves. The places where the rest of the Gloucester fleet of 1880 was built will appear in the following statement:

Essex, Mass.	218	Bristol, Me.	3
Gloucester, Mass.	133	Belfast, Me.	2
Salisbury, Mass.	9	Damariscotta, Me.	2
East Boston, Mass.	5	Brunswick, Me.	2
Newburyport, Mass.	5	Harpswell, Me.	1
Danversport, Mass.	4	Yarmouth, Me.	1
Chelsea, Mass.	3	Wells, Me.	1
Salem, Mass.	2	Portsmouth, N. H.	1
Quincy, Mass.	2	Middletown, Conn.	3
Medford, Mass.	1	East Haddam, Conn.	1
Rockport, Mass.	1	Essex, Conn.	1
Ipswich, Mass.	1	Chatham, Conn.	3
Annisquam, Mass.	1	Noank, Conn.	1
Duxbury, Mass.	1	New London, Conn.	1
Dorchester, Mass.	1	Bridgeport, Conn.	1
Wellfleet, Mass.	1	East Haven, Conn.	1
Bath, Me.	36	New York	3
Boothbay, Me.	13	New Jersey	1
Kennebunk, Me.	9	Total	475

As soon as Essex and Gloucester had adopted the fast schooner every other fishing town along the whole coast did the same from necessity, and the new boats superseded not only the bankers, but also the pinks, for shore fishing; so that after 1850 a complete revolution was effected in the character of the fishing fleet of the whole Atlantic coast. Except on the Chesapeake, where a distinct class of vessels, peculiarly local, had been evolved, old fashions lingered only in a few scattered and out of the way places. The fast schooners added greatly to the prosperity of all the fishing towns; the American fishing fleet multiplied rapidly, and the capital invested in fast vessels yielded a far larger return than that put into the slower craft that preceded them. The vessels owned in large towns were provided generally by fishing merchants, who would put the profits of one year into a new schooner, to be added to their fleet the next, and who would fit out annually from three to twelve, and even as many as twenty vessels; but the masters of most of the schooners had shares in the craft they sailed, and hundreds of them came in course of time to possess and sail their own vessels. Builders, sailors, and merchants all became prosperous after the new impetus given to the business by the clipper class of schooners; the fishing towns were filled with neat and comfortable residences, owned by them; and their operations gave rise to shops, lofts, and mills, which made employment for thousands of men in the various arts that a large fishing fleet calls into action. Nearly all the fishing towns in New England made their own sails, rigging and cordage, anchors, and outfit, a contract for a new vessel, therefore, meaning work for nearly all the shops in town. The majority of the villages were supplied with small marine railways, on which regularly twice a year all the vessels of the town were hauled up out of the water for calking and painting and such other repairs as circumstances demanded; and thus there was work both winter and summer. This state of affairs continued, especially in New England, until the operation of the new fishery treaty with Canada brought a blight upon the business by admitting Canadian-caught fish to the United States free of duty.

The early schooners, both bankers and clippers, were from 20 to 40 tons register. The size increased with the growing accumulations of capital, and since 1860 the majority have been built of from 60 to 90 tons register, the fair average being about 75 tons, but many from 100 to 140 tons.

It is remarkable that, while the form and the rig of the schooners have been greatly improved, the manner in which they have been framed and built has scarcely changed in the last hundred years. The measurements, scantling, etc., of a 75-ton schooner are as follows:

DIMENSIONS AND SCANTLING. Length, 76 feet, from the outside of planking at the bow to the after side of the stern-post, measured along the deck; breadth from outside to outside of planking, 22 feet; depth of hold, 7 feet 8 inches, and molded depth from under side of plank-sheer (top of beam), 8 feet 6 inches; keel, 70 feet long; molded with shoe of 6 inches, 18 inches, and sided 10 inches; stem, 12 feet long, sided 15 inches; stern-post, 10 feet long, sided 15 inches; knee to stern-post on keel, 4 feet 3 inches high, about 12 feet long on keel, and sided 10 inches; keelson, 10 inches square. The ceiling of the hold is 2 inches thick, except on the turn of the bilge, where a few streaks are laid 3 inches thick, and except just under the beams (the clamps), where they are also 3 inches. The outside planking is 2½ inches, with 3-inch fender streaks. The beam knees are sided 5 inches and molded 10 inches in the throat. Beams are 9 inches wide, tapering from 7 inches deep in the center to 5 inches at the ends. Carlines are 4 inches by 6; decking, 3 inches thick. Frames, double, are 14 inches wide and 8 deep over the keel, the depth or molding of the frames tapering thence to the plank-sheer, where it is 4 inches. At the plank-sheer only one of the timbers of each frame rises to form the bulwark of the schooner, this timber, or stanchion, being sided 5 inches and molded 3; bulwark, 2 feet high amidships, 2 feet 6 inches forward; sheer of vessel, 22 inches.

SPARS AND SAILS. Length of foremast, 69 feet; length of mainmast, 70 feet 6 inches; length of mast-heads, 6 6/12 and 6 10/12 feet; length of topmasts, 35 feet; length of poles of topmasts, 6 feet; rake of masts, ⅝ inch to the foot; the masts bury below deck 8 feet 6 inches; from knight-heads to center foremast, 21 feet; from center foremast to base of mainmast, 27 feet; from center mainmast to center of taffrail, 36 feet; length of bowsprit outboard, 21 feet; center line of bowsprit strikes stern-post above keel 4 feet; length of jib-boom outside cap, 13 feet; length of fore boom, 23 feet; length of main boom, 57 feet; length of fore gaff, 23 feet; length of main gaff, 25 feet.

The spars, with the bill for labor in making them, cost about $300.

Mainsail: Hoist, 46 feet; foot, 55 feet; head, 24 feet; after leech, 60 feet; containing 2,015 square feet of area and 410 yards of canvas.

Main gaff topsail: Hoist, 36 feet; after leech, 31 feet; foot, 24 feet; area, 350 square feet; canvas, 70 yards.

Foresail: Hoist, 46 feet; head and foot, 22 feet; after leech, 51 feet; area, 940 square feet; canvas, 190 yards.

Fore gaff topsail: Hoist, 36 feet; after leech, 34 feet; foot, 23 feet; area, 340 square feet; canvas, 70 yards.

Staysail: Fore leech, 15 feet; after leech, 36 feet; head, 31 feet; foot, 24 feet; area, 550 square feet; canvas, 115 yards.

Jib: Fore leech, 60 feet; after leech, 44 feet; foot, 46 feet; area, 840 square feet; canvas, 175 yards.

Flying-jib: Fore leech, 68 feet; after leech, 40 feet; foot, 32 feet; area, 350 square feet; canvas, 75 yards.

Jib-topsail, or balloon jib: Fore leech, 84 feet; after leech, 42 feet; foot, 50 feet; area, 805 square feet; canvas, 165 yards.

Riding-sail, or lug-sail: Area, 450 square feet; 90 yards of canvas.

Total sail area, 6,640 square feet, or 1,360 running yards of canvas, to which add about 60 yards for linings; cost of the suit, about $570.

[The sails vary in area somewhat on different vessels of the same tonnage, as the masts are planted at slightly different distances apart and the topmasts are shorter or longer, but the variation is seldom more than 50 yards of canvas either way.]

Blocks, etc.: 16 double and 46 single blocks; 24 6-inch and 8 4-inch dead-eyes; 36 21-inch and 16 10-inch mast hoops; 24 24-inch, 30 18-inch and 40 16-inch jib-hanks; 2 topmast balls. Average cost of blocks, etc., for a two-topmast schooner, about $140.

A schooner of this size will carry, in addition to what is mentioned below, two chains from 30 to 45 fathoms long each, if fitted out for mackerel fishing; but if fitted out for cod or halibut fishing she will have from 225 to 425 fathoms of best $8\frac{1}{2}$-inch or $8\frac{3}{4}$-inch manila cable and three anchors, one of them being carried on deck for use in case one of the others should be lost. The following is the hemp standing rigging, the table giving the circumference and the fitted lengths ready to go on the vessel:

	Lengths in feet	Circumference in inches
Jib stay	88	$8\frac{3}{4}$
Foremast shrouds, each	$54\frac{1}{2}$	$6\frac{3}{4}$
Mainmast shrouds, each	$56\frac{1}{2}$	$6\frac{3}{4}$
Bowsprit shrouds, each	28	5
Spring stay	$25\frac{2}{3}$	5
Flying-jib stay	108	$4\frac{1}{2}$
Flying-jib guys, each	$35\frac{1}{2}$	4
Foretop-mast back stays, each	86	3
Maintop-mast back stays, each	88	3
Foretop-mast shrouds, each	32	$2\frac{3}{4}$
Foretop-mast stay	129	$2\frac{3}{4}$
Maintop-mast shrouds	32	$2\frac{3}{4}$
Maintop-mast stay	38	$2\frac{3}{4}$
Bowsprit foot-ropes, each	24	$2\frac{3}{4}$
Main-boom foot-ropes, each	26	$2\frac{1}{2}$
Counter stay (foretop-mast)	37	$2\frac{1}{2}$
Maintop gallant stay	41	2
Foretop gallant stay	133	2
Flying-jib foot-ropes, each	15	$2\frac{1}{4}$
Jib topping-lift	36	3
Fore-boom topping-lift pendant	24	3
Main topping-lift pendant	57	$4\frac{1}{2}$
Main-boom topping-lift pendant	30	$4\frac{1}{2}$
Flying-jib topping-lifts pendant	15	$3\frac{1}{2}$

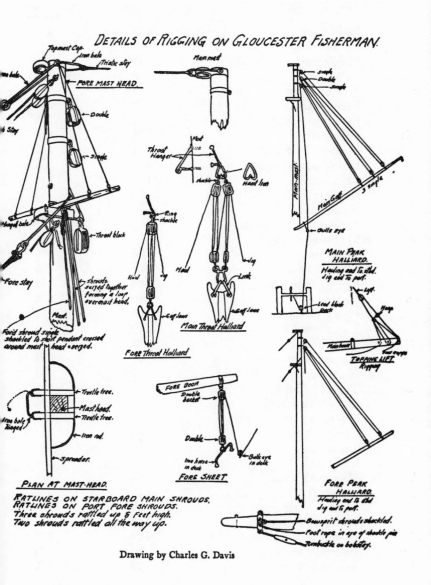

DETAILS OF RIGGING ON GLOUCESTER FISHERMAN.

Drawing by Charles G. Davis

The following are the circumferences and lengths of the manila running rigging:

	Lengths in feet	Circumference in inches
Main sheet	132	3
Cat stoppers	27	3
Main topping-lift runner	18	3
Fish-hook	12	3
Fore and main lanyards, each	30	3
Fore-peak halliards	318	2¾
Fore-throat halliards	264	2½
Fore sheet	96	2¾
Main-peak halliards	324	2¾
Main-throat halliards	270	2½
Jib halliards	180	2½
Jib sheet	60	2½
Jib downhaul	87	2
Main-staysail halliards	165	2½
Main-staysail sheet	60	2½
Main-boom tackle	108	2½
Flying-jib halliards	198	2¼
Flying-jib downhaul	105	1¾
Jib topping lift	156	2¼
Flying jib sheets, each	60	2¼
Fore staysail halliards	120	2¼
Topsail sheet	114	2¼
Crotch tackles, each	48	2¼
Main topping-lift, fall	96	2¼
Topsail halliards	114	2
Main-peak downhaul	126	1¾
Fore-boom topping-lift	156	2
Fore-peak downhaul	60	2
Topsail back	60	2
Reef tackle	96	2
Main-peak whip	144	2
Fore-peak whip	138	2
Jib-peak whip	138	2
Jib-topsail halliards	258	1¾
Jib-topsail downhaul	108	1½
Jib-topsail sheet	72	2½
Topsail clew-line	138	1¾

Weight of tarred hemp, 1,330 pounds; weight of manila cordage, 890 pounds. Cost, about $440, including rigger's bill of $100 for fitting and setting up.

The practice has been in vogue for the builder to contract to furnish only the hull and the spars of the vessel, the sails being furnished by another contractor. The cordage is bought by the owner from the manufacturer or from a ship-chandlery store, and is fitted to the vessel by a rigger, whose bill is almost exclusively for labor, and the chains and anchors are bought from either a shop or a store. The fine carpentry work on the cabins is done by a joiner; the iron ballast, often costing $500, is purchased from the mill, and when the sails, rigging, cabins, chains, anchors, and ballast have been purchased the main features of the outfit of a fishing schooner have been provided, the rest of the outfit consisting of a large lot of small articles, costing in all from $400 to $600.

The following statement, taken from the books of a leading sail-maker in a fishing town in New England, shows the yards of canvas in schooners of different sizes, the first cost, the yearly amount spent for repairs of sails, and length of time the suits of sails last:

In what fishery	Tonnage of schooner	Yards of canvas in sails	Cost of suit	Yearly amount for repairs	Life of a suit of sails Years
Halibut, the year round	95	1350	$600	$100	2
Mackerel and herring, the year round	93	1338	600	70	2½
Halibut, the year round	83	1380	570	100	2½
Mackerel and herring, the year round	83	1380	570	50	2½
Mackerel, the season	80	1349	650	50	3
Bank fisheries, the season	75	1360	570	100	3
Mackerel and shore, the season	72	900	470	80	2
Bank fisheries, the season	65	850	570	83	3
George's banks, the season	60	800	500	70	2
Do	56	750	450	60	2½ to 3
George's banks and shore, the year round	48	700	340	50	2½ to 3
Shore, the year round	40	640	300	40	2½
Do	32	550	250	40	2½ to 3
Do	28	500	240	30	2½ to 3
Do	26	460	200	30	2½ to 3

The differences between vessels of nearly the same size are due to the lack of foretop-mast on some of them, and to the use of light canvas in some cases and of heavy canvas in others.

Many of the fishermen sail with no foretop-mast, this being thought to be a snugger and safer rig, the rolling and pitching of a fishing boat being severe upon all the top hamper. In such cases the "top bills" of the vessels are lessened somewhat.

The manner of building a 75-ton schooner in the New England yards is as follows: All the plank, and a good deal of the square lumber, such as is used in keelsons, beams, and stern-posts, are bought from the lumber-yard in the town, or in the most favorable market near by and sent to the town by coasting vessel or by railroad. The frame timber is obtained in two ways: Either it is bought at the nearest saw-mill in the flitch, that is, in heavy plank sawed only on two sides, the bark of the tree remaining on the other two edges, and drawn to the yard on wagons or sleds, according to the season, when the crooked pieces of the frame, stem, etc., are hewn from it with broadaxes; or the cheap pine board patterns of the crooked pieces are given to a contractor, who makes a business of getting out frames in the woods in Delaware, Maryland, or Virginia. In that case the contractor goes to the scene of his operations in the winter time, fells the trees, hews the frames from the trunks on the ground on which they fall, marking each separate piece when finished, and brings the whole frame to the yard in New England by coasting vessel in the spring. The contractor pays about $3, but sometimes from $4 to $6 per thousand board feet for the white oak standing in the woods, and it costs him about $9 a thousand to fell the trees and hew out the frames, besides an additional charge for hauling out of the woods. Freight to the north is about $7 a thousand, and by the time the timber is delivered in the ship-yard the frame has cost the builder about $34 per thousand board feet. The white pine used for decking and houses costs him about $35 a thousand, and the pitch-pine, for beams, keelsons, and other uses, $25 a thousand.

The keel is stretched on a series of blocks made of cheap

SAILS AND RUNNING RIGGING OF A FISHING SCHOONER

timber, and such of them as have to be split out are usually hemlock or spruce. The declivity toward the water is usually about five-eighths of an inch to the foot. A keel 73 feet long would be made of two pieces, with the ends united by a horizontal beveled joint, or scarf, about 6 feet long, strongly bolted with round iron. Owing to the fact that single sticks of timber of the right curvature long enough to reach from the keel to the main rail cannot be obtained for the ribs of the vessel the frames have to be made of several pieces. A frame is composed of eleven pieces, the first being the "floor timber," 7 inches wide and 8 inches deep, tapering toward the ends, which is laid across the keel, extending each way as far toward the bilge as the natural crook of the log from which it is cut will allow. Abutting against each end of the "floor timber" is another curved stick, or "futtock," which carries the sweep of the frame farther on upward, and against the end of that another futtock, or "top timber," as in the illustration on page 16, which carries it to the plank-sheer on either side of the vessel, the frame tapering gradually from the keel to the plank-sheer. This collection of pieces makes one-half of the frame. In front, and strongly fastened to them by treenails of oak or locust, are the pieces composing the other half of the frame, which break joints with the pieces first mentioned. There are, first, two "navel timbers" abutting over the keel; then a "futtock" adjoining each navel timber; then a "stanchion," which rises to the main rail and supports the planking of the bulwark of the vessel. As the frame is thus double, it measures over the keel 14 inches by 8. The pieces are laid together and treenailed on the ground, and the completed frame is then raised to its place by a derrick and held up by shores.

In a schooner of 75 tons there are about 27 frames, spaced 24 inches from center to center, the first one being set up about 6 feet from the stem at the water-line. After these frames are set up, and each is fastened to the keel with 1-inch iron bolts about 2 feet long, the stem, with the hawse timbers and knight-heads bolted to it solidly, is raised and bolted to the keel. Then the stern-post is set up, the deadwood is placed at the stem and stern, upon which the extreme forward and after frames, or "cants," are stepped, and then the keelson is laid, bolts 1 inch thick and about 20 inches long are driven through each frame into the keel, and these bolts often go clear through the keel and are clinched on the under side by spreading the ends with a hammer. The forward cants are usually four or five in number, and are of the same size as the frames of the "square body," so called; but the bottom ends are tapered to suit the model of the vessel, and are bolted with ⅞-inch iron to the deadwood. There are five or six after cants, which are secured in the same way. After the frames are all up, three sets of ribbons, or strips of wood, are run around the vessel lengthwise and nailed to the frames, to hold them steady and in proper position while being planked, one of these ribbons being fastened at the head of the navel timbers, another on the bilge, and the third at the gunwale. The planking and ceiling generally go on at the same time, but in many cases the ceiling is put in first, and is fastened with spikes. The planking is fastened to the frames with oak or locust treenails, 4 in each frame, one-half of the treenail going through frame and ceiling, and is clinched at each end by driving wooden wedges into the treenail. The ends of the planking are fastened by two 5-inch spikes of galvanized iron and one ⅝-inch galvanized iron bolt, going through, and clinched inside over an iron ring. Each plank of the "bends" is bolted to every set of timbers, this being called "bend bolting." The beams are put in about 4 feet from center to center, and are bolted to the clamps, or piece of thick ceiling, with ¾-inch iron, there being four ¾-inch bolts through each lodging knee into the beam and about six through the body of the knee into the side of the vessel. The deck planking is laid nearly straight fore and aft, but aft it follows the sweep of the sides of the vessel somewhat. The decking is 3 inches thick, 5 or 6 inches wide. Two 5-inch spikes are driven through each plank into every beam, the heads countersunk, and the holes plugged with wooden plugs set in white lead. On the top of the main rail, at the bow, is placed a wooden chock 5 inches high, tapering to 3 inches aft, and 5½ inches thick, tapering to 4 inches aft. This chock extends from the bow to the fore-rigging. The taffrail varies from 14 to 18 inches in width on the main rail; the top rail is 9 inches wide. The houses are the last thing built. The whole of the top and outside of the vessel is duly planed, the deck oiled, the hull calked and painted, and the schooner is then launched. It was more frequently the case in 1880 that fishing schooners were launched before the spars were set.

If there were ship-chandlery stores and sail and rigging lofts in the town the new schooner was placed alongside of a wharf and fitted out at once, but in many towns near cities as large as Rockland, Portland, Gloucester, Boston, and New York the schooner was placed in tow of a tug and sent to the city, where she got her spars, sails, rigging, anchors, hawsers, boats, and all the paraphernalia of her outfit. It cost from $50 to $100 to tow a new schooner to the nearest large city, but, as a rule, outfits could be purchased there relatively so cheap as to warrant this expense. The use of the steam tug since 1860 has extinguished the sail and rigging lofts, anchor shops, and chandlery stores of a large number of vessel-building towns along the Atlantic coast by concentrating the outfitting business in the large cities.

From first to last, about thirty distinct trades are concerned in the collection of the material for a fishing schooner and the construction of a vessel. The largest part of the cost is for material. Fishing schooners were built in 1880 for from $55 to $65 per register ton. The cost of a 75-ton vessel was about $5,000; the amount paid out in the ship-yard for labor of building was about $1,900.

The outfit of such a vessel for a five-weeks' mackerel trip for a crew of master and 14 men was:

1 seine, costing $850.
40 hogsheads of salt, $70.
1 seine-boat, $225.
400 barrels, $400.
4 barrels of flour.
2 barrels of beef.
100 pounds of pork.
120 pounds of sugar.
25 gallons of molasses.
½ barrel of beans.
25 pounds of dried apples.

25 pounds of cornmeal.
10 gallons of kerosene.
10 pounds of coffee.
50 pounds of lard.
60 pounds of butter.
10 bushels of potatoes.
1 bushel of peas.
10 pounds of rice.
50 pounds of oatmeal.
Other small stores, costing about $40.

INDEX

319

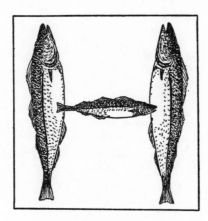

HADDOCK